For Dummies
BESTSELLING
BOOK SERIES

Annuities For Dumm...

P9-EEE-459

Sheet

Determining What You Need Your Annuity to Do

When you're considering an annuity, you need to seriously evaluate your personal situation to determine what type of annuity you should get, or even whether you should get one at all. Before you start looking for an annuity, consider the following points carefully, and keep them in mind when you're ready to go shopping. For more information, see Chapter 5 to determine whether you should get an annuity, and review the Part II chapters to pick the best type for you.

- **Assess your needs.** After you estimate your living expenses in retirement and identify all sources of income, you'll know whether you'll need an income annuity.

- **Consider your options if you don't have a traditional pension.** Like most people, you may not retire with a traditional pension. But you can use an income annuity to build a do-it-yourself pension.

- **Get familiar with your "risk tolerance."** Determine what risks you can tolerate and which ones you can't. For example, if a 500-point drop in the Dow doesn't deprive you of sleep, then you probably don't need a life annuity.

- **Expect trade-offs in risk and reward.** Annuities are insured investments, which means they protect you from some of the risks that accompany investing. But greater safety often means smaller gains, so some risks may be worth taking.

- **Count on living longer.** Don't assume you'll die young — most people underestimate their lifespan by several years, and half of all 65-year-old Americans will live past age 83. Look at annuities that can help with extended retirement funding.

- **Protect the wife.** Women tend to outlive their husbands, and therefore have a much greater risk of running out of money during their lifetimes. That's why prudent couples buy "joint-and-survivor" life annuities.

- **Protect yourself from inflation.** The rising cost of living can erode your purchasing power in retirement. An income annuity with an inflation rider or a variable income annuity can help.

- **Look at how much you need to spend.** An advanced life deferred annuity (ALDA) is an inexpensive way to guarantee yourself an income in late retirement while pumping up your spending power in early retirement.

- **Get a discount for less-than-ideal health.** If you think you'll have a shorter-than-average lifespan, check out "impaired risk" annuities. They'll give you bigger-than-average monthly payments.

Annuities For Dummies®

Cheat Sheet

Becoming — and Remaining — Annuity Savvy

You need to be aware of the latest annuity trends when buying an annuity and making sure it continues to benefit you in the best way possible. The following checklist shows the most important things for you to track and keep in mind in the world of annuities. Refer to it often.

- ✔ **Recognize that the annuity world changes.** For example, deferred annuities used to be purchased mainly as a tax dodge by people in the upper tax brackets. In the future, income annuities will likely be purchased by baby boomers who want a guaranteed lifelong paycheck. Keep on top of the trends, and you'll be able to make adjustments to ensure that your annuity stays on top of them, too.

- ✔ **Understand how "survivorship credits" (mortality credits) work.** When the owner of a life annuity dies, his or her assets are distributed as so-called survivorship credits to the owners who go on living. That's the biggest benefit (and for some, the biggest drawback) of life annuities. See Chapter 4 for more information.

- ✔ **Get creative with your annuities.** You may be able to maximize your income in retirement with a combination of two or three annuities. This path takes research and planning, but it can pay off! See Chapter 15 for more information.

- ✔ **Decide how much money to keep outside an annuity.** When you buy an annuity, leave some money in more liquid investments so you can meet emergency expenses. If a salesman urges you to put all your money into an annuity, get a second opinion.

- ✔ **Plan for trade-offs in risk and reward.** Annuities are insured investments, which means they protect you from some of the risks that always accompany investing. But insurance costs money, and the fees can eat up a good chunk of your returns. See Chapter 17 for more information on how to head off or reduce these types of problems.

Shopping for a Contract

When you're ready to sit down and really start looking for a contract, make sure this list is on hand and cover every option it gives you, so you can be certain you're staying on top of the game. See Chapter 11 for information on contract structuring, and Chapter 16 for tips on finding an annuity.

- ✔ **Find an annuity-savvy adviser.** Income annuities aren't yet widely used, so not many advisers or brokers understand them. Try to locate a professional who does.

- ✔ **Look for a strong insurer.** Always buy your annuity from a financially strong insurance company with "Superior," "Excellent," or "Strong" ratings from the major rating agencies.

- ✔ **Read the prospectus before you buy an annuity.** Annuity contracts offer guarantees, and guarantees are always accompanied by complex exclusions and restrictions that may appear only in fine print.

- ✔ **Buy direct and save money.** If you're the self-reliant type, you can save big by purchasing your annuity direct from an insurance carrier or from a no-load mutual fund company like Vanguard or Fidelity.

- ✔ **Buy only what you understand.** Some annuities are more complex than others. Don't buy one (or any other financial product) that confuses you. What you don't know may come back to haunt you.

- ✔ **Be wary of excessive fees.** Variable annuities offer attractive options, but the options aren't free. Try to get the benefits you need at a reasonable price.

For Dummies: Bestselling Book Series for Beginners

Annuities

FOR

DUMMIES®

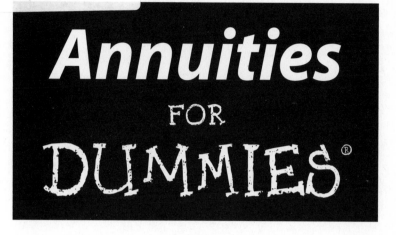

by Kerry Pechter

BICENTENNIAL
1807
WILEY
2007
BICENTENNIAL

Wiley Publishing, Inc.

Annuities For Dummies®

Published by
Wiley Publishing, Inc.
111 River St.
Hoboken, NJ 07030-5774
www.wiley.com

Copyright © 2008 by Wiley Publishing, Inc., Indianapolis, Indiana

Published by Wiley Publishing, Inc., Indianapolis, Indiana

Published simultaneously in Canada

For general information on our other products and services, please contact our Customer Care Department within the U.S. at 800-762-2974, outside the U.S. at 317-572-3993, or fax 317-572-4002.

For technical support, please visit www.wiley.com/techsupport.

Wiley also publishes its books in a variety of electronic formats. Some content that appears in print may not be available in electronic books.

Library of Congress Control Number: 2007941625

ISBN: 978-0-470-17889-8

Manufactured in the United States of America

10 9 8 7 6 5 4 3 2 1

WILEY

About the Author

Kerry Pechter is the senior editor of *Annuity Market News*. As a reporter who writes about annuities and the annuity industry full-time and as a former marketing writer who specialized in annuities at The Vanguard Group, he brings both an outsider's and an insider's perspective to the writing of this book.

A financial journalist for many years, Kerry has written for the *New York Times*, the *Wall Street Journal*, the *Los Angeles Times*, and many other national and regional publications. His previous books include two career guides, *A Big Splash in a Small Pond: How to Get a Job in a Small Company* (Fireside) and *An Engineer's Guide to Lifelong Employability* (IEEE). He is a graduate of Kenyon College.

Dedication

To my family — my supportive and resourceful wife, Lisa Higgins; my three wonderful daughters, Hannah, Ariel, and Mattea; my brother, David, and his wife, Jean; my sister, Carol, and her husband, Andy; and my parents, Allen and Dorothy.

Author's Acknowledgments

The community of people who think about, write about, create, and sell annuities is a relatively small one. Many of its members patiently guided me through the intricacies of these odd but necessary insurance products when I was figuratively climbing stairs in the dark.

A special thanks goes to Noel Abkemeier, Jeremy Alexander, Lisa Bennett, Garth Bernard, Scott DeMonte, Howard Drescher, Jerry Golden, Pem Guerry, Kelli Hueler, David Macchia, Moshe Milevsky, Lisa Tibbitts, Tamiko Toland, John Ziambras, the folks at NAVA (Mark Mackey, Deborah Tucker, and Kathleen McKee), and to the media relations professionals at dozens of insurance companies who cheerfully responded to my last-minute requests for information.

I'm grateful to Adam Reinebach and Lee Barney, the publisher and editor of *Annuity Market News,* respectively, for supporting this project and for sharing my editorial values. I am also indebted to my former colleagues at The Vanguard Group, who taught me the true fundamentals of investing.

Thanks to my agent, Marilyn Allen, my acquisitions editor, Stacy Kennedy, and my project editor, Natalie Harris, for recognizing the value of publishing this book and welcoming me into the fold. I'd also like to thank my friend and fellow Dummies author, Russ Wild, for his indispensable help. Finally, I owe a huge debt to Jesus Salas for his wise counsel.

Publisher's Acknowledgments

We're proud of this book; please send us your comments through our Dummies online registration form located at www.dummies.com/register/.

Some of the people who helped bring this book to market include the following:

Acquisitions, Editorial, and Media Development

Project Editor: Natalie Faye Harris

Acquisitions Editor: Stacy Kennedy

Copy Editor: Pam Ruble

Technical Editor: Ron Hanson

Editorial Manager: Christine Meloy Beck

Media Development Manager: Laura VanWinkle

Editorial Assistants: Leeann Harney, David Lutton, Erin Calligan Mooney, Joe Niesen

Cartoons: Rich Tennant (www.the5thwave.com)

Composition Services

Project Coordinator: Katie Key

Layout and Graphics: Reuben W. Davis, Alissa D. Ellet, Melissa K. Jester, Christine Williams

Proofreaders: Jessica Kramer, Bonnie Mikkelson

Indexer: Broccoli Information Management

Publishing and Editorial for Consumer Dummies

Diane Graves Steele, Vice President and Publisher, Consumer Dummies

Joyce Pepple, Acquisitions Director, Consumer Dummies

Kristin A. Cocks, Product Development Director, Consumer Dummies

Michael Spring, Vice President and Publisher, Travel

Kelly Regan, Editorial Director, Travel

Publishing for Technology Dummies

Andy Cummings, Vice President and Publisher, Dummies Technology/General User

Composition Services

Gerry Fahey, Vice President of Production Services

Debbie Stailey, Director of Composition Services

Contents at a Glance

Table of Contents

Introduction

· ·

*T*he oldest members of the baby-boomer generation reached age 60 in 2006. Every year for the next 18 years, millions of these former rock-and-rollers, flower children, peaceniks, backpackers, Yuppies, do-it-yourselfers, suburbanites, and Mr. Moms will reach this milestone and begin riding off into their sunset years. I'm a boomer. Perhaps you are, too.

Boomers and later generations have good reason to be curious about annuities. Millions of these folks will have no other guaranteed income in retirement than the soon-to-be-underfunded Social Security program. They may have savings — trillions overall — but they need a financial tool that can help turn decades of savings into lifetime income streams. Annuities, when used wisely, can fill the bill.

Think of annuities as investments with insurance features or insurance with investment features, depending on the particular contract. For people in their prime earning years, these insurance features can make as much sense as training wheels at the Tour de France. But for people in their 50s — whose financial priority is no longer speed but safety and whose savings' interest isn't great enough to live off of — those training wheels can be appealing.

You may have heard about annuities with costs and complexities that are downright prohibitive. But, as I show you in this book, the right annuity (or combination of annuities) can help you squeeze more retirement income out of your savings than any other financial tool. The right annuity can assure you a decent income, no matter how long you live.

About This Book

If ever a candid, consumer-driven book about annuities has been needed, the time is now.

Thousands of companies have replaced their traditional pension plans with defined contribution plans like 401(k)s. As a result, their millions of employees will be cobbling together their own pensions rather than relying on their employer's pension-fund managers. Yet these employees have no equivalent of Home Depot, or *This Old House*, or even a user's guide to help them.

Several books have been published on annuities, but they aren't aimed at do-it-yourselfers; they're written for professionals (financial advisers, tax experts, and public-policy mavens) who specialize in pensions and retirement issues.

In addition, most of these books give fairly short shrift to the annuity's unique ability to generate guaranteed lifetime income.

Annuities For Dummies, in contrast, is written and designed for the average person, and it focuses a lot of attention on the income-generating aspect of annuities. Like all the *For Dummies* books, this one has an open architecture that lets you read the contents in any order. Its bold headings and eye-catching icons tell you exactly what you're reading and how the details relate to the big picture. You don't have to dig very far to find the information you need.

Annuities are pretty simple when you can clear away all the technicalities and legalities. Basically,

1. **You put money into them** — a little at a time or all at once. This is the *accumulation phase.*

2. **The money appreciates** — you hope — by earning interest or through capital gains.

3. **You take money out** — all at once, at your own pace, or in the form of a regular income. This is the *income phase.*

Note: The tax breaks and insurance guarantees associated with annuities tend to complicate matters because they have all sorts of conditions and restrictions. But in this book, I try to keep the larger picture firmly in view.

I suggest you don't ask whether annuities are good or bad. The right questions are

✔ Would I feel safer in retirement if I had insurance against certain financial risks like running out of money?

✔ How can I make sure I buy the right annuity for my particular needs?

✔ How can I make sure I buy an annuity that doesn't cost too much?

This book answers these questions in language that most people with a bit of investment experience — the typical baby boomer with a 401(k) plan, for instance — can understand. For casual reading or future reference, *Annuities For Dummies* is your DIY guide to the strange but potentially rewarding world of annuities.

Conventions Used in This Book

When this book was printed, some Web addresses may have broken across two lines of text. If that happened, rest assured that I haven't put in any extra characters (such as hyphens) to indicate the break. When you want to use one of these addresses, just type exactly what you see, pretending that the line break doesn't exist.

What You're Not to Read

If you're in a hurry to read through a chapter (although I hope you'll read every bit of information in the book — the more you know, the better!), you can take some shortcuts. For example, you don't have to read the text preceded by the *Technical Stuff* icons in order to understand the subject at hand. You'll also see *sidebars,* text in gray boxes. Sidebars are merely *asides;* the information is interesting but not critical to the text. You can safely skip it.

Foolish Assumptions

When an author sits down to write a book, he tries to envision the people — or sometimes a single person — to whom he's speaking. In the process, he makes certain assumptions about that audience. In writing this book, I've made a few assumptions that may apply to you:

- ✔ You're looking ahead toward your retirement years, and you'd like to make them more financially secure.

- ✔ You know a fair amount about saving and investing for retirement (perhaps through your employer-sponsored retirement plan), but you know little or nothing about annuities.

- ✔ You want to participate in the financial decisions that affect you. Even if you leave the details to a financial adviser, broker, or insurance agent, you still want to understand what's going on and whether your adviser is taking you in the right direction.

- ✔ You're a bit skeptical. You've heard or read some negative media about annuities, including lawsuits against salesmen or companies that allegedly prey on retirees.

- ✔ You tend to be a risk-averse investor. You understand that the stock market isn't just a roller-coaster ride for thrill seekers but also a place where prudent people can take steps to protect themselves against its volatility.

How This Book Is Organized

Here is a general overview of how the book's contents are separated into parts.

Part I: Annuities: A Blend of Insurance and Investment

Part I defines annuities and lays an informational foundation for what's to come. The text includes a high-altitude view of annuities and their place within the larger context of retirement security. It also descends to the microscopic level for a close-up view of an annuity's internal parts. After reading Part I, you should know whether an annuity is right for you.

Part II: Identifying the Main Types of Annuities

In Part II, I devote an entire chapter to each of the major types of annuities. Chapters 6, 7, and 8 focus on the most common annuities for *accumulating* wealth. Chapters 9 and 10 concentrate on annuities that are typical for *spending* wealth in retirement. In some ways, all annuities are alike. But in other ways, the five types of annuities are so dissimilar that having a common name can seem downright misleading.

Part III: Making the Most of Your Annuity

When you purchase and own an annuity contract, you make a lot of intermediate decisions — or at least help your financial adviser make them. This section shows you where those decisions arise and how to make them. Ultimately, no two annuities are alike because annuity owners customize their contracts to match their particular needs and preferences. Your satisfaction with your annuity will depend on how carefully you customize it.

Part IV: Navigating the Annuity Superstore

With dozens of insurance companies offering annuities and dozens of ways for buying them, finding the right annuity at the right price isn't necessarily easy. In Part IV, you meet the insurance carriers who manufacture annuities, the channels through which annuities are sold, and the agents and brokers who sell them. I also provide resources for reliable annuity information on the World Wide Web. To spare you from finding out the hard way, I point out some annuity pitfalls you'd be wise to avoid.

Part V: The Part of Tens

Whenever you need instant information about annuities, you can turn to these lists. Suppose you have an appointment with a broker to talk about annuities; use Chapters 18, 19, and 20 for quick prep work. If you find time for Internet research, Chapter 21 can show you where to start surfing.

Also, check out the three appendixes:

- Appendix A provides research tips and background information on several of the largest insurance companies.
- Appendix B explains the reimbursements that state guaranty associations make to annuity owners whose insurance companies go bankrupt.
- Appendix C contains a good chunk of IRS Publication 939, *General Rule for Pensions and Annuities*, to further help you with your research.

Icons Used in This Book

Throughout this book, you find icons that alert you to especially useful tidbits of information. If they were in a more formal book, they'd sound like editorializing, but I use them to *tell it like it is*.

When you see this icon, look for useful advice that can probably save you time or money or both!

I try to make each chapter as independent as possible. But occasionally I need to remind you of a fact from another part of the book. You'll see this icon whenever something bears repeating.

The world of annuities can be like an evil golf course — full of rough patches, water hazards, and sand traps just waiting to add strokes to your score. This icon points them out.

Number crunching may not be your favorite pastime, but make note of the numbers that come up with this icon, because you can use them to your advantage.

You can skip this stuff if you want to, but if you really want to get down and dirty with annuities details, dive in.

Where to Go from Here

Feel free to dive into this book wherever the headings catch your interest or wherever the table of contents directs you. The *For Dummies* books are designed for use as references as well as narratives. (They're not just for beach reading!)

If you don't know anything about annuities, definitely read Part I. If you're already conversant with annuities, however, try skipping straight to Chapter 15. If you're in the throes of deciding whether to buy an annuity, definitely read Chapters 4 and 5. And if you're ready to shop for an annuity or call a broker, cut right to Part IV.

Part I

Annuities: A Blend of Insurance and Investment

The 5th Wave   By Rich Tennant

"The first thing we should do is get you two into a good annuity. Let me get out the 'Magic 8 Ball' and we'll run some options."

In this part . . .

*H*ere you learn that annuities are investments with money-back guarantees of one kind or another. They include elements of both insurance and investment products. I define annuities, identify their internal parts, and explain how they work. You discover that income annuities are the most efficient way to convert a limited sum of money into a retirement income stream that you (or you and your spouse) can't outlive. I reveal their unique contribution to retirement security: *survivorship credits.*

Chapter 1

Making Sense of Annuities

*M*any people confidently walk the financial high wire of life without a safety net. Others, especially those who are approaching retirement, feel more secure when a net is there to catch them — just in case the tightrope snaps.

If you prefer a financial safety net and you're willing to pay for one, then consider an annuity. Put simply, annuities are investments with money-back guarantees. Imagine a typical investment in stocks or bonds; then imagine that same investment with a guarantee that you'll get your money back with interest after (or over) a certain time period. That's an annuity.

Of course, annuities aren't quite that simple. Most annuity brochures and prospectuses contain enough disclaimers, footnotes, and contingencies to keep a dozen lawyers busy. But it's useful, at least at first, to ignore the complexities of annuities and take a high-level snapshot of what they are and how they work.

To resume the circus metaphor, an annuity is both a tightrope and safety net; it's an investment and insurance against the loss of that investment. Annuities aren't always as exciting as the investment alone (like a tightrope walker without a net), but they're not as risky. If you're in or near retirement, you might find such a trade-off appealing.

In this chapter, I give you the basics by explaining what annuities are, what they do, how they work, who should buy them, and so on. In the interest of full disclosure, I also share my own opinions about annuities, because my opinions inevitably shape this book.

Annuities: Older Than You (Probably) Think They Are

Because people don't know how long they'll live, they don't know how much money they'll need to support themselves for the rest of their lives. The history of annuities is the search for a solution to that problem.

Annuities have existed for at least 1,800 years. In ancient Rome, contracts called *annua* promised a stream of payments for a fixed number of years or for life in return for an up-front payment. Speculators who sold insurance for Mediterranean shipping ventures sometimes offered these insurance contracts to the public.

Wealthy Romans often willed their heirs or friends an income for life. Because tax collectors needed to know how much that income would cost the benefactor's estate, they also needed to know how long those heirs or friends were likely to live. In AD 225, a Roman judge named Ulpanius produced the first known mortality tables. By his reckoning, a 30-year-old Roman man would live until age 60, on average. Any man over age 30, he concluded, had an average life expectancy of 60 years minus his current age.

William Shakespeare is said to have invested a large part of his wealth near the end of his career in an "annuity-like arrangement." In pre-Renaissance Europe, both the Church and assorted annuity dealers sold life annuities to raise funds. As early as 1540, the Dutch government sold annuities to finance wars and public works, just as modern governments sell bonds.

In the 1600s, special annuity pools called *tontines* operated in France. In return for an up-front payment, purchasers of tontines received a lifetime income. As purchasers died over time, their income was divided among the survivors. The last purchaser to die collected the remaining money. Tontines were eventually banned — partly because they gave the last two or three survivors a motive to kill each other!

Edmund Halley, the famous astronomer, used the birth and death records of an isolated German town to create the first modern set of mortality tables. He surmised that if the town had 600 30-year-olds but only 300 57-year-olds, a 30-year-old's average life expectancy must be 27 years. He published his tables in 1693, but they weren't widely used for another century.

The first record of annuities in the United States is from 1759, when the Corporation for the Relief of Poor and Distressed Presbyterian Ministers and Distressed Widows and Children of Ministers was chartered in Pennsylvania. In 1812, the Pennsylvania Company for Insurance on Lives and Granting Annuities was founded.

After the stock market crash of 1929, many people turned to guaranteed annuities as a safer place to put their retirement savings. The modern era of annuities began in 1952, when TIAA-CREF (the educators' retirement fund) offered the first group variable deferred annuity — a precursor of other employer-sponsored retirement savings plans.

Individual annuities (which are purchased by individuals from insurance companies) flourished after the tax reforms of 1986, when deferred annuities became the only remaining financial product that allowed people to save and invest unlimited amounts on a tax-deferred basis. As of 2007, Americans have saved more than $1 trillion in annuities, along with the trillions they hold in employer-sponsored retirement plans and other accounts.

Today, many economists and finance professors (not to mention life insurance companies) hope that the baby boomer generation, whose oldest members are just beginning to retire, will rediscover the original purpose of annuities and use them to turn their 401(k) accounts and IRAs into guaranteed lifetime income.

Should You Get an Annuity?

So, should you get an annuity? This is a not a simple question. The only sensible answer is that certain annuities are right for certain people. If you recognize yourself in any of the following categories, then you should definitely explore annuities further:

- ✔ **People in high tax brackets** often like deferred annuities because they can contribute virtually any amount of money to the plan and still defer taxes on the gains for as long as they like.

- ✔ **Middle-class couples in their 50s who are earning $100,000 or less and have a savings of $250,000 or more but no pension** should like income annuities. They have a 50-percent chance that one of them will live to age 90.

- ✔ **Financial advisers** sometimes put their wealthy clients' money in variable annuity subaccounts (mutual funds) instead of conventional (taxable) mutual fund accounts so that they can defer taxes on any gains they realize when buying and selling fund shares.

- ✔ **Pessimists** — otherwise known as *Cassandras, doomsayers,* and *bears* — who believe that the gigantic, highly leveraged house of cards (the United States' financial system) may collapse at any time, should like the guarantees that annuities provide.

- ✔ **Women** are much more likely to need annuities than men. It's true. Women live significantly longer and are therefore at greater risk of running out of savings.

Single or widowed women are more likely to be poor in old age than single or widowed men. Many people expect that, in the future, as birth rates in developed countries (the United States, Japan, and much of Europe) fall, and the number of elderly citizens rises, a retirement financing crisis will occur. Women will probably bear the brunt of that crisis.

For more on this topic, see Chapter 5.

Raising Your Awareness

As I mention earlier in this chapter, I hope this book raises your awareness of annuities and makes you a reasonably savvy consumer of these complicated but useful financial tools. And although I try not to prejudice you for or against them, I do share my point of view, make judgments, and draw conclusions.

So, as you read, don't be surprised when you hear elements of my credo more than once:

- ✔ **Costs matter.** John C. Bogle, the founder of The Vanguard Group and the best friend an individual investor can have, has said it loudest, "Costs matter." Don't expect annuities to be cheap; guarantees are expensive. But be vigilant about the annual costs, fees, and expense ratios you'll pay, particularly if you buy a deferred variable annuity. See Chapter 8 for more information.

- ✔ **Don't invest in a contract you can't understand.** Many annuities are highly (and sometimes necessarily) complex. They may have moving parts that can change your costs from year to year, and they often function in counterintuitive ways. Many annuity prospectuses defy comprehension entirely. If one contract makes no sense to you, investigate another.

- ✔ **The survivorship credit is the core strength of annuities.** Income or immediate annuities distribute the assets of deceased contract owners to the remaining owners, thus enhancing the income of all surviving contract owners. This often-neglected feature makes an annuity an annuity, and some experts think it should get more attention.

- ✔ **Creative combinations of annuities should be explored.** The question is not, "Should I buy an annuity?" The question is, "Is there an annuity or a combination of two or three annuities that can give me the financial security I need in retirement?" A creative mixture of deferred and immediate annuities can often do the trick. For tips on how to work this magic, see Chapter 15.

✔ **The best annuities are yet to come.** Many of today's annuities are prototypes of better annuities to come. As more baby boomers retire and recognize that they need guaranteed lifetime income, they'll demand cheaper, more attractive annuities. For more information on new types of annuities that are just around the bend, see Chapter 15.

Mortality pooling (see the sidebar "Survivorship credits — the unique aspect of annuities" later in this chapter) allows all annuity owners not only to receive lifelong income but also to maximize the amount of income they receive from a fixed amount of money while living. For instance:

• If a 65-year-old man retires with $300,000 and wants it to last at least as long as he lives, research shows that he can safely withdraw about 5 percent a year ($15,000) from age 65 until around age 90.

• If the same man buys a single life annuity with $300,000 at age 65, he can receive more than $25,000 a year for life, no matter how long he lives. To protect his beneficiaries, he can buy an option that guarantees payments for a certain number of years or until he dies, whichever is longer.

Annuities guarantee a pension-like income for life better than any other financial product. There is no more efficient tool for converting a specific sum of money into a monthly income that lasts as long you live — even if you're still kicking at 105.

So why don't more people buy annuities when they retire? There are lots of reasons, which I describe at length in Chapter 4. But it's likely that more people will buy annuities in the future. People are living longer and saving less. Fewer employers provide pensions. Social Security benefits may be trimmed back. Millions of people will replace their lost pensions and benefits with annuities.

Seeing How Annuities Work

Annuities are intended to help you save for retirement and supplement your retirement income. To encourage this practice, Uncle Sam lets you defer taxes on the growth of your annuity. And to discourage you from spending your annuity assets before retirement, the IRS penalizes you for any withdrawals from annuities and other tax-deferred investments before you reach age 59½.

Various types of annuities can make your retirement more secure by helping you:

✔ **Save for retirement.** Before you retire, fixed deferred annuities (including CD-type annuities, market value-adjusted fixed annuities, and indexed annuities) allow you to earn a specific or adjustable rate of interest on your money for a specific number of years, tax-deferred. They're also a safe place to park money during retirement. See Chapter 6.

✔ **Invest for retirement.** Before you retire, variable deferred annuities (a basket of mutual funds, essentially) allow you to invest your savings in stocks or bonds and still defer taxes on all the capital gains, dividends, and interest that mutual funds usually throw off every year. See Chapter 7.

✔ **Distribute your savings.** Most baby boomers who retire with six-figure balances in their employer-sponsored retirement plans aren't sure how fast or slow to spend their savings. An immediate annuity or a variable deferred annuity with guaranteed lifetime benefits can provide structure to the process. See Chapter 8.

✔ **Insure against longevity risk.** Just as life insurance insures you and your family from the risk of dying early, an income annuity or an advanced life deferred annuity (ALDA) can insure you against the risk of living so long that you run out of money. See Chapter 10.

✔ **Manage your taxes.** Everybody with a big 401(k) or 403(b) plan will retire with a massive income-tax debt to the government. A life income annuity allows you to spread that tax liability evenly across your entire retirement. See Chapter 15.

The strength of an annuity's guarantee depends on the issuer's ability to pay you back. Every insurance company receives ratings for financial strength from the major rating agencies (A.M. Best, Fitch, Standard & Poor's, and Moody's Investors Services). *Note:* Do business only with carriers who have an all-A rating. (See Appendix A for more on these ratings.)

Note: To understand the functions of annuities better, you need to look at the types of annuities — and there are several. Please review the chapters in Part II to understand the types of annuities and what they can do for you.

The annuity purchase process

Like some other vital commodities (think air, gasoline, or even money itself), annuities are both ubiquitous and invisible. You don't smell, hear, or taste annuities, yet they're all around you. For example:

✔ Social Security benefits, pensions, and structured settlements of personal injury lawsuits are all annuities.

✔ Many state lottery jackpots are paid out as annuities.

✔ Thousands of university employees contribute part of their paychecks to group retirement annuities.

But the annuities in this list aren't the focus of this book. Instead, I focus on the individual annuities that people purchase from insurance companies or their designated representatives. Here's a rough description of the sales process:

You probably buy your annuity from a licensed insurance agent, broker, or financial adviser. Standing directly behind these intermediaries are brokerage firms (for brokers and financial advisers), marketing organizations (for independent insurance agents), or the insurance companies themselves (in the case of career insurance agents). ***Note:*** Insurance agents aren't licensed to sell variable annuities. (See Chapter 16 for more about this licensing.)

The transaction includes these steps:

1. You meet with the agent or broker to discuss your finances and choose a suitable product.

2. You complete an application and the agent or broker submits it to the contract issuer for approval.

3. After your application is approved, you send the contract issuer a check for the minimum amount (every carrier sets its own minimum initial premiums) or more.

4. The carrier sends you your contract.

   You have 10 to 30 days to reconsider your decision and send the contract back for a refund.

5. If you decide to keep the annuity, put the contract in a safe place. Shoeboxes, filing cabinets, desk drawers, and safe-deposit boxes are among the preferred destinations (but not necessarily in that order!).

Be sure to check out Chapter 16 for more on the sales process.

Important participants in the annuity food chain include:

✔ **Annuity issuers:** Only insurance companies issue annuities. Hundreds of issuers are out there, but the 25 largest firms — household names like The Hartford, MetLife, and Prudential — account for about 90 percent of all annuities sold each year.

Some insurers are publicly owned and some are mutually owned. The two types may have different cultures, attitudes, and slightly different products:

- Publicly owned firms are owned by their stockholders.

- Mutually owned firms are owned by their customers.

Look for a company whose view of risk and reward matches your own.

✔ **Annuity distributors:** Distributors serve as middlemen between the carriers and the producers (see the next bullet). In many cases, they employ or supervise the producer, making sure the producer complies with insurance and investment laws. Distributors include

- *Wirehouses* (Large, established full-service brokerages like Merrill Lynch and Morgan Stanley; so called because their ancestors were among the first to use the telegraph or "wire")

- Independent broker-dealers like Raymond James and LPL (Linsco/Private Ledger) Financial Services

- Banks like Bank of America and Wachovia that sell annuities through their branches

✔ **Annuity producers:** Years ago, most insurance companies employed an army of career agents to represent their products. Although carriers like AXA Equitable, New York Life, and others still employ these "captive" agents, many insurers now rely entirely on independent agents, brokers, and bank officers to sell their annuities.

These independents can recommend any annuity they want. In practice, they may steer you toward their list of preferred products or carriers. Be aware that a producer may earn a higher commission or a free trip to Cancun for selling certain products. Feel free to ask the producers about their rewards. See Chapter 19 for more questions you should ask.

✔ **Direct marketers:** Some (but not all) insurance companies sell no-load (that is, no sales commission) contracts directly to the public. If you're the self-reliant type and don't need an agent or broker to explain annuities to you, you can buy your annuity direct and save that added commission cost.

No-load mutual fund companies like Vanguard, Fidelity, and T. Rowe Price also sell no-load annuity contracts over the phone or Internet or by mail. Their contracts are issued by third-party insurance companies.

Relatively few people buy annuities direct. Most people need intermediaries to explain annuities and help them choose the right one. There's nothing wrong with that. But you can save big by cutting out the salesman.

Chapter 16 contains even more information on how to acquire annuities, so please flip to that chapter when you're ready to know more.

Getting your money out of an annuity

Putting money into an annuity is relatively easy. Getting money out is "sticky" — that is, more complicated.

Annuities are "sticky" for a reason. The benefits of fixed deferred annuities, variable annuities with guaranteed living benefits, and income annuities all depend on your agreement not to touch your money for a while. To discourage you from taking out your money until the "cake is baked," in a sense, insurance carriers and the government both charge fees or levy penalties on early withdrawals.

But insurance companies and the IRS aren't totally inflexible about withdrawals. For instance, you can withdraw 10 percent of most fixed annuities every year without a penalty. The newer income annuities allow emergency lump-sum withdrawals and provide for almost unlimited withdrawals to pay for nursing home care. You can tailor an income annuity so that, if you die before receiving at least as much as you paid for your annuity, your beneficiaries will recover the difference. For more details, see Chapter 13.

Understanding the dual nature of annuities

Think of annuities as the financial world's version of the platypus, the egg-laying mammal that's part duck, part beaver. They're neither pure investments nor pure insurance; instead, they have one foot in the investment world and one foot in the insurance world. I've also heard them compared to the Osprey — an aircraft that can hover like a helicopter and fly like a plane.

Ospreys don't hover as well as helicopters and don't fly as well as planes, but no other vehicle in the world does both. Similarly, annuities aren't the most lucrative investments and they don't insure you against every financial disaster. But, for the right candidate, they can offer an attractive blend of earnings and safety that few other readily available financial products can match.

Part investment, part insurance

An annuity is an *investment* because you give a sum of money to a financial institution with the hope that you'll get back more than you put in. Your investment — in this case, a *premium* — can range in size from $2,000 to over $2 million. The financial institution, usually an insurance company, puts your money in its general account (if you buy a fixed annuity) or in a separate account (if you buy a variable annuity).

An annuity is also *insurance* because a small portion of your premium buys a guarantee (the exact nature of the guarantee varies with the type of annuity). For example:

- In fixed annuity contracts, your guarantee is the rate of return for a certain number of years.
- In the latest variable annuity contracts, your guarantee is the locked rate of return.
- With an immediate annuity, the guarantee is your income.

Risk reduction versus risk taking

Annuities are all about trade-offs between risk and return. The guarantees reduce your risk of losing money, but the fee for the guarantee generally reduces the potential growth of your investment. **Note:** That's not always the case, but the principle holds true — lower risk brings lower returns.

If anybody tries to convince you that an annuity lowers your risk without curtailing your potential return, put your hand on your wallet and slowly back away. There are no free lunches.

Survivorship credits — the unique aspect of annuities

When you buy an annuity for lifetime income, you throw your money into a pool with money from thousands of other annuity owners your age. This is *mortality pooling;* Social Security and corporate pensions are based on the same principle.

With annuities, an insurance company puts the money into its own interest-bearing account or into a separate account where your money goes into subaccounts (mutual funds) that a professional fund manager oversees. All owners then take an annual income from that pool.

Each month (or quarter, if you prefer) you receive a payment consisting of three elements:

- A little bit of your principal
- A bit of the pool's investment growth
- A bit of the money left behind by fellow annuity owners who have died

This amount is your *survivorship credit* or *mortality credit.*

Of course, this income depends on (is "contingent upon," the lawyers might say) certain circumstances:

- If you die early, you may not receive as much as you put in.
- If you live exactly to your life expectancy, you get back exactly what you put in, with interest.
- If you live past your life expectancy, you get back much more than you put in.

True annuities serve two purposes: They guarantee you an income for life (or a specific number of years), and they maximize your income rate while you're alive.

Chapter 2

Using Annuities to Meet Retirement Challenges

In This Chapter

▶ Identifying the financial risks of retirement

▶ Coping with longevity, investment, and planning risk

▶ Understanding your role in retirement planning

For most baby boomers, retirement will be different from the way it was for previous generations. The disappearance of company pensions and the replacement of defined benefit plans by defined contribution plans will have a profound effect on the way the boomer generation copes with retirement. Sure, many people will still have pensions, but not nearly as many as before.

As a result, ordinary people in their 50s and 60s who know nothing about finance will need to deal pragmatically with sophisticated questions of longevity risk, investment risk, and planning risk that used to be the province of professional pension managers. It's a precarious situation.

To insure against those risks and convert their savings into do-it-yourself pensions, many boomers will turn to annuities. The annuities won't necessarily be cheap, and some people will need help understanding them. But the alternative — an epidemic of poverty among the very old — is unthinkable.

This chapter describes the most common financial risks that tend to vex people over age 55, and shows you which annuities can help you hedge against those risks. Sure, there are risks involved in purchasing an annuity. You could pick the wrong one, or you might overpay for it. But you're a boomer. You can wade through the risks, if you're well prepared.

Calculating Retirement Risks and Solutions

In 2006, the Society of Actuaries (the mathematicians who calculate insurance premiums) took a close look at the risks baby boomers would face in retirement. After identifying the risks, the actuaries estimated the extent of those risks and suggested financial products that offered protection against them. Table 2-1 shows the findings of their study.

Chances are you'll be vulnerable to at least three of the financial risks in this chart. (Health risks are financial risks, indirectly.) You can ignore those risks, self-insure against them by increasing your savings, or consider insuring yourself against them with one of the products described in the third column.

Table 2-1	Retirement Risks and Remedies	
Risk	*Potential Size of Risk*	*Products for Risk Transfer*
Outliving assets	At age 65, 30 percent of women and almost 20 percent of men can expect to reach age 90	* Immediate annuities (joint and survivor) * Deferred annuities that pay income starting at age 75 or later
Loss of spouse	Women may spend 15 years or more in widowhood, with a declining standard of living	* Joint and survivor life annuities that pay income as long as either spouse is living * Life insurance
Decline in function	Nursing-home costs may exceed $70,000 per year	* Long-term care (LTC) insurance * Annuity/ LTC hybrids
Healthcare and medical expenses	Medical costs not covered by Medicare can exceed $1 million per couple	Medical insurance
Inflation	From 1980 to 2005, annual inflation ranged from 1.1 to 8.9 percent, averaging 3.3 percent; medical costs rose 6.4 percent a year on average	Annuities with cost-of-living adjustments

Excerpted from The Society of Actuaries' "Key Findings and Issues: How Americans Understand and Manage their Retirement Risks" in its 2005 Risks and Process of Retirement Survey Report.

How can you minimize your risk of running out of money in retirement? Research shows that if you put one-fourth of your money in a fixed income annuity and keep the rest mainly in stocks, your risk will be much lower than if you buy no annuity and keep your money mainly in bonds.

Back in December 2001, two leaders in the field of retirement research, John Ameriks and Mark Warshawsky, along with Robert Veres, a journalist, published an article in the *Financial Planning Association Journal* that examined the risk of running out of money during retirement.

The researchers offered the hypothetical portfolios of two investors (I'll call them "Smith" and "Jones"):

- Smith put 20 percent of his money in stocks, 50 percent in bonds, and 30 percent in short-term liquid assets such as money market funds.

- Jones used 25 percent of his money to buy a fixed income annuity, and then put 64 percent in stocks and 11 percent in bonds.

In retirement, Smith and Jones started drawing their money at an inflation-adjusted rate of 4.5 percent a year. Then, in what's called a *Monte Carlo simulation,* the researchers ran the two portfolios through software that showed how they'd perform over 40 years and in thousands of hypothetical stock market scenarios.

The result? Jones was much better off. Both strategies kept a 65-year-old retiree safely afloat until age 85. But by age 90, Smith ran out of money in 25 percent of all possible outcomes. Jones ran out in only 2.2 percent of the outcomes.

By age 95, Smith ran out of money in 67 percent of the cases, but Jones ran out in only 5.4 percent. The apparent lesson: A portfolio that focuses on stocks and annuities is safer in retirement than a portfolio that focuses on bonds and cash.

Let me repeat: *stocks and annuities are safer than bonds and cash.* This assertion runs counter to conventional wisdom, which says that bonds are safer than stocks. But, in retirement, the returns from bonds may be too low to sustain you over the long term.

Annuities, by covering your basic expenses, allow you to invest the rest of your savings more aggressively. The result: more money for you to spend or bequeath. Suppose, for instance, that you and your spouse have $300,000 in savings, $34,000 in Social Security income, and household expenses in retirement of $50,000 a year.

If you spent $200,000 on a fixed-payout income annuity that paid $16,000 a year for life and then invested the rest of your savings in stocks, you'd have a secure income of $50,000 and $100,000 in stocks. On the other hand, if you put your $300,000 in bonds earning $15,000 a year in interest, you'd have an income of $49,000, no liquid assets and no significant chance for growth. You might feel richer for still having $300,000 in bonds, but you couldn't spend it without reducing your source of annual income.

In the rest of this chapter, I discuss the three main types of risks in retirement, along with suggestions for the types of annuities that might help control those risks.

Countering the Main Risks of Retirement

A number of surveys have tried to measure how well Americans are prepared for retirement, how well they understand the risks they face, and how anxious they are about the future.

Generally, the surveys have shown these results: Most people are not well prepared for retirement; they underestimate some risks and overestimate others; and they're unaware of a few of the most important risks.

The most common retirement risks tend to fall into three main areas:

- **Longevity risks:** The hazards of aging
- **Investment risks:** The uncertainty of the financial markets
- **Planning risks:** The chance that people will make mistakes with their money

In the following sections, I first talk about each type of risk. Then I explain how specific annuities can reduce those risks and provide greater peace of mind in retirement.

Longevity risks

"You can be young and poor but you can't be old and poor, and that's the truth," wrote Tennessee Williams in *A Glass Menagerie*. Everyone faces the risk of living long enough to run out of savings. Public annuities (Social Security), group annuities (traditional pensions), and individual annuities are the only investment products that can relieve you of that risk.

Outliving your savings

When you're young, you worry about dying young — if you think about mortality at all. But when you're older, you face the risk of living too long and running out of your savings; technically, this is *longevity risk*. Most Americans aren't aware of these statistics:

- ✔ At age 65, men have a 50-percent chance of living past age 81.
- ✔ At age 65, women have a 50-percent chance of living past age 84.

The World-War-II generation relied on a combination of Social Security and company or government pensions to provide a guaranteed lifelong income. In contrast, most baby boomers have only one source of guaranteed lifelong income (Social Security), and they're generally living longer than their parents. End result? Boomers are more likely to run out of money before they die.

Losing a spouse

As married couples get older, they inevitably worry about the spouse who outlives the other. The surviving spouse loses a guide and a caregiver. In addition, for two-income couples, the death of one spouse can mean a decline in Social Security benefits. Similarly, if the recipient of a corporate or government pension dies, the surviving spouse may stop receiving benefits.

Most surviving spouses are women. Women live an average of two years longer than men, and 46 percent of women over age 65 are widows. In contrast, only 14 percent of men over 65 are widowers, according to LIMRA International, the life insurance research organization. As the last to die, women are much more likely to run out of money in old age than men.

Requiring long-term care

Today's retirees know that if they live long enough, they'll probably need nursing-home care. According to the Society of Actuaries, about 60 percent of pre-retirees and 50 percent of retirees worry that they won't be able to afford the care they need. Even if they do have substantial savings, they face the risk that nursing-home costs will eat up the resources they'd prefer to leave to their children.

Good nursing-home care costs as much as $150 to $200 a day today, and it may cost much more in the future. One solution is to buy long-term care (LTC) insurance, but it can be prohibitively expensive. So far, the insurance industry has not come up with a truly affordable solution. Regardless of whether people buy LTC or reserve part of their savings for future care, the mere possibility of nursing-home expenses will affect their finances throughout retirement.

Using annuities to insure against longevity risk

Annuities are the *only* financial product that can provide you with guaranteed lifetime income and insure against the risk of outliving your money. In fact, several types of annuities can help you turn a limited amount of savings into an income that never stops. Check out these four examples:

- ✔ **Variable deferred annuities with living benefits:** This annuity is a vehicle for tax-deferred investing that has been around for about half a century (see Chapter 8). But in the past few years, insurance companies have reinvented it as a way to provide one person or a married couple with *living benefits* that include guaranteed lifelong income for one or both of them.

  Some products allow you to invest, say, $200,000 at age 55; they guarantee that, if you don't touch the money for ten years, you'll receive at least $20,000 a year for life — with the option to dip into your savings for large purchases or nursing-home expenses. You can arrange for the income to last until you die or, for a higher fee, until both you and your spouse have died.

- ✔ **Fixed and variable immediate annuities:** Immediate annuities provide guaranteed income for life — either for a specific period or for as long as both spouses are alive (see Chapter 8).

  Note: Immediate annuities provide more income than deferred variable annuities with living benefits because you receive income from three sources: your investment in the annuity, the earnings on your investment, and the *survivorship credits* you receive by outliving other annuity owners.

  A *fixed* immediate annuity pays a preset monthly income every month for life, or for two lives, or for a specific period.

  A *variable* immediate annuity also pays a monthly income, but the payments fluctuate with the market value of the underlying investments (think of these as clones of mutual funds).

- ✔ **Annuity and long-term care insurance combinations:** A number of companies now guarantee you an income for life or nursing-home coverage for a specific number of years in return for your lump sum investment. Essentially, they're high-deductible LTC insurance; the deductible is paid by the money in the annuity. (Chapter 15 has more info on this combo.)

  For years, the different tax treatments of annuity income and nursing-home benefits delayed the development of these products. (The income is taxable; the benefits aren't.) But the Pension Protection Act of 2006 cleared that obstacle away. Genworth Financial, Lincoln Financial, and several other insurance companies now offer LTC/annuity hybrids.

- ✔ **Advanced-life deferred annuities:** Also called *longevity insurance,* this annuity pays you an income only if you live beyond a specific advanced age such as age 80 or 85. It's the cheapest way to ensure that you'll always have an income. (See Chapter 10 for more on these annuities.)

Investment risks

Every investor experiences *investment risk*, the volatility of the financial markets. When you're young, you can laugh off the ups and downs of the market because, over the long run, the market has always risen. When you're older, however, time is no longer on your side. You're more vulnerable.

The risk of a market crash

Americans became reacquainted with the risks of investing in equities in early 2000, when the Internet bubble of the late 1990s collapsed and stocks averaged a one-third loss of value. Before 2000, people thought the market would gain 25 percent a year forever.

Retirees used to play it safe by putting their money in bonds or bond funds. But today's soon-to-be retirees are often advised that they'll run out of money if they don't invest in stocks. The downside? When you rely on stock investments for retirement income, you experience *market risk*. That's not a bad thing — risk is the source of returns. But it's a factor that must be considered and controlled.

Sequence of returns risk

Here's a risk you may not be aware of and may not want to know about: *timing risk* or *sequence-of-returns risk*. To a great extent, the ability of your savings to last until you die depends on *when* you decide to retire. For example:

- ✔ A person who retired in 1970 (a prosperous year in itself) was headed for trouble. His stock investments were reduced to pocket change by the 1974 to 1975 recession.
- ✔ An investor who retired in 1980 (a dismal year economically) rode the 1982 to 1999 bull market to financial glory.

The five years immediately before and after you retire are the most vulnerable years for your savings. A serious bear market during that time can put you in a financial hole that you don't have time to earn your way out of. One insurance company calls this period the *retirement red zone.*

Consider, for instance, someone who retired in August 2000 with $200,000 in shares of Vanguard 500 Index Fund, whose price follows the performance of the stocks of the 500 largest U.S. companies. From September 2000 to September 2002, the share price of that fund fell from $140 to $75, reducing a $200,000 investment to a $107,000 investment.

It wouldn't have been so terrible had the retiree not needed that investment for living expenses, because the price of 500 Index shares eventually recovered. But the retiree was forced to sell many of his shares while they were losing or had lost value. A combination of forced withdrawals plus declining values can devastate a retiree's resources.

Inflation risk

Over the past 25 years, the Consumer Price Index has doubled. To put it in another way, the cost of living today is twice what it was in 1982. During your retirement, inflation will shrink your income, in real terms, by about 3 percent each year. Unless you plan to reduce your standard of living, you'll have to find a way to replace your lost buying power.

Insuring against investment risks with annuities

Annuities can insure you against the threat of market risk and sequence-of-returns risk. You can also purchase annuity riders that reduce or eliminate inflation risk. Here's how:

✔ **Fixed deferred annuities:** Suppose you're 55 years old and lie awake at night worrying that your life savings of $250,000 (invested mainly in stocks) may be cut in half by a bear market. A fixed deferred annuity can help you get the sleep you need.

At today's rates, you can park your money in a 10-year fixed annuity that pays 5 percent. At age 65, you can be certain (assuming you bought your contract from a rock-solid insurer) that you'll have about $407,000 ($250,000 grown at a compounded rate of 5 percent for 10 years) waiting for you.

✔ **Variable deferred annuities:** The latest variable deferred annuities offer living benefits that insure you against both market risk and sequence-of-returns risk. Depending on the contract, you can purchase options that guarantee the following:

- The safety of your principal

- A minimum return

- A minimum amount of annual withdrawals

- A minimum annual payout for life

- Annual payouts that keep pace with inflation

If the market tanks, you exercise the option. If your investments do well, you at least purchased peace of mind. (See Chapter 8 for details.)

✔ **Fixed immediate annuities:** To insulate yourself from worry about the stock market, you can buy a fixed immediate annuity that pays you (or you and your spouse) the same amount every month for life.

In 2007, a 65-year-old man could receive about $710 a month in guaranteed lifetime income for every $100,000 he put in a fixed annuity. (A joint and survivor life annuity for a husband and wife, both age 65, would pay about $615 a month.) Some single premium immediate annuities (SPIA) offer annual payment increases to offset inflation.

Planning risk

Over the next 20 years or so, millions of baby boomers will retire with trillions of dollars in savings, but they may have no idea how to reinvest it, ration it over time, or protect it from taxes.

A person's inexperience, in itself, poses a more serious threat to his financial security than any real or imagined market crash. Many people will have to rely on their broker, adviser, or insurance agent for advice — but that advice won't be free. The sooner you start preparing for retirement — and you should start no later than five years before you stop working — the better off you'll be.

Having no income plan

Few employer-sponsored retirement plans offer advice or options for converting savings into retirement income. Many people will leave their plans with a lot of money but no strategy for investing it, protecting it from taxes, or spending it. Without a strategy, an employee may withdraw her money in one lump sum, fail to roll it into an IRA, *and* lose 25 percent of it to taxes in the first year. Obviously, the absence of an income plan raises the risk of running out of savings during retirement.

Overspending

A vast amount of research shows that if you spend more than 4 to 5 percent of your savings every year during retirement, you run a pretty high risk of running out of money. But 5 percent of, say, $300,000 (which is more than most boomers will retire on) is only $15,000. The temptation will be great to spend at a much higher rate, especially during the first years, when you're healthy and eager to travel.

Under-spending

Conversely, many people run the risk of spending too little of their savings out of fear that they may live to age 100, as did my grandmother, Rose (Mayer) Pechter! By rationing too conservatively, people deprive themselves of pleasures that, in retrospect, they could have afforded. Some behavioral economists believe that baby boomers are so conditioned to save that they'll be reluctant to spend during retirement.

The risk of a bequest

The desire to leave money to children can lead to inefficient retirement income planning. Parents may not be sure how much they can spend without eating into the money they hope to leave to their children or grandchildren. As a result, the parents risk overspending or under-spending.

For baby boomers, an unprecedented challenge

Every generation experiences retirement differently. When I was growing up, it wasn't unusual to see elderly grandparents living with their children and grandchildren.

One friend's uncle, a World War II veteran with polio who carved wooden warships for us, lived with my friend for years. Throughout high school, another friend shared a small bedroom with his widowed grandfather. A third friend's dying grandmother spent her last months not in a nursing home but in a spare bedroom in his home.

The next generation — the post-World-War-II generation — seemed to fare better financially. In the middle-class neighborhood of tidy brick-and-frame row homes where my wife and I first lived, most of our neighbors were elderly couples who, thanks to Social Security and pensions from careers of labor in the local mills and factories, could afford to live on their own in retirement.

For the 77 million baby boomers, retirement will be a new adventure. Between 1983 and 2007, the number of defined benefit plans (traditional pensions) in the United States fell from 175,000 to only 25,000. As a result few boomers will have pensions to supplement Social Security; they'll only have the money they saved in tax-deferred 401(k) and 403(b) plans.

The challenge for those who are pension-less — including those who have ample savings — will be to convert those savings into do-it-yourself pensions. Annuities can help them do it.

Insuring against planning risk with annuities

Annuities are a tool for converting your retirement into the pension you wish you had. They're designed to relieve the risk of overspending and under-spending.

- ✔ **Variable deferred annuities:** As Chapter 7 explains, today's variable deferred annuities offer a variety of structured ways to withdraw your money from savings during retirement.

  With one interesting option, you can decide to receive 5 percent of your savings every year for life at age 65, 6 percent at age 70, or 7 percent at age 75. When you die, your children will receive the remaining funds in your account.

- ✔ **Fixed and variable immediate annuities:** Immediate annuities can make your retirement decisions very simple:

  1. You decide how much income you'll need in addition to Social Security during retirement.

  2. You calculate the premium cost of an annuity that generates that much income.

  3. You subtract the cost of the premium from your total savings, give half of the remainder to your kids — today, not when you die — and keep the rest for your own whims and emergencies.

Chapter 3

Dissecting an Annuity

Zvi Bodie, the esteemed professor of finance at Boston University, once noted that most people are no more curious about the way financial products work than they are about the way their DVD players work. "People just want the gizmo to do what it's supposed to do," he said, and "not sit there blinking at them."

It's true. There's no reason for you to take an academic interest in annuities. But an annuity is a more serious purchase than a DVD player — especially if you intend to rely on it for your monthly income when you're 70 or 80 years old. You need to understand them well enough to know if an agent or broker is, as Sky Masterson put it in *Guys and Dolls*, "squirting cider in your ear."

This chapter is intended to demystify annuities a bit. I start with general concepts and then examine the distinctions among various types of annuity contracts. In the last section, I discuss the most complicated *and* popular product — the deferred variable annuity. After you read this chapter, no broker will be able to snow you.

Examining the Elements of Annuities

Whether they're fixed or variable, immediate or deferred, all annuity contracts share the same basic DNA. In this section, I acquaint you with the components that you'll find in every annuity you come across.

Getting to know the participants

Every annuity has an owner, an annuitant, beneficiaries, and an issuer.

The owner

The owner of an annuity is just that — the owner. This person

- ✔ Pays the premiums
- ✔ Signs the application
- ✔ Agrees to abide by the terms of the contract
- ✔ Decides who the other parties of the contract will be
- ✔ Can withdraw money or even sell the annuity (depending on the type of contract or the stage it's in)
- ✔ Is liable for any taxes that are due

Two people can own an annuity contract jointly. The owner should be a person, but it can also be a trust that represents the interest of a person. If one owner dies, the joint owner, like a copilot, takes the helm. A corporation can't own an annuity.

Depending on the contract, the owner may be able to change the *annuitant* (see the following section) after buying the annuity. The owner can pass ownership over to someone else, but a taxable event (where the owner ponies up the income taxes on the contract's gains) may result. That is, the owner may have to pony up the income taxes on the contract's gains.

The annuitant

The annuitant is the person on whose life expectancy the annuity payments will be calculated. If and when the owner decides to start taking a guaranteed lifetime income from the annuity, the size of the (typically monthly) annuity payments are based on the annuitant's age and life expectancy — not the owner's.

For instance, if the owner is 68 years old but the annuitant is his 65-year-old wife, then the insurance company will assume that it will make monthly payments to her for about 19 years, which is the life expectancy of a 65-year-old woman. (Keep in mind, however, that insurance companies may base annuity payments on the life expectancies of annuity purchasers, who tend to live longer than average.)

In most annuity contracts, however, the owner and the annuitant are the same person. In fact, if they are not the same person, and one of them dies, trouble can result. This leads us into the complicated area of annuity "structure," which I cover in detail in Chapter 11.

The beneficiaries

A *beneficiary* is the person designated to receive assets upon someone else's death. When filling out an annuity contract application, the owner names his own beneficiary and also the annuitant's beneficiary. The owner and the annuitant can be each other's beneficiary (which simplifies matters); no one can be his or her own beneficiary. Chapter 11 contains a complete discussion of the rights and responsibilities of beneficiaries.

The issuer

The insurance company that issues the contract and puts itself on the hook for any guarantees in the contract is the *issuer*. **Note:** I use *issuer* and *carrier* a lot in this book because both words are briefer than *insurance company*. All three have the same meaning.

Always look for an issuer that's rated *Excellent, Superior,* or *Very Good* by the ratings agencies, such as A.M. Best and Fitch. A high rating suggests — but doesn't guarantee — that the issuer will fulfill its promises and that you'll get your money back.

Common elements of all (or most) annuities

All annuities have a free-look period, a death benefit, guarantees, and annuitization options. Most of them also have surrender periods. Deferred variable annuities have accumulated unit values (AUVs). In the next few sections, I give you the basic information you need on all these elements.

Free-look period

When you buy an annuity, you have between 10 and 30 days to cancel the contract after you receive it in the mail. This *free-look period* gives you (or someone who has your best interests at heart) a final chance to opt out of the purchase. The period is especially useful for frail senior citizens who have been pressured into buying a contract.

Some immediate annuity contracts let you cancel your contract within the first six months, and some fixed annuity contracts let you opt out during a brief window at the beginning of each contract year. For more information, see Chapter 6.

Death benefit

If the owner of the contract dies (or, in some contracts, if the annuitant dies), his or her beneficiary receives a "death benefit." Depending on which death benefit option the owner chose when he bought the contract, the death benefit may be equal to:

- ✔ The value of the investments in the contract when the owner or annuitant dies.
- ✔ The amount of the original investment, if it's higher than the value of the investments when the owner or annuitant dies.

> ✔ The highest value of the contract on any contract anniversary, if it is higher than the original investment or the value of the investments when the owner or annuitant dies.

If the owner of an annuitant-driven contract dies, his or her beneficiary receives the current value of the contract, not the death benefit. Similarly, if the annuitant of an owner-driven contract dies, his or her beneficiary receives the current value of the contract.

Insurance companies measure time by *contract anniversary* years, not by calendar years. So, if you buy your contract on June 17, that's your contract anniversary. The date is important because some contracts sell an option to mark the account value up to its peak value on a contract anniversary. This distinction explains why contracts purchased only a few months — or even a few days — apart can have significantly different values as the years pass.

Surrender periods

Most, but not all, annuities have *surrender periods*, a span of time when the issuer may levy a contingent deferred sales charge (CDSC) if the owner withdraws too much money too soon.

CDSCs are a necessary evil to discourage withdrawals. If investors could cancel their contract at any time, the carrier would lose the commission money it paid to the agent or broker before it could earn the money back by deducting the annual mortality and expense risk (M&E) fee from the contract.

All deferred fixed annuities have CDSCs; so do most deferred variable annuities that are purchased from agents or brokers. If you bought from a salesperson (rather than directly from a carrier or a mutual fund company) and that salesperson earned a commission, your contract has a CDSC.

Surrender periods are not the impenetrable firewalls between you and your money that the popular press makes them out to be. There is generally no surrender charge on:

> ✔ Withdrawals of 10 percent or less of a deferred annuity's value every year
>
> ✔ Withdrawals taken to satisfy your required minimum distribution (RMD). These are the withdrawals Uncle Sam requires you to take from your tax-deductible retirement accounts, such as traditional IRAs and employer-sponsored retirement plans, after you reach age 70½. (See Chapter 10 for more on RMDs.)
>
> ✔ Withdrawals taken to pay for nursing-home care

Annuitization options

To *annuitize* a deferred annuity means to convert the value of the investments in the contract to a guaranteed income stream for

- ✔ A specific number of years
- ✔ The rest of your life
- ✔ As long as you or your spouse is living

Just as nature designed women to bear children but not all women do, all deferred annuities are designed for eventual annuitization but not all owners do. In fact, more than *90 percent* of deferred annuity owners do not annuitize. Many deferred annuity owners don't even know that they have the option to annuitize.

People who *do* want income from an annuity typically buy an *immediate* annuity (see the later section "Immediate annuities"). To continue the birth metaphor, buying an immediate annuity is a bit like adopting an infant instead of going through a pregnancy.

Even those people who already own a deferred annuity usually exchange their deferred annuity for an immediate annuity rather than annuitize their deferred annuity. Why? Because, by shopping around among carriers that offer immediate annuities, they can usually get higher monthly payments than the issuer of their deferred annuity offered.

Confusing, isn't it? (You may want to read the preceding two paragraphs more than once!) For a full discussion of annuity income options — including the length of payments, recipients of payments, and places the premium is invested during the payment period — see Chapter 8.

Guarantees

All annuities offer guarantees. That's why people buy them. An annuity will offer one or more of the following:

- ✔ A guaranteed rate of return on an investment
- ✔ A guarantee against loss of principal
- ✔ A guarantee that, if the owner dies during a bear market, his beneficiary will be protected from financial loss
- ✔ A guaranteed income in retirement

Because of their guarantees, annuities are more accurately called contracts than investments.

Telling One Annuity from Another

In the beginning, there was just one kind of annuity contract, with two stages. In the first stage — the accumulation stage — you contributed to the contract, as you would to a bank account. In the second stage — the income stage — you converted your contributions savings to a monthly income in retirement.

In practice, this holistic ancestral annuity evolved into two specialized sub-types:

- Deferred annuities, which were contracts that stayed in the accumulation stage indefinitely, with the assets growing tax-deferred

- Immediate annuities, which were contracts that skipped the accumulation stage and started paying out income shortly after the owner made a large, lump-sum investment

Annuity evolution didn't stop there. Depending on the type of deferred annuity you bought, your money could *accumulate* at

- A fixed rate (if the money was invested in an insurance company's bonds)

- A variable rate (if it was invested in mutual funds, called subaccounts)

- An indexed rate (if returns were linked to a market index)

If you bought an immediate annuity, on the other hand, the level of monthly *income* could be

- Fixed (if the money was invested in the insurance company's bonds)

- Variable (if the money was invested in subaccounts)

Over the years, certain types of annuities have become more popular than others. Today, for a variety of reasons, deferred variable annuities are by far the most popular, with Americans holding more than $1 trillion in them. Deferred fixed annuities are next in popularity.

As for immediate annuities, Americans buy only a few billion dollars worth of them each year, but that's expected to change as baby boomers look for ways to convert their savings to guaranteed retirement income.

Deferred annuities

As mentioned previously in this chapter, a deferred annuity is a tax-deferred investment or savings vehicle that stays in the accumulation stage, and will only rarely be converted to income through annuitization. There are three major types of deferred annuities, *variable, fixed, and indexed:*

✔ A deferred *variable* annuity pays the owner whatever the return happens to be on her underlying investments in subaccounts (which are similar to mutual funds).

✔ By contrast, a deferred *fixed* annuity pays the owner a guaranteed rate of return for a specific period of time. The rate may be guaranteed for as little as one year or as long as ten years.

✔ Another type of fixed deferred annuity — an *indexed* annuity — works very differently. It pays one of two rates, depending on which is higher: a minimum guaranteed rate or a rate that's tied to the performance of a stock market index.

Immediate annuities

In contrast to deferred annuities, an immediate annuity (also called an *income* or *single premium immediate annuity* or *SPIA*) is purchased with the intent to turn it into income within a year. The purchase of an immediate annuity is irrevocable. There are two main types, variable and fixed:

✔ With an immediate *variable* annuity — in my opinion, a product that hasn't gotten the attention it deserves — your income fluctuates along with the value of your subaccounts (stocks, bonds, cash, or fixed rate). You can manage your money in these subaccounts, but you can't withdraw lump sums.

✔ On the other hand, a *fixed* immediate annuity pays you a fixed amount during retirement. You can opt to have your payments inflation-adjusted by *front-loading* them (they start lower and end higher than payments that aren't inflation-adjusted). Other than that option, you don't manage your money at all.

Note: Under many contracts, you can have it both ways. In a *combination* annuity, part of your money is in the fixed account and part is in the subaccounts.

Other subgroups of annuities

Each of the types of annuities I describe in the previous sections can be further categorized, depending on the number of payments used to buy them and the tax status of the premium. In addition, they may be purchased on a group basis or individually.

Single versus flexible premium

You purchase a *single premium deferred or immediate annuity* with one big payment that can range from as little as $2,000 to $1 million or more. In contrast, a *flexible premium* contract lets you make ongoing contributions, just as you make contributions to your employer-sponsored plan.

Qualified versus nonqualified

An individual *qualified* annuity is a contract that you purchase with the savings in your tax-deductible IRA or employer-sponsored retirement plan. A qualified annuity may also be part of an employer-sponsored retirement plan, and you can buy it with direct, tax-deductible contributions to the plan. A *nonqualified* annuity is purchased with savings that you *have* paid income taxes on.

The differences between these two types of annuities are significant:

- ✔ **With a qualified annuity,** at age 70½, you must take out RMDs (which equal the value of your account divided by your life expectancy). All of your withdrawals become part of your taxable income the year that you withdraw them. (See the earlier section, "Surrender periods," in this chapter for more on RMDs.)

- ✔ **With a nonqualified annuity,** you do not have to take RMDs; you only owe income tax on a portion of your withdrawals. (See Chapter 14 for more information.)

Individual versus group annuities

Just as there are individual and group health insurance plans, there are also individual and group annuities. Note these differences between the two types:

- ✔ Anyone can buy an individual annuity, either direct from an insurance company or through a bank, brokerage, or insurance agency. You can use qualified or nonqualified money to buy an annuity, although the rules may be different.

- ✔ Generally, you can't buy a group annuity unless the retirement plan sponsored by your employer or professional organization offers one. Contributions to an employer-sponsored group annuity will be tax-deductible. Some employers now offer annuities within their retirement plans. Some plans allow participants to buy a little bit of guaranteed lifetime income (like $10 every month starting at age 65) with every contribution.

Annuity fees

Because of their insurance features, annuities generally entail higher costs than conventional investments, which lack insurance features. The costs of fixed deferred and fixed immediate annuities are usually incorporated into the guaranteed payout or "quote" that the insurance carrier offers you when you buy one of them. They are never stated separately. But the costs of any variable annuity are specified in the prospectus.

A fixed annuity's fees are included in the *quote* — the interest rate a deferred annuity pays or the monthly payment of an income annuity.

Variable annuity costs are often regarded as outrageous. So why do people buy them? Back in the 1990s, Americans poured hundreds of billions of dollars into variable annuities because stocks were rising and because variable annuities offered a chance to defer taxes on investment gains. The flow of new money into variable annuities has cooled since then. But the enhancement of variable annuities with lifetime withdrawal benefits has sparked new interest in these products, despite their costs. (See Chapter 7 for a more detailed discussion of all aspects of variable annuities.)

The following bullets pertain to the fees of *deferred* variable annuities. *Immediate* variable annuities charge some of the same fees, but very few immediate annuities are sold each year. (All these fees are deducted in tiny amounts every day from the value of your contract.) The data excludes surrender charges because you don't pay them unless you exceed the annual withdrawal limit. ***Note:*** The fees below are listed in the order in which you are likely to encounter them when reading the annuity prospectus.

✔ **Mortality and expense risk fee:** This is the largest fee of your annuity contract. It ranges from 0.20 to about 1.75 percent a year ($20 to $175 per $10,000 in premium).

   On the surface, this fee pays the carrier for taking the risk that you and your fellow annuity owners will live longer than expected or that the carrier's expenses will increase dramatically. But, as far as I can tell, the M&E charge actually reimburses the carrier for the distribution costs — the commission to the seller and the wholesaler or broker-dealer.

✔ **Administration charge or contract maintenance fee:** This fee may be a dollar amount (like $25 a year) or an expense ratio (like 0.15 percent, which amounts to $15 for every $10,000 invested).

✔ **Investment management fees:** These fees vary. For example, they can be

   • As low as 0.10 percent per year for an investment in an index fund or exchange-traded fund.

   • As high as 2 percent for a subaccount that's actively managed by a fund manager (as opposed to a computer).

   • As high as 5 percent for extremely risky subaccounts that try to multiply gains by investing borrowed money (the cause of most market crashes).

✔ **Rider/option fees:** Today's most popular deferred-variable-annuity options are guaranteed living benefits. They cost 0.25 percent to 0.60 percent for a single person and as much as 0.80 percent for a married couple.

The death benefit can range from no charge to 0.60 percent and may be higher for older contract owners. The more generous the death benefit — for instance, one that gives your heirs the highest value your account ever achieved — the more it costs.

✔ **12b-1 fees:** These fees are levied on existing investors in a mutual fund (or a variable annuity subaccount) but pay the fund's costs of marketing to new investors. Mutual fund companies won the right to levy these expenses about 30 years ago, when the industry was too broke to promote itself. The slump is over but the fees remain, costing their investors billions of dollars a year.

Fortunately, many variable annuity contracts have subaccounts that don't charge 12b-1 fees. Check the prospectus to find out.

✔ **Other fees:** Sometimes subaccount managers farm out their tasks to other fund managers. (This is frequently the case when the subaccount is a *fund of funds* — that is, a mutual fund consisting of other mutual funds.) The costs of hiring those other managers may be passed along to you in the form of *other fees* and can be as high as 0.35 percent per year.

The Life Cycle of All Annuities

Technically, every annuity has two phases: *accumulation* and *income*. During the accumulation phase, you put money in the account (paying all at one time or making a series of payments), and it grows tax-deferred. During retirement, you initiate the income stage by converting it to an irrevocable income stream.

In practice, as I mention earlier in this chapter, it usually doesn't work that way. Most people who buy deferred annuities never formally convert them to income; they just take withdrawals during retirement. And a handful of people buy immediate annuities after age 59½ and start receiving income right away.

The *purchase stage* I describe below isn't an official contract stage. I've added it to the beginning of the cycle to articulate the initial steps in acquiring an annuity.

1. **The purchase stage** (typically starting at age 45 or so):

   • Meet with a trusted agent/broker/adviser to explain your needs; give her time to research the annuity products available in your state.

   • Study the various prospectuses or brochures your broker obtains from the wholesaler, broker-dealer, or carrier; choose the best product.

Where do your expense dollars go?

Insurance companies use your fees to pay their bills and to generate profits for their shareholders if the company is publicly held. Here's where some of your expense dollars go:

- **Compliance:** Insurance is a highly regulated industry. It is overseen by state and federal watchdogs that require a constant stream of reporting to demonstrate that the company is compliant with the law.

- **Customer service:** Any large financial service company employs thousands of people who work at computer terminals, answer telephones, respond to policyholder questions and complaints, resolve problems, and execute routine transactions.

- **Financial reporting:** If the insurer is publicly owned, it must continuously report its financial activities to its shareholders and to the Securities and Exchange Commission.

- **Information systems:** Insurance companies have terabytes of policy information that have to be stored and managed by mainframe computers and computer networks.

- **Marketing:** The carrier may buy millions of dollars worth of advertising on television and the radio and in magazines and newspapers each year.

- **Research and development:** The biggest insurance companies employ squads of actuaries and product developers to invent new kinds of annuities and other insurance products.

- **Risk management:** To protect themselves from market volatility, annuity issuers employ sophisticated hedging strategies that involve the continuous buying and selling of options.

- **Training:** Because the world is constantly changing, financial services companies continually retrain their employees to use new types of technology, represent new types of products, or employ new ways to market to the public.

- **Wholesaling:** Besides paying commissions to those who sell their contracts (independent agents, brokers, and financial advisers), insurers must maintain small armies of wholesalers to promote their products to their frontline sales force.

- Fill out the contract application; if it's a deferred variable annuity, choose the subaccounts (mutual funds), riders (options), and services you want.

- Wait while your application is submitted to the insurance company for approval.

- Sign the approved application and provide a check for the purchase premium.

2. **The accumulation stage** (lasting from purchase until after age 59½):

- Manage your subaccounts. If it's a deferred variable annuity, make periodic contributions; if it's a fixed annuity, wait until the term ends and, if you want, roll it into a new contract.

- Take withdrawals if necessary, knowing that withdrawals may be subject to a surrender charge, income tax, and a 10-percent federal penalty tax if you are under age 59½.

- If you purchased a "guaranteed accumulation benefit," watch to see whether your account value surpasses or falls short of it. If your account balance falls short, you can exercise your option to take the guaranteed amount.

3. **The income or distribution stage** (starts at age 59½ and lasts indefinitely). Do only one of the following:

   - Take withdrawals from your contract as needed without converting the assets to a guaranteed irrevocable income stream.

   - Exercise your guaranteed withdrawal benefit, if you purchased one, to receive a guaranteed income for life while maintaining access to your money.

   - Convert your annuity assets to a fixed or variable guaranteed income stream for one of the following: life; either of two lives; or a certain period.

   - Transfer the assets of your deferred fixed or variable annuity to an immediate income annuity and receive guaranteed income for one of the following: life; either of two lives; or a certain period.

Chapter 4

Weighing the Pros and Cons of Annuities

*B*efore you buy an annuity, you should consider all of their advantages and disadvantages. Distinguishing between an annuity's pros and cons isn't always easy, however, because in many cases the pros *are* the cons, and vice versa.

To complicate matters, different annuities — deferred and immediate, variable and fixed — have different pluses and minuses. Ironically, the best feature that annuities offer — the survivorship credit — is the aspect that's most commonly neglected.

But don't lose sight of the bigger picture. Annuities are effective tools for achieving a financially secure retirement. The question is whether, in your situation, they can deliver that benefit more conveniently and efficiently than competing tools.

Annuities don't exist in a vacuum. You always have to compare them to alternative or competing products, and you have to factor in your own needs and preferences. Even when annuities are good, they may or may not be right for you.

Such disclaimers aside, my goal for this chapter is simply to identify the pros and cons of annuities in general and of specific types of annuities in particular. I also show you how annuities measure up against their closest competitors. (For further details about each type of annuity, see Part II.)

By the end of this chapter you'll know why people buy annuities (to take advantage of tax deferral and lock in guaranteed returns or income) and why they don't (to avoid the fees, complexity, and, in some cases, barriers to using their own money). After you read this chapter and Chapter 5, I think you'll know whether an annuity is right for you.

Evaluating Annuity Pluses

Annuities offer two types of benefits: tax-related and investment-related. To put it another way, annuities generally fall into either of two categories — deferred and immediate — and each has its own benefits. Deferred annuities help you save for retirement by letting you defer taxes on your gains and by reducing your investment risk. Immediate annuities help you squeeze the most retirement income out of your savings.

For an overview of the different types of annuities, please see Chapter 3.

Assuring income after age 59½

Annuities are the only financial product that you can use to convert savings to guaranteed lifetime income. You can use different types of annuities to accomplish this. You can

- Contribute regularly throughout your life to a deferred fixed or variable annuity and invest your contributions wisely; then reverse the stream and convert your savings to a guaranteed fixed or variable (fluctuating) retirement income.

- Take money from another source (for example, the sale of conventional investments, the sale of a business, the savings in a rollover IRA), plop it into a new fixed or variable income annuity (also called an *immediate* annuity), and start drawing your fixed or variable retirement income from it within a year.

- Contribute money (gradually or all at once) to a deferred variable annuity with a guaranteed lifetime withdrawal benefit (GLWB); this entitles you to lifelong income that's usually a percentage of your account value or a specific guaranteed minimum account value.

- Buy bits of retirement income with a portion of your biweekly tax-deductible contributions to your employer-sponsored retirement plan.

    For instance, a small but growing number of plans allow participants to purchase, say, $10 a month in future income with each contribution (just as workers build up Social Security income with payroll tax deductions).

- Purchase *longevity* insurance (advanced life deferred annuities — ALDAs). This relatively inexpensive annuity pays you a guaranteed life-time income only if you live past a specific age, such as 80.

Key benefits of deferred annuities

Deferred annuities come in two basic flavors: variable and fixed. A person in a high tax bracket can use a deferred variable annuity to invest in stock mutual funds without worrying about paying taxes on his or her investment gains until many years later. People usually invest in deferred fixed annuities to get a guaranteed rate of return.

Tax deferral

When you buy a deferred annuity, you can let the money grow without paying taxes on the interest until years later — ordinarily after age 59½. The IRS allows this tax deferral in order to encourage you to save for retirement.

Assuming that your tax rate during retirement will be lower than your tax rate while you're still working, you ultimately pay less in taxes by deferring them. Calculations show that you'll have more money in a tax-deferred account after 20 or 30 years (even after adjusting for the income taxes you must eventually pay) than in a taxable mutual fund account, where you pay taxes each year on the capital gains, interest, and dividends.

Even though you can't deduct contributions to a deferred annuity from your taxable income the way you deduct them with a traditional IRA or employer-sponsored retirement account, annuities offer other advantages. For instance, you don't have to start taking money out of a deferred annuity at age 70½ as you do with deductible accounts. This feature gives the money even longer to grow tax-deferred.

Before buying a deferred annuity, contribute as much as you can to your tax-deductible retirement savings accounts, such as traditional IRAs or employer-sponsored retirement plans.

Factors that make tax deferral more effective include the following:

- ✔ Large contributions
- ✔ High income tax bracket while working
- ✔ Maximum benefit from tax deferral
- ✔ Ten years or more of accumulation
- ✔ Low fees
- ✔ Continuing contributions
- ✔ Low income tax bracket in retirement

Unlimited contributions: A key benefit of deferred annuities

As I note in the preceding bullets, tax deferral works best for people who can sock away a lot of money for a long time. You can contribute as much as you want to a deferred annuity, but most insurance companies reserve the right to review contributions over $1 million in advance (in part, to prevent large-scale money laundering), but they don't specifically discourage large deposits.

Contributions to all annuities are unlimited. But unlimited contributions are a selling point of deferred annuities, not income annuities. Tax deferral may enhance income annuity payouts somewhat, but I have never seen anyone tout that as a benefit of income annuities.

Reducing investment risk

As I remind you throughout this book, annuities are *contracts*, not *investments*. There's an important difference between the two:

- ✔ Investments involve risk. When you buy stocks, for example, you face the chance that the prices of your stock or of all stocks will rise or fall. When you buy bonds, you face the risk that interest rates may rise and reduce the sale price of your bonds. In fact, investors actively seek investment risks in order to get rewards.

- ✔ Contracts involve the transfer of risk from you to another party. When people buy annuities, they buy guarantees that transfer their risk of losing money to an insurance company. Annuity buyers actively seek to limit investment risk.

Annuities permit financial risk and reduce it at the same time. Owning an annuity is a little like applying the gas and the brakes at the same time while driving. (This, I believe, greatly adds to the public confusion about annuities.) But that's precisely why people buy annuity contracts: as tools to control risk rather than avoid it altogether.

For instance, when you buy a deferred variable annuity contract, you usually put most of your money in stock mutual funds. That's risky. But you can add a rider to your contract guaranteeing that if you contributed $100,000 to your annuity at, say, age 55, you're guaranteed an income of at least $10,000 a year for life starting at age 65 — even if the stock market crashes in the meantime. That reduces your risk. The guarantee won't be free: In this example, it would cost you about $600 a year over ten years. (For more on variable annuities, see Chapter 7.)

Death benefits

When you buy a deferred annuity, you pay a small annual fee for a death benefit that ensures your beneficiaries a certain minimum if you die while the contract is in force. The more you pay for the death benefit (you may have up to three or four options), the richer the benefit. As a side note, I've never seen market research proving that consumers choose annuity contracts based on the death benefit.

Advantages of income annuities

The benefits of income annuities are the same as the benefits of Social Security or a corporate pension. They help you create do-it-yourself pensions, and can maximize income during retirement while ensuring that monthly checks will arrive as long as you (or your spouse, if you want) are living. In sum, they deliver financial peace of mind in retirement.

Survivorship credits

Income annuities give you a benefit you can't get simply by drawing from your savings in retirement. It's called *survivorship credits* or *mortality credits*.

Consider 100 commandos who are embarking on an extremely dangerous yearlong mission. Only one out of five will return alive, and all are equally at risk. Before they ship out, they each agree to put $1,000 in a pool and to invest the pool in stocks.

A year later, the pool has grown to $110,000. When the 20 survivors return, they each receive $5,390, which consists of

- ✔ **$1,000:** Their original investment

- ✔ **$390:** Their share of the $10,000 growth, minus investment expenses

- ✔ **$4,000:** Their survivorship credit — each survivor's share of the money forfeited by the soldiers who didn't return

In another example closer to home, a cohort of 65-year-olds buys life annuities. Over their lifetimes, each contributor receives a monthly payment consisting of three components: returned principal, investment gains, and a share of the money relinquished by those who die earlier.

The active ingredient in both of these examples is *mortality pooling.* This is insurance at work, and it's the unique advantage of a classic life annuity.

To the extent that you plan to use your savings for retirement income (rather than, say, European vacations or an inheritance for your kids) *and* to the extent that you think you'll live past age 85, mortality pooling is the most efficient way to maximize your retirement income and guarantee an income for life.

Obtaining peace of mind!

People who own income annuities say they like the security that comes from a regular paycheck — just like the peace of mind that Social Security and traditional company pensions provide. Do you remember the public response to proposals that would have changed and possibly undermined the Social Security system a few years ago? Many middle-class people protested.

Most people don't like the ongoing disappearance of traditional pensions either, but they can't do much about it. Annuities can provide the safety and security that many people yearn for in retirement.

A retirement distribution method

Are you one of the millions of Americans who have compiled six-figure nest eggs in their employers' retirement plans but don't know how to convert them to income? An income annuity that pays out a blend of principal, earnings, and survivorship credits somewhat evenly over your entire future may be the most efficient way to turn your savings into income.

Suppose you're a 65-year-old man with $500,000 in savings. To generate a lifelong, risk-free income from your savings, you can invest it in government bonds and draw 5 percent a year ($25,000). At death, the residual half-million dollars will go to your beneficiaries. Although you can dip into principal along the way, those withdrawals will reduce your interest income.

Alternately, if maximum income is your goal, you can buy a life annuity with the $500,000. You receive $42,000 a year for life, risk free. At your death, your heirs will receive nothing. If that's too stark a choice, try this: Put $300,000 in a life annuity that pays about $25,000 a year and put the remaining $200,000 in stocks — for potential growth, or a villa in Tuscany, or your kids.

Note: This example is simplified for clarity. Taxes, fees, interest rate movements, stock market fluctuation, and your choice of contract options all add more nuances to these numbers.

Confronting the Annuity Negatives

Every benefit of annuities has a corresponding drawback. On the one hand, they provide tax deferral. On the other hand, their gains are eventually taxed at a higher rate. They offer guaranteed returns and income, but in return you often have to give up complete control of your money. As I noted at the beginning of the chapter, an annuity's pros *are* its cons.

The nature of insurance utility

As you ponder the pros and cons of annuities, remember that they're a form of insurance, and like all insurance they let you use your scarce financial resources more effectively. For instance, if you rely on a car to commute to work, you can't afford to be without it. To offset the risk that an accident might deprive you of your car, you have a choice. You can put $30,000 in escrow so you can buy a new car right away. (That's called self-insuring.) Or you can buy insurance for $3,000 a year. The insurance, in effect, frees up $27,000 for other purposes and limits your potential cost to only $3,000.

An income annuity also frees up money and limits your potential cost. Suppose you're worried about living to age 90, because longevity runs in your family. You can self-insure by saving more, which is like putting money in escrow for a new car. Or, with far less money, you can buy a life annuity that pays out as long as you live. That's like buying car insurance. Annuity analysts have calculated that it takes 40 percent more savings to self-insure against living to age 90 than it does to buy a life annuity.

You already own an income annuity

Anyone who has worked and paid payroll taxes in the United States for a number of years owns an annuity from the Social Security Administration. Although its financing is different from that of individual annuities and its payment is proportionately higher to people in lower income tax brackets, Social Security provides almost every worker with a true annuity.

If you're still working, you own a *deferred* Social Security annuity; if you're past age 62, you can convert that annuity to income. But Social Security payments aren't huge, and you may very well need another layer of guaranteed income in order to feel secure in retirement. Your decision to buy an annuity in addition to Social Security will depend on how much guaranteed income you feel you need and on your risk tolerance — your ability to cope with the uncertainties of investing.

Higher expenses than mutual funds

Although inexpensive annuities are not hard to find, high fees are common in the world of deferred variable annuities — mainly because commission-earning brokers or agents sell most of them. The insurance fees, distribution costs, investment fees, and rider fees of today's deferred variable annuities can easily exceed 3 percent. In other words, if the investments in your variable annuity are worth $200,000, you're probably paying around $6,000 a year in fees.

If you're saving for retirement, that 3 percent per year is a severe handicap (or *haircut,* as people in finance sometimes call it). For example, $10,000 in a mixture of low-cost, tax-efficient Vanguard index funds that total less than 1 percent in annual costs but have a 9-percent growth rate will grow to about $47,000 after 20 years. In contrast, a variable annuity portfolio with a 3-percent load will only grow to $32,000 in 20 years. Fees eat the heart right out of your returns.

You don't have to pay high fees for a variable annuity. You can follow these guidelines to keep your costs low:

- Buy your contract directly from an insurance company or a no-load mutual fund company (like Fidelity, Vanguard, or T. Rowe Price).
- Skip the riders (options) you don't think you'll need or use.
- Avoid subaccounts (which resemble mutual funds) that have high fees.

On the other hand, you may like the options well enough to pay for them. For example, the added fees might pay for

- The guidance you receive from a broker
- The bonus you get when you sign the contract
- The guarantees of minimum accumulation or withdrawal
- The active management of subaccounts

These are the annuity world's equivalent of a sunroof, side airbags, an extended warranty, and a global positioning system. If the options are important to you, they may be worth their price.

Immediate (income) annuities also have fees, but the fees are built into the price, so they aren't as apparent. Sales commissions and investment management costs are also lower for immediate annuities, which reduces your fees.

Depending on the insurance company's costs (and perhaps its desire to make a sale), you may be asked to pay anywhere from $140,000 to $150,000 for a $1,000-a-month lifelong income. But you'll never get an explanation for the variance. As with any other product, even the brand's prestige can affect the price. (No single company consistently offers the lowest price, so you have to shop around when buying an immediate annuity.)

Reduced liquidity and control

Annuities offer guaranteed benefits, but insurance companies can't provide those guarantees unless they can count on having your money long enough to collect fees and earn interest. In many cases, it's a trade-off: The longer you relinquish access to your money, the more generous the guarantees. The trade-off is that annuities offer less flexibility and access to your money *(liquidity)* than riskier investments.

To back up these restrictions, most deferred annuities (especially fixed deferred annuities) have surrender periods (a length of time after the sale of an annuity when you will be penalized for making excessive withdrawals), and traditional immediate annuities are generally irrevocable. (That is, after you convert your money to income, you can rarely convert it back.) Even the government restricts access, penalizing everyone under age 59½ who withdraws money from a deferred annuity (unless they qualify for a hardship withdrawal).

You can avoid the deferred variable annuity surrender periods by buying contracts without surrender periods (yes, they're out there), and you can avoid the irrevocability of income annuities by buying a deferred variable annuity with a guaranteed lifetime withdrawal benefit. (See Chapter 7 for a more complete discussion of these limitations.)

Annuity earnings are taxed as ordinary income

Eventually you have to pay income taxes on the gains in your deferred annuity contract. If your taxable income is around $160,000 or higher, your gains on the investments in your annuity will be taxed at 33 or 35 percent. In contrast, the big profits on that single stock you bought 20 years ago and sold last year will only be taxed at the capital gains rate of 15 percent — more than a 50-percent savings.

Even more painful, if you bequeath that appreciated stock to your children, its cost basis is *stepped up* to its current value at your death. This means your children don't owe any taxes on it *if* they sell it at that same price. But inheriting the profits in your deferred annuity is a whole different story; your children will owe all the income tax you didn't pay. They do not necessarily have to pay the tax all at once, however. For details, see Chapter 14.

The difference between income tax rates and the long-term capital gains rate only makes a big difference for retirees with very high incomes. According to *2007 Tax Facts on Insurance and Employee Benefits* (National Underwriter, 2007), a retired couple filing jointly with an enviable taxable income of $100,000 will owe less than 20 percent in income taxes. In short, it's misleading to suggest that annuity income will be taxed at much higher rates than long-term capital gains.

Little transparency but several moving parts

Insurance is a proverbial black box. No one but the managers and actuaries are privy to the many different formulas and factors that go into the pricing of products. So, when an issuer of income annuities offers to pay you $671 per month from age 65 until you die in exchange for a one-time premium of $100,000, you have no idea how the carrier arrived at those figures. It's a mystery.

You could call the issuer back next month and the payout may have risen to $678 or dropped to $659. You still wouldn't know why. The carrier may reduce its quote simply because it already wrote enough income annuity contracts for 65-year-olds in your state for that particular month and wants to discourage further purchases. Go figure.

Then there are the *moving parts* (variable factors, such as interest rates or fees, that may change after you purchase your contract) in deferred annuities. These are a few examples:

✔ When you buy a fixed deferred annuity that guarantees a rate for only the first year, you don't know what the rate might be in subsequent years.

✔ An issuer of indexed annuities reserves the right to change the formula for crediting gains to you. Your profit potential may go down as a result.

✔ The managers of a deferred variable annuity may indirectly reduce your potential for gains when taking steps to reduce your risk of loss.

   If you elect a guaranteed minimum accumulation benefit (GMAB) rider on a deferred variable annuity, for example, the carrier may reserve the right to shift your money from stocks to bonds when stock prices are falling. This limits your losses, but also limits your ability to use falling stock prices as an opportunity to buy at bargain prices.

The benefits of today's popular deferred variable annuity contracts — which offer guaranteed lifetime income and access to your principal if you need it — require complex financial engineering and entail many different restrictions. The rules are always in the prospectus, but they can be extremely difficult or even impossible to understand.

Adverse selection

Healthy, wealthy, well-educated people — those with the longest life expectancies — are the most likely to seek out and purchase income annuities. People with low incomes and poor health tend not to buy income annuities. In the insurance world, this bias is called *adverse selection* because it can drive up the cost of insurance. It's comparable to a situation where only those with suicidal tendencies buy life insurance.

To compensate for this distortion, insurance companies have to charge more for life annuities than they would if random members of the population bought annuities. Carriers have no choice but to keep premiums high. If just 1,000 annuity owners who receive $1,000 a month start living an average of one year longer than mortality tables predict, the carrier will come up short by $12 million!

If income annuities were priced fairly for people with average life expectancies — as if *everyone* were buying life annuities — the annuities would be a bargain for people with superior health. However, by compensating for adverse selection, insurance carriers make life annuities more expensive for people with merely average mortality risk. This is a defect in the pricing of life annuities. Some insurance companies do discount income annuities for people with serious chronic illnesses, but that's as close as the industry comes to health-based pricing.

Comparing Annuities with Their Competition

As I note at the start of the chapter, annuities don't exist in a vacuum. Every financial strategy involves trade-offs. Are the net benefits of annuities greater or smaller than the net benefits of competing products? That answer depends on the situation and the matchup. (It also depends on you — as I explain in Chapter 5.)

Deferred fixed annuities versus CDs

Deferred fixed annuities and certificates of deposit (CDs) are both tools for saving and earning interest on savings. The biggest difference is that the annuities offer tax deferral and CDs do not.

For example, the pros of deferred fixed annuities include

- Tax-deferred gains
- Unlimited contributions
- Low risk; backed by insurer
- Guaranteed rates

The cons of deferred fixed annuities include

- ✔ Low transparency; the interest rates offered by some deferred fixed annuities may decline after first year
- ✔ Low liquidity

The pros of CDs include

- ✔ Guaranteed rate
- ✔ Low risk; backed by Federal Deposit Insurance Corp.

The cons of CDs include

- ✔ Gains that are subject to current taxation
- ✔ Low liquidity

It's easy to compare CDs to deferred fixed annuities because the interest rates are readily available. Fixed annuity rates are posted on the Internet (see Chapters 17 and 21 for specific sites) and CD rates are posted in the lobbies of banks.

It's best to buy fixed annuities when long-term interest rates are significantly higher than short-term interest rates; that's when they usually offer higher rates than CDs. I would avoid buying a fixed annuity whose rates are not guaranteed for the length of the term, however. For more on deferred fixed annuities, see Chapter 6.

There are lots of different bond rates, depending on whether you're borrowing for 3 months, 3 years, or 30 years. The difference between the 3-month rate might be tiny or huge, positive or negative. Rate levels, and the differences between rates, determine the ever-changing interest rate climate.

Deferred variable annuities versus mutual funds

Deferred variable annuities and mutual fund accounts are both ways of investing in mutual funds and building up your retirement savings. In this case, you're trying to maximize the growth rate of your retirement savings.

The pros of using a deferred variable annuity are

- ✔ Tax deferral on unlimited contributions
- ✔ Death benefit
- ✔ Option for guaranteed living benefits

The cons include

- ✔ Generally high fees
- ✔ Low liquidity until age 59½
- ✔ Gains taxed as ordinary income

Those are quite a few serious cons! But compare them to the pros and cons of mutual funds. The pros of mutual fund accounts are

- ✔ Generally low fees (although both Vanguard and Fidelity market variable annuities whose total fees are lower than the average mutual fund fee)
- ✔ High liquidity
- ✔ Transparency

Not bad. But now look at their cons:

- ✔ Subject to current taxation (unless you hold them in an IRA or employer-sponsored retirement plan)
- ✔ Stock market risk
- ✔ No income options or guarantees

As a *savings* tool, mutual fund accounts generally grow faster than annuities because of their lower fees. However, as a *retirement income* tool, variable annuities now offer payout options that ordinary mutual funds don't offer. (Let's ignore the impact of tax deferral for the moment, because many people hold mutual funds in tax-deferred retirement accounts.)

So keep your savings in cheap-as-possible mutual funds until you get close to retirement, and then buy your retirement income tool — either a variable annuity with guaranteed income options (Chapter 8) or an income annuity (see the next section).

All of this really comes down to personal decision. What would you buy: a $22,000 certified used car, or the exact same used car for $20,000 without a $2,000 service contract? When you're playing roulette in Las Vegas, do you put your chips on red or black? Would you rather have a 100 percent chance of winning $50 or a 50 percent chance of winning $100? It's your choice.

Income annuities versus systematic withdrawals

When you reach retirement, you'll probably weigh the benefits of income annuities against the benefits of a "systematic withdrawal plan." Both are time-honored ways to derive a clear, icy stream of retirement income from that glacier of savings it took you a lifetime to accumulate.

Systematic withdrawal plans (also known as SWIPS) are nothing more than strategies for keeping your savings in a blend of stocks, bonds, and money market accounts and withdrawing money as needed, usually from the money market account first. SWIPs offer

- ✔ Liquidity
- ✔ Maximum benefit for beneficiaries
- ✔ Low costs; gains taxed at low capital gains rate

And here are the cons:

- ✔ Exposure to market risk in old age
- ✔ No system for generating retirement income
- ✔ No benefit from mortality risk pooling

Now, take a look at an income annuity (either fixed or variable). The annuity pros are

- ✔ Peace of mind
- ✔ Reduced investment risk; survivorship credits
- ✔ A retirement distribution strategy

And the cons are

- ✔ Lack of liquidity
- ✔ Reduced benefit for beneficiaries
- ✔ Adverse selection; high prices

Overall, income annuities generally appeal to investors who want the peace of mind that comes from a guaranteed retirement paycheck and who fearlessly embrace the concept of survivorship credits. SWIPs appeal to people who can laugh in the face of market uncertainty and don't need that guarantee — or who have so much money that they needn't worry about running out. In my own case, I'd probably put part of my money in an income annuity, and keep the rest "in play." Or I'd buy a ladder of fixed income and fixed deferred annuities. For more on the creative use of annuities in retirement, see Chapter 15.

Chapter 5

Deciding Whether an Annuity Is Right for You

*W*ho should own an annuity? I've struggled to find a short, simple answer to that question, but I haven't been able to dredge one up. No single type of person needs an annuity, and no single type of annuity is right for everybody.

I can generalize, however. Annuity buyers tend to be upper-middle-class people in their 50s or 60s — far from rich but by no means poor — who want tax deferral on their savings, a safe return on their investments, and/or guaranteed income during retirement.

Interest in annuities is growing fastest among that third group — the ones seeking retirement income. As affluent baby boomers approach retirement with swollen 401(k) accounts, they'll need income annuities to help convert their savings into lifelong paychecks.

 Not everybody needs an annuity. It depends on your age, the size of your portfolio and, even more importantly, your attitude toward investment risk and your faith in the financial markets. If you lose sleep every time stock prices plunge or the Fed raises interest rates, then I suggest you find out more about annuities.

Who Should Own an Annuity?

In this section, I point out ten types of people who are more likely than most to benefit from annuities. If you see yourself in any of these brief portraits, investigate further. I also identify the kinds of annuities each type of person might use. For more about each type of annuity, see the chapters in Part II.

You find a heavy emphasis here on people who can benefit from income-producing annuities. Using annuities for long-term investment purposes is, frankly, a bit "last century." Going forward, I believe, most annuities will be purchased by retired baby boomers to provide them with lifelong income.

Boomer couples with 401(k) or 403(b) accounts

Imagine a couple, John and Gerri Springer. He's 56 years old; she's 53. They both work full time, and so far their two 401(k) plans are worth a combined $361,000. Neither John nor Gerri has a defined benefit pension, and they don't currently own any annuities. They hope to have their mortgage paid off by the time John turns 65.

Healthy and fit, the Springers would like to travel after they retire, and they've got pent-up desires to improve their home. But they're not sure how much they can afford to spend in retirement. They're also looking for a way to minimize the income tax on their tax-deferred savings.

Until they retire, the Springers should keep contributing as much as they can to their 401(k) accounts — at least enough to receive all of their employers' matching contributions. After they retire, they'll have ample time to think about annuities.

The possibilities are fairly endless. They could buy an immediate income annuity that, with Social Security, could cover their basics expenses and guarantee income for life. Or they could build a ladder of fixed deferred and fixed immediate annuities, like the ones described in Chapter 15.

An advanced life deferred annuity (ALDA) may ease their fear of overspending during early retirement. Any of these annuities can help them spread out their tax liability. If they want guaranteed income plus complete access to all of their assets, a deferred variable annuity with living benefits might fill the bill.

Uncle Sam places a provision in tax-deferred retirement plans that, in a sense, forces Americans to use them like annuities. Starting at age 70½, participants must take annual Required Minimum Distributions (RMDs) from their savings. (Each required distribution equals the value of the retirement account, divided by the plan owner's life expectancy, in years; see Chapter 14). But keep in mind that RMDs don't guarantee you an income regardless of how long you live; annuities do.

Women

Rita Goldberg is a 94-year-old widow living in a south Florida retirement community — and she's not even the oldest in her coven of Mahjong players. Lucky for her, she's got a life annuity. Back in 1982, when risk-free Treasury notes paid a lofty 12 percent, her late husband, Sam, put $200,000 in a joint-and-survivor life annuity with a 100 percent survivor benefit. Every month, Rita still gets a check for $2,600 to supplement Social Security and other savings.

Women, above all, should find out as much as they can about income annuities. On average, 65-year-old women live two or three years longer than 65-year-old men. After age 85 or so, women significantly outnumber men. Women are likelier to run out of money before they die (that's called *longevity risk)* than men and, therefore, they're more likely to benefit from either:

- ✔ **A *life* annuity:** The irreversible conversion of a lump sum into a lifetime income. Also known as a life income annuity, an immediate annuity, or a SPIA — a single premium immediate annuity.

- ✔ **A *guaranteed lifetime withdrawal benefit:*** A deferred variable annuity rider that can be used to provide income for life, even if the financial markets tank.

If you're a married female boomer, you should do your homework on annuities. The law of averages says that you will outlive your husband. You may need an annuity far more than he will.

The middle class and the affluent

John Knoll, a retired federal judge, has $1.6 million in savings, owns homes in Weston, Connecticut, and Martha's Vineyard, Massachusetts, and dabbles in commercial real estate. With half of his investable assets in safe municipal bonds and the other half in growth stocks, plus a government pension, he doesn't need an annuity.

Neither does Knoll's 61-year-old gardener, Bob Veldt, though for different reasons. He keeps all of his modest savings of $71,000 in a money market fund, in case of emergencies. In retirement, he'll supplement Social Security by working part time as a handyman.

But Mike Sturges, who owns the car wash where Judge Knoll's car is detailed, might gain a lot from annuities. Now in his 50s, he hopes to sell his business at age 60 and retire to rural North Carolina with about $600,000 in savings.

Instead of putting 40 percent of his money ($240,000) in bonds and reaping $12,000 a year in interest, he could receive a guaranteed $20,000 a year for life by putting the same 40 percent in an immediate income annuity. Or he could take 10 percent of his money and buy an ALDA to cover his expenses after age 80 — if he lives that long.

People like Mike Sturges — not rich but hardly poor — are prime candidates for annuities. Wealthier individuals, like John Knoll, can afford to self-insure. They'll never run out of money. Less advantaged people, like Bob Veldt, don't have enough surplus wealth for an annuity to make sense. But Sturges has enough liquid assets to put some in income annuities (for peace of mind), some in stocks (for growth), and still keep some in a money market (for splurges and emergencies).

As a general rule, people who are still working shouldn't consider a deferred annuity (unless it's a retirement annuity through workplace contributions) until they've contributed the maximum to a tax-deductible IRA or an employer-sponsored retirement plan. *Note:* In 2007, the IRA limit was $4,000 for people under age 50 and $5,000 for age 50 or over. Participants in retirement plans could make deductible contributions up to $15,000.

Here are some thoughts on wealth and annuities:

✔ **Under $250,000 in savings:** In the annuity industry, there are several schools of thought regarding new retirees with less than a quarter million in savings. For instance, some believe that people with less than $250,000 in savings are unlikely candidates for variable income annuities (where your assets are invested in mutual funds).

Fidelity Investments suggest that no one put more than 30 percent of his or her investable wealth in an income annuity; 30 percent of $250,000 ($75,000) would generate only about $500 a month in income at current rates.

Others say that if someone needs an extra $1,500 a month in retirement just to cover basic expenses, then he should put the whole $250,000 into an income annuity.

✔ **$250,000 to $1 million in savings:** As I noted above with regard to Mike Sturges, these folks can benefit from several types of annuities or combinations of annuities. By putting half of their money in income annuities, for instance, they give themselves the freedom to take bigger risks with the rest of their money, or spend without fear that they'll end their days living on condensed soup and soda crackers.

✔ **Over $1 million:** People with significant assets face little risk of running out of money, so they are not especially good candidates for income annuities. If they expect to be in a high tax bracket in retirement, they're better off investing in taxable accounts than in tax-deferred annuities, because their gains will be taxed at the long-term capital gains tax rate instead of their income tax rate.

But wealthy people shouldn't rule out annuities. Like all of us, they're vulnerable to health risk. They often worry that an extended illness and extraordinary nursing-home expenses could consume the assets that they had planned to leave to their children or to charity. The new generation of combination income annuity/long-term care insurance products, just now coming on the market, may give them the peace of mind they're looking for.

Retirees who don't have a defined benefit pension plan

This probably means you! Between 1995 and 2005, the number of corporate-defined benefit plans fell by half. In the future, even more companies are expected to convert their pensions to defined contribution plans such as 401(k) plans. The disappearance of such plans is expected to drive the demand for income annuities over the next two decades. Bottom line? If you're not covered by a traditional pension plan at work, you can use an income annuity to create a do-it-yourself pension.

People with rugged genes

While hiking near Ouray, Colorado, a few years ago, my wife and I met a snowy-haired couple with alpenstocks in their grips, rucksacks on their backs, and big smiles on their faces. They were retired university professors, both in their mid-80s, still flush with health. They were poster children for life annuities.

Obviously, the longer you live, the more you need lifelong income and the more you get out of it. Statistically, some segments of the population average longer lives — the same 20 to 30 percent of the United States' population who receive life's related blessings: affluence, good healthcare, a college education, and a supportive family. Of course, no one knows how long he or she will live, but that's where annuities come in — to insure you against that uncertainty.

People who buy life income annuities voluntarily tend to live about 10 percent longer than people who don't buy annuities. That's because people with average or below-average health avoid annuities entirely. This phenomenon is called *adverse selection*. (Will you live longer if you buy a life annuity? Certainly the incentive is there.)

Knowing that the average annuity customer will live longer than the average American, insurance companies raise the prices of life annuities to budget for those extra years of payments. But, in a kind of vicious cycle, higher rates inevitably make annuities less financially appealing for people with lower life expectancies.

Here's an analogy. Suppose the National Basketball Association raised the official height of the rim to 12 feet from its current 10 feet to adjust for the increased average height of today's players. For those more than 7 feet tall, the change might seem fair. But few players less than 6 feet tall would get much playing time.

Higher annuity rates put less-healthy people at a similar disadvantage, discouraging them from using annuities at all. Some insurance companies have begun to offer "impaired risk" annuities, which offer higher payouts to people with serious illnesses, such as heart disease or diabetes. But such products are not widely used.

Note: Defined benefit pension plans and Social Security don't suffer from adverse selection because they're not voluntary. Everyone, sick and healthy, is in the pool.

Market bears and other pessimists

Bill Nielsen and Mark Zeffrey are next-door neighbors. They both live in four-bedroom Colonials. They both drive Toyota Camrys. And at age 59, they both have about $400,000 in savings and neither has a pension. But they differ in one respect. Bill predicts a rosy economy ahead. Mark thinks our financial system is on the brink of collapse.

Two emotions are said to govern a person's attitude toward money and drive the financial markets: fear and greed. If, like Mark, you're more fear-driven than greed-driven — that is, if you believe that America's budget deficit, trade deficit, and credit-card binge will eventually unhinge the economy and topple the stock market — you may be a candidate for an annuity.

You don't have to be paranoid to have this fear. The fact is, everyone eventually faces *sequence-of-returns* risk — the chance that an ugly 1974-like recession will occur shortly before or after you retire and cut the heart out of your savings.

One way to eliminate sequence-of-returns risk is to buy a deferred variable annuity with living benefits. As of mid-2007, there are several contracts on the market promising that if you invest, say, $100,000, at age 65 you can draw an income of at least 5 percent of $200,000 ($10,000) a year for life. If the market crashes in the meantime, you're protected from the worst of it. For details, see Chapter 8.

Even if you're not apocalyptically inclined, you may like deferred fixed annuities because they're even safer than bond mutual funds. You can lose money in a bond fund, but the value of a deferred annuity is guaranteed. Then in retirement, you may also want an income annuity because it can generate more current income than bonds. (Although safe government bonds can pay 5 percent a year, the same investment in an equally safe income annuity may pay more than 8 percent a year.)

Neither the very young nor the extremely old

Your age has a big impact on which annuity to consider and whether to consider one at all. At any age, however, your choice is complicated by trade-offs. For instance, buying a deferred variable annuity in your 20s or 30s to save for retirement gives you the benefit of three or four decades of tax-deferred, compounded growth. But the 10-percent federal penalty for withdrawals from a deferred annuity before age 59½ puts a stiff barrier between you and your money. In addition, you may have to pay certain rider fees — such as death benefit riders or guaranteed withdrawal benefit riders — for many years before you use the option, if you use it at all.

On the other hand, buying an annuity when you're young can make a lot of sense *if* you can do it through a group annuity plan whose expenses are low. For instance, university employees can contribute to TIAA-CREF retirement annuities on the installment plan and then convert their savings to an annuity when they retire. Some retirement plans such as the Genworth Clear Course plan allow employees to buy chunks of future income with contributions to the plan.

In addition, insurance companies are aiming their latest generation of income-generating deferred annuities at people in their mid-50s. Under the terms of one new product from Prudential, a 55-year-old can buy a deferred variable annuity with a $200,000 purchase premium and be guaranteed that, starting at age 65, he can withdraw $20,000 a year for the rest of his life — even if his original investment shrinks to zero along the way. (For more on deferred variable annuities with lifetime withdrawal benefits, see Chapter 7.)

Although you can be too old to qualify for certain kinds of annuities or their riders, it generally makes sense to postpone purchasing an immediate life annuity. With each passing year, the *survivorship credits* (also called *mortality credits*) become larger. Survivorship credits, which I discuss in Chapters 1, 4, and 18, are the core principle and the main attraction of a life annuity.

Researchers in Frankfurt, Germany, have suggested that at about age 60, the survivorship credit is large enough to justify an income annuity in place of bonds. At about age 75, the credit justifies an income annuity in place of stocks.

People who want to turn a tax bite into bite-sized pieces

If you've inherited the money in a tax-deferred retirement account or have money in a deferred variable annuity, you'll owe income tax on either all or part of the money. But you can avoid paying the tax all at once by converting the money to an income stream and spreading your tax burden over several years or over the rest of your life.

Those seeking less-expensive long-term care insurance

Many people worry about living so long that all of their savings (and their children's inheritance) will be swallowed up by nursing-home expenses. Today, full-time care can easily cost $50,000 to $75,000 a year.

For a variety of reasons, long-term care insurance has been a flawed product. However, the Pension Protection Act of 2006 will make it possible to combine annuities and long-term care insurance into a single product starting in 2010. The law will allow owners of these products to apply annuity assets to their long-term care expenses tax free. The cost of a combined product is expected to be lower than the cost of buying the two types of insurance separately. So far, such products can't be purchased with money from a traditional IRA or an employer-sponsored retirement plan.

People without beneficiaries

Many parents avoid income annuities because they think they'll forfeit the remaining money to an insurance company instead of passing it to their beneficiaries or heirs. But that's a myth — or at least a misleading generalization. You can look at it this way: If you *don't* have beneficiaries, you have one less worry about annuities!

Preparing for the "Suitability" Test

Suitability is perhaps the biggest current buzzword in the world of variable annuities. That's because state insurance regulators have discovered that some brokers and insurance agents have been selling fixed or variable deferred annuities to people for whom such contracts are *unsuitable* — usually because the unsuspecting customer is too old to benefit from owning a long-term investment, especially if there's a surrender period.

Who owns nonqualified deferred annuity contracts?

In 2004, The Association for Insured Retirement Solutions (NAVA; formerly the National Association of Variable Annuities) surveyed owners of nonqualified annuities (annuities purchased outside of tax-qualified retirement plans). Typical owners were solidly middle class with at least a high school diploma and an average household income under $75,000. The median value of their annuity was about $100,000. Here are a few of the survey's findings:

✔ Women owners of nonqualified annuities outnumbered men 56 to 44 percent, but men owners of *variable* nonqualified annuities outnumbered women 53 to 46 percent.

✔ Annuity owners are well educated: Forty-six percent had an undergraduate college degree or higher, 16 percent attended college without graduating, and 29 percent graduated high school but did not attend college.

✔ The average age of annuity owners was 66; they bought their annuities, on average, at age 50. Only 14 percent were under age 54, and more than one-third were over age 72.

✔ More than half (58 percent) of the owners were retired, and half of their spouses were retired. Less than 30 percent were still working, and 8 percent were employed part time.

✔ Business owners, company officers, professionals, and supervisors accounted for 54 percent of nonqualified annuity owners. The next largest group (19 percent) included blue-collar workers, support staff, and service workers.

✔ Most annuity owners aren't rich. Only 18 percent had household incomes over $100,000. Even among those who were still working, almost half earned less than $75,000. Three-fourths of retired owners had household incomes under $75,000, which means the income tax rate on their first $31,000 was only 15 percent and on the next $44,000 was 25 percent.

More than 80 percent of the owners gave the following two reasons for owning a nonqualified annuity:

✔ "To have a financial cushion" (in case they live too long)

✔ "To avoid being a financial burden on their children"

To reduce or eliminate unsuitable sales, state regulators and FINRA (the Financial Industry Regulatory Authority; formerly the National Association of Securities) have begun to require that

✔ All purchasers of new or replacement annuities must complete and sign a *suitability assessment* form when they complete the annuity application form.

✔ The salesman must submit this form with the contract application to his supervisor for review before sending the paperwork to the annuity provider.

Assessing suitability

The suitability assessment form has two purposes:

- ✔ To make sure the purchaser knows what she's getting into
- ✔ To prevent the insurance company from a sale that may lead to prosecution or a lawsuit

The typical questions on the assessment form ask for the following information:

- ✔ Your age
- ✔ Your tax bracket
- ✔ Your risk tolerance
- ✔ The range of investments you own
- ✔ How soon you expect to need the money that's going into the annuity

If you're swapping one annuity for another, you may also be asked to write the costs and benefits of the two contracts side by side.

What sets off the alarms

Alarms should go off, figuratively, if any of the following is true:

- ✔ You're over age 70.
- ✔ The annuity will monopolize most of your liquid assets.
- ✔ Your tax bracket is too low for you to benefit from tax deferral.
- ✔ The replacement annuity doesn't leave you significantly better off (think costs, benefits, and liquidity) than the one you had before. This applies if you are being urged to swap an existing contract for a new contract through a *1035 exchange*.

Agents and brokers have been prosecuted and sued in several states for, essentially, convincing older people to move their money from one annuity to another in a transaction that only benefits the salesman. Suitability forms are designed to eliminate that practice.

Just who owns immediate income annuities?

In 2002, the American Council of Life Insurers conducted a survey of 460 owners of immediate annuities (you exchange a large lump sum of money for a monthly, quarterly, or annual income stream for a specific number of years or for the rest of your life). Immediate annuity owners tended to be non-wealthy retirees who apparently used their annuity income to supplement income from Social Security, part-time employment, and other investments.

Age

<60	9 percent
60 to 69	18
70 to 79	42
80 and older	31

Employment status

Retired	80
Employed	15
Not employed	5

Marital status

Married	44
Widowed	41
Single	15

Annual income

<$25,000	22
$25,000 to $49,999	42
$50,000 to $99,999	30
>$100,000	6

Annual annuity income

<$5,000	41
$5,000 to $9,999	29
$10,000 to $19,999	17
>$20,000	13

Part II
Identifying the Main Types of Annuities

The 5th Wave   By Rich Tennant

"I was looking for an annuity that came with a rate that was fixed, not neutered."

In this part . . .

Although all annuities share a common history, they've evolved into several distinct products. Each type has its own purpose, characteristics, and audience. In these five chapters, I explain the difference between *deferred* and *immediate* annuities and what makes an annuity *fixed* or *variable.* Note the chapter titles; they tell you what each type of annuity does best.

Chapter 6

Saving with Fixed Annuities

....

In This Chapter

▶ Understanding how fixed annuities work

▶ Getting to know the types of fixed annuities

▶ Sizing up the pros and cons of different types

▶ Making your move: Purchasing that fixed annuity

▶ Maintaining your annuity

....

*Y*ears ago, before the invention of credit cards and mutual funds, people *saved*. If they wanted to buy something big — a house, a diamond, or a dream vacation — they put money in a *savings* account, where it earned *interest*. The money grew slowly but steadily, and when the day of purchase finally arrived, voilà! They paid cash.

A fixed deferred annuity is the insurance industry's version of a savings account. It helps you earn a modest rate of interest safely, and allows you to postpone the payment of income taxes on your earnings for as long as you want. (***Note***: For simplicity, I call these fixed annuities. Don't confuse them with fixed *income* annuities, which I cover in Chapter 8.)

In this chapter, I acquaint you with the major and not-so-major types of fixed deferred annuities. I explain their pros and cons, and tell you where you can buy them. If you're approaching retirement or recently retired, fixed annuities are a great way to protect your savings from the unpredictability of the markets.

How Fixed Annuities Work

When you buy a fixed deferred annuity, you're indirectly lending money — without taking the risk that the borrower won't pay you back. The process is fairly simple. In most cases, you hand a check to an agent, who sends it on to an insurance company. The insurer promises that your money will earn a certain rate of interest for at least the first year.

When it receives your money, the insurance company adds it to its *general account* (where it pools most of its incoming premiums). It invests that money as it sees fit — usually in safe government securities or high-quality corporate bonds that pay a slightly higher rate of interest than the insurance company pays you.

The difference between the rate the carrier earns and what it pays you is known as the *spread*. The wider the spread, the more money the carrier makes. If one of the carrier's creditors defaults on its bonds, that's the carrier's problem, not yours. The carrier *has* to pay you back. It gave you a guarantee.

The carrier pays you *compound* interest on your premium, which means that

- In the first year, you earn interest on your investment.
- In the second year, you earn interest on your investment plus your first year's interest.
- In the third year, you earn interest on your investment plus your first year's interest and your second year's interest, and so on.

It's a snowball effect that's often described as the *magic* of compound interest. At the end of the *term* (for example, one, three, five, seven, or ten years), you take your money out.

What makes a fixed annuity?

Fixed annuities sometimes offer higher interest rates than competing investments, such as CDs or short-term bond mutual funds, because the insurance carrier puts your money in longer-term bonds, which typically offer a better return than short-term bonds. Whenever fixed annuities pay higher rates than other safe investments, they're worth considering.

Characteristics of fixed annuities include:

- **Guaranteed principal:** You can't lose your money unless the insurance company fails, which is unlikely if it has a strong financial rating.
- **Guaranteed minimum interest rate:** Your money never earns less than this rate, even if the insurance company reserves the right to reduce the rate it gave you in the first year.
- **Annual withdrawals:** Most contracts let you withdraw up to 10 percent of the value of the annuity (your original investment plus interest) every year with no penalty. If you're younger than age 591/2, however, you may owe an Internal Revenue Service penalty.

✔ **Surrender period and surrender charges:** This is the waiting period (one to ten years in most cases) during which you can't withdraw more than 10 percent of your money per year without a penalty or adjustment.

Surrender charges are also called *contingent deferred sales charges.* The first-year charge often equals the number of years in the surrender period; then the charge declines by 1 percent per year. For instance, a seven-year annuity may have a first-year charge of 7 percent, a second-year charge of 6 percent, a third-year charge of 5 percent, and so on.

✔ **Death benefits:** If you die while owning the annuity, your money (including the interest you've earned up to your death) goes to the beneficiaries identified in your contract. If you want, you can change the beneficiary after you buy the contract.

✔ **Income option:** You can convert the value of the fixed annuity to a guaranteed income stream (regular payments to you) for a specific number of years or for as long as you (or you and your spouse) are living. *Note:* The "deferred" in *deferred annuity* indicates that the owner is postponing the decision to convert the annuity's value to income. It isn't a reference to tax deferral.

✔ **Premium requirements:** The minimum initial investment for a fixed annuity ranges from $2,000 to $100,000. You can purchase a *single-premium* contract with one payment or a *flexible-premium* contract with ongoing payments. If you send in more than one premium, each premium may require the purchase of a separate contract.

Don't confuse these fixed annuities with *immediate fixed annuities* where you pay a lump sum for a fixed monthly payment that can last the rest of your life, a specific number of years, or as long as you or your spouse is living.

Fixed annuities have their pitfalls. For example, you may find yourself trapped for years in an investment that pays you less and less interest every year if you

✔ Neglect to read the fine print on the contract

✔ Are lured into a bad contract by the offer of a big, upfront bonus

✔ Get bad advice

But, when handled with care, fixed annuities can be valuable because

✔ Your money is safe.

✔ You can delay paying taxes on the interest you earn.

✔ You have virtually no upper limit on contributions.

✔ They often — but not always — offer higher interest rates than competing investments.

✔ Like bonds and bond mutual funds, they can reduce the overall risk of your investment portfolio.

Protection from two kinds of risks

Why not just buy bonds on your own? Because you take two risks:

- ✔ **Default risk:** The chance that the loan you made (by buying bonds) won't be paid back — not good.

- ✔ **Interest rate risk:** The chance that interest rates will go up after you buy your bond. In this case, your bonds (which pay the old rate) are worth less than new bonds (which pay the higher rate) — also not good.

In contrast, when you buy a fixed annuity and follow all the rules of the contract, the insurance company assumes one or both of these risks for you.

Your only worry is that the insurance company itself may fail. But that's why you buy a fixed annuity only from a company whose financial strength is rated "A" or better by rating agencies such as Fitch, A.M. Best, and Standard & Poor's. (For more info on these ratings, see Appendix A.)

Examining the Main Types of Fixed Annuities

The two most common types of fixed deferred annuities are *single-year guarantee* contracts and *multi-year guarantee* contracts. (I prefer the multi-year contracts, because you know exactly what you'll get over the term of the contract.) Either type of fixed annuity can be *market value-adjusted* (MVA), and I include a separate section devoted just to that category.

Single-year guarantee fixed annuity

The single-year guarantee fixed annuity is like an adjustable rate mortgage in reverse. With this annuity, the insurance company promises to pay you a certain rate of interest for one year. But each year until the contract expires, the insurance company can raise or (more commonly) reduce that interest rate. The new rates are called *renewal rates*.

At the end of the surrender period, the contract expires. You have to buy a new contract or roll over to it.

Be sure you understand your actual rate; an agent or broker may throw a lot of different terms at you, including all or most of the following:

✔ **The base rate:** The interest rate the company pays you the first year

✔ **The bonus rate:** The bonus the company adds to the interest rate in the first year

✔ **The current rate:** The base rate plus the bonus rate

✔ **The current yield:** The interest rate your money will earn over the entire term of the contract if the company does not lower its base rate

✔ **The guaranteed yield:** The lowest possible interest rate you can earn

✔ **Renewal rates:** The rates after the first year

A table of renewal rates can tell you whether the company has a history of raising, lowering, or maintaining the base interest rates of its single-year guarantee contracts after the first year.

Ask your agent or broker for a renewal rate table, or look up the contract's interest rate history at a Web site like `annuityadvantage.com`. See Figure 6-1 for a sample rate table at AnnuityAdvantage.com (Rate histories are routinely provided to annuity salesmen, but not necessarily to customers.)

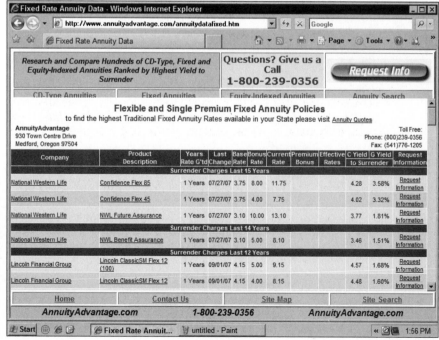

Figure 6-1: A table of fixed annuity rates, as shown at Annuity Advantage. com.

The bonus rate only lasts for the first year. For example, Web sites like annuityadvantage.com or annuity.info have lists of single-year guaranteed products that offer first-year bonuses of two, five, seven, and even ten percentage points on top of its *base rate* the first year.

Sounds sweet, but what happens after the first year? Generally, the rate gradually falls from year to year, enabling the company to recover the cost of the bonus. It's not unusual for the base rate on a single-year guarantee annuity to decline between 0.10 and 0.25 of 1 percent per year after the first year.

Also, the guaranteed yield for a bonus annuity is usually lower than the guaranteed yield for a multi-year guarantee (MYG) annuity, so the bonus annuity rate potentially has farther to fall.

Multi-year guarantee (MYG) fixed annuity

An MYG fixed annuity is like a fixed-rate mortgage in reverse. You give a specific amount of money to an insurance company, and the insurer guarantees that your investment will earn a specific rate of compound interest for a specific number of years.

MYG annuities are often called *CD-type annuities* or *tax-deferred CDs* because they serve the same purpose as a certificate of deposit (CD; a security purchased at a bank that pays a fixed rate of interest for a specific number of months or years).

The beauty of MYGs is their transparency. What you see is what you get. You know the rate of interest your money will earn and how long it will earn that rate. So, if you want to buy a $30,000 boat in ten years, you can plunk down $19,500 today in a ten-year MYG annuity that pays 4.5 percent. In ten years, you can pay cash for the boat *and* have enough money left over for dinner for two at the marina.

Investment advisers often recommend MYG fixed annuities over single-year guarantee contracts because MYG contracts are more predictable. There's no risk that the insurance company will reduce the interest rate after the first year.

Market value-adjusted (MVA) fixed annuities

In the earlier section, "How Fixed Annuities Work," I note that insurance companies assume your interest-rate risk when you buy a fixed annuity. That's not always the case. With a *market value-adjusted* (MVA) fixed annuity, you assume the interest-rate risk. In return, the insurance company can afford to pay you a slightly higher interest rate than it pays on *non-MVA* annuities (*book value* annuities)

If MVA annuities pay a higher rate, why buy anything else? Because, if interest rates go up and you decide to break an MVA contract to take advantage of a fixed annuity that offers the new rate, you'll pay a bigger penalty than if you broke a book value contract.

The MVA triggers two penalties when you withdraw too much money (over 10 percent, in most cases) from your annuity during the surrender period. Typically:

✔ You have to pay a surrender charge (for example, equal to the number of years left in the surrender period)

✔ Your account value is adjusted

  • Downward if interest rates have risen since you bought your annuity

  • Upward if rates have declined

Keep in mind the effects of interest-rate risk. Suppose you buy a $10,000 bond that pays 5-percent interest per year. Your bond has a face value of $10,000 and a *yield* (rate of return) of 5 percent. But then calamity occurs. The Federal Reserve's Board of Governors raises interest rates to 6 percent. Immediately, the market price of your bond drops.

Why does your bond lose value when rates rise? Because no one wants to pay $10,000 for a bond with a 5-percent yield when he can buy a $10,000 bond with a 6-percent interest rate! Trust me on these numbers — your 5-percent bond will fetch about $9,260 on the open market when 6-percent bonds are selling for $10,000. The important principle to remember is this: When interest rates rise, the market prices of existing bonds fall.

When you buy a fixed annuity, the insurance company buys bonds with your money, seeking to earn a higher rate than it promised to pay you. If interest rates rise, the market price of the carrier's bonds will drop. If you choose that moment to withdraw some or all of your money, the insurance company will have to sell some of those depressed bonds — at a loss — in order to pay you.

The insurer will try to recover that loss from you. If you own a non-MVA annuity, the insurer will charge a surrender fee. If you own an MVA annuity, the insurer will charge a surrender fee *and* deduct its loss from the value of your contract. Here's an example. Suppose you bought a $10,000 MVA fixed annuity, and the insurance carrier took the money and bought a bond paying 5 percent. Then rates immediately went up to 6 percent, and the value of the carrier's bond dropped to $9,260. (See the earlier discussion of bond prices.) If you decide to withdraw all your money, the carrier will reduce (adjust) the value of your contract to its new market value ($9,260), and charge you, say, a $300 surrender fee. You'd get a check for only $8,960.

Is that bad? Only if you break the contract. If you leave your money in for the entire term, you enjoy the fact that MVA fixed annuities pay a higher rate than book value fixed annuities. MVA contracts offer a better return because the contract issuer — the carrier — won't take a loss if you decide to pull money out when interest rates rise. *You* will. Lower risk for the carrier always translates into higher returns for you, and vice versa.

What if prevailing interest rates went *down* by 1 percent right after you bought your contract? In that case, the value of the carrier's bond (which still pays the earlier, higher rate of interest) would go *up* to, say, $10,800. (Bond prices and interest rates move in opposite directions.) If you withdrew all of your money at that moment, you'd get $10,800, minus your surrender fee. Would that be a reason to break the contract? Yes — but only if the surrender fee is less than $800, and only if you can find a better place to put your money. Also, if all other safe investments are paying 1 percent less per year than your annuity paid, you may want to leave your money where it is.

Don't be unduly distracted by surrender charges or MVAs. As long as you don't try to withdraw more than 10 percent of your money per year during the surrender period, the charges and adjustments don't matter much. If you think you may need your money before the end of the surrender period, don't buy a fixed annuity in the first place! For more about bonds, see *Bond Investing For Dummies* by Russell Wild (Wiley).

"Floating-rate" and "pass-through rate" contracts

Unlike any of the other fixed annuity contracts described so far, a few fixed annuity contracts offer interest rates that *float* from month to month. In other words, if interest rates go up a bit, you earn a little more that month. If interest rates go down, you earn less. Certain floating-rate fixed annuities give you a 30-day window once a year to take withdrawals without a penalty or a market value-adjustment.

You may also find annuities that offer *pass-through rates* of interest. Instead of paying you a fixed rate and keeping whatever interest it can earn on your money, the insurance company pays itself a fixed margin — perhaps 2 percent — and gives you the rest of the interest it can earn by investing your money. These annuities can be attractive because there's no upper limit on the amount of interest you can earn.

In these contracts, the insurance company typically tries for the highest possible returns by investing in *junk bonds* (bonds that offer higher interest rates than government or high-quality corporate bonds because the bond's issuer — the borrower — isn't as good a credit risk). To attract lenders, high-risk borrowers have to offer to pay their lenders higher interest rates.

These two types of fixed annuities have potentially higher returns — and higher risk — than conventional fixed annuities. But why add risk to a fixed annuity, whose principal virtue is safety? If you want more risk (and more reward), consider investing a larger percentage of your money in stocks. See Table 6-1 for more details and comparisons.

Table 6-1   Comparing the Two Main Types of Fixed Annuities

	Surrender Period	*First-Year Bonus*	*Renewal Rates*	*Market Value-Adjustment*	*Availability*
Single-year guarantee fixed annuity	Yes	In most cases; as high as 10 percent	Yes	Optional	Varies by state
Multi-year guarantee *CD-type* fixed annuity	Yes	In some cases; typically 1 percent	No	Optional	Varies by state

Comparing MYG fixed annuities to CDs

When shopping for a safe place to earn interest on spare cash, compare the rates on MYG fixed annuities to the current rates for CDs. Depending on market conditions, one may pay a significantly higher interest rate than the other. Table 6-2 shows how these two types of low-risk investments differ.

Table 6-2   A Comparison of Multi-Year Guarantee Fixed Annuities and Certificates of Deposit

MYG Fixed Annuities	*Certificates of Deposit*
Issued by an insurance company and sold by an insurance agent, broker, banker, or financial adviser.	Issued by and sold at a bank.
Assets are guaranteed by the by strength of the insurance company.	Up to $100,000 per depositor is insured the Federal Deposit Insurance Company (FDIC).
Grow tax-deferred; you pay no income tax on earnings until their withdrawal.	Interest is taxed as ordinary income for the year it's earned.

(continued)

Table 6-2 (continued)

MYG Fixed Annuities	Certificates of Deposit
Initial deposits range from $1,500 to $100,000.	Minimum investments start as low as $500.
When owners die, assets go to their beneficiaries without passing through probate court.	When owners die, assets become part of their estates and pass through probate court.
Withdrawals up to 10 percent each year usually have no surrender charge; withdrawals before age 59½ may be subject to a 10-percent federal penalty.	Withdrawals are penalized.
Option to annuitize assets (convert money to a guaranteed lifetime income).	No annuitization option.
Offer higher rates than CDs when long-term interest rates are higher than short-term interest rates.	Often offer higher rates than a fixed annuity when long-term rates are close to or lower than short-term interest rates.

Pros and Cons of Fixed Annuities

Fixed deferred annuities offer safe, but low, returns and tax deferral. Risk-averse investors buy them when they offer higher interest rates than CDs, when the stock market is declining or appears headed for a fall, and when they've already parked as much money as possible into other savings vehicles, like employer-sponsored retirement plans.

Here's a roundup of their pros and cons. First, I list the reasons why people buy fixed annuities. Then I list the reasons why people tend to shy away. Fixed annuities are neither good nor bad: They're either right for your particular needs or they're not. Only you can decide.

The pros include:

✔ **Safety:** Buying a fixed annuity with an MYG (see the preceding section) and holding it for the entire term is a safe, conservative way to grow your money. It's even safer than a bond or shares in a bond fund because a bond's price or the share prices of a bond fund can fall in response to rising interest rates.

✓ **Tax deferral:** Annuities, like IRAs and 401(k) plans, grow tax-deferred. You earn interest each year, but you don't pay taxes on it. The advantage? Your savings grows faster than it would if your gains were taxed every year.

The longer you defer taxes, the better — especially if you expect to be in a lower tax bracket in retirement.

✓ **Stable rates:** When you buy an MYG fixed annuity, you know its annual interest rate and the exact worth of your investment at the end of the term. As long as you don't make withdrawals, the result is entirely predictable.

✓ **Higher returns when bond-yield curve is steep:** A steep bond-yield curve occurs when bonds of longer maturities (like a ten-year Treasury bond) pay higher rates of interest than bonds of shorter maturities (like a three-month Treasury bill). At such times, fixed annuities often pay higher interest rates than CDs.

✓ **If the owner dies, the assets avoid probate:** It's hard to get excited about a benefit triggered by your own demise, but annuities are famous for them. If you die while owning a fixed annuity, your money goes straight to the beneficiaries on your contract. Because the money doesn't become part of your estate, it doesn't go through *probate* (the legal process), where creditors and relatives can lay claim to it.

✓ **The option to annuitize:** Like all annuity contracts, a fixed annuity can be converted to a retirement income stream. Although this option is the defining feature of annuities, few people know about it or care about it and even fewer use it.

The cons include:

✓ **Low liquidity:** Generally, if you take more than 10 percent of your money out of your fixed annuity during any single year of the surrender period, you pay a charge. You can avoid charges by buying a fixed annuity with a short surrender period or by using other sources of cash for emergencies.

Contracts with longer surrender periods typically pay higher rates, but don't be lured into tying up your money for longer than you can afford to.

✓ **Uncertain returns:** With single-year guarantee fixed annuities, you don't know the exact interest rate after the first year.

From what I've seen of renewal-rate histories, the rates on these contracts either stay the same or decline gradually after the first year. Rates are especially likely to fall if the annuity offers a first-year bonus.

✓ **Lower returns when bond-yield curve is flat:** When the yield curve is flat — that is, when long-term interest rates are the same or lower than short-term rates, as they were during the mid-2000s — you may get a better rate from a CD. (You can find an illustration of the yield curve in the business section of the Sunday *New York Times*.)

✓ **Federal penalty for early withdrawal:** If you withdraw money from a fixed annuity before age 59½, you may have to pay a penalty (10 percent of the amount withdrawn) to the IRS. *Note:* Under certain circumstances such as illness, you can withdraw money from an annuity before this age without a penalty. You may also be able to withdraw the money penalty free by taking Substantially Equal Period Payments, or SEPPs, over a minimum of five years.

The penalty is Uncle Sam's way of discouraging Americans from using annuities and other tax-deferred investments for anything but saving for retirement.

Buying a Fixed Annuity

You can buy a fixed deferred annuity almost as easily as you can pick up a gallon of milk or order a pizza. Because they are not registered securities, like stocks or bonds, insurance agents can sell them. You can buy them at the branch office of the bank where you keep your checking account, or the brokerage where you keep your mutual funds. You can eliminate the middleman and buy them direct from a financial services company like Vanguard or Fidelity. You can even shop for them on the Internet and order one over the phone.

Buying from an agent or broker

Most people buy their fixed annuities from independent insurance agents who sell the products of several insurance companies. But you can also purchase fixed annuities from *captive agents* (full-time employees of an insurance carrier), bankers, brokers, and financial advisers. Because fixed annuities are insurance products and not securities (such as stocks, bonds, and mutual funds), they can be sold by agents who have insurance licenses but not securities licenses.

The agent or broker may search through an annuity database to find a product that fits your needs, or she may recommend one of the annuities that she's most familiar with. In some cases — and you may never discover this — the seller may be paid a direct or indirect incentive to sell certain products.

In any case, be prepared to ask the seller the following questions before you buy:

✓ What is the interest rate?

✓ How many years is the interest rate guaranteed?

✓ How does the rate compare to the rates of other fixed annuities?

✔ How good is the rate compared to CDs?

✔ Does the annuity have a market value-adjustment?

✔ How long is the surrender period?

✔ How much can I withdraw each year without a penalty or adjustment?

✔ What financial rating does the insurance company have?

✔ What will the contract be worth at the end of the surrender period, assuming that I make no withdrawals?

✔ Can I get my money out without a penalty if I become seriously ill?

The following are questions you should ask yourself:

✔ Can I benefit from tax deferral?

In other words, when I withdraw money from my annuity, will my income tax bracket be lower than it is today?

✔ Do I intend to convert the contract to an income stream in retirement?

✔ Can I afford to cover a financial emergency without dipping into my annuity?

✔ Do I know and trust the agent? Is he likely to act in my best interest or in his own?

Unscrupulous insurance agents sometimes try to sell annuities to elderly individuals who have no need for a long-term investment. To prevent such abuses, regulatory agencies now insist that an annuity be a *suitable* investment for the purchaser. During the course of a sale, the seller should offer a *suitability assessment* form to help determine whether a fixed annuity is right for you.

To calculate the future value of your fixed annuity or to compare payouts of different annuities, use the following formula:

$$FV = P(1 + r)^n$$

The *FV* equals the future value of your annuity, *P* stands for the amount of your initial investment, *r* stands for the guaranteed interest rate, and *n* stands for the number of years until the end of the surrender period.

If a person puts $10,000 into a five-year fixed rate annuity that pays 4.30 percent per year, the equation is

$$\$10,000 \times (1.43)^5 = \$12,343.$$

You can calculate future value with a pocket calculator or one of the many compound interest calculators on the Web at sites like moneychimp.com or investopedia.com.

A word about fees

Fixed annuities do charge fees, but you don't pay them directly; they're built into the contract's interest rate. A company with lower fees can, in theory, afford to offer a higher rate.

What about commissions? Think of the insurance company as the manufacturer of the annuity and the brokerage as the distributor. A broker who sells you a $100,000 fixed annuity issued by an insurance company may earn

- ✔ A 2-percent commission ($2,000)

- ✔ Another 0.80 percent ($800) for incidental costs

- ✔ A trailing fee equal to 0.10 percent (starting at $100) every year you own the contract

The insurance company pays these fees and commissions out of the spread (the difference between what it earns by investing your money and what it pays you). You don't see the fees, and they shouldn't necessarily matter much to you. The important number is the interest rate that the insurance company promises to pay you.

The fixed annuity calculator at `finance.cch.com` even estimates the difference that a tax deferral can make on the growth of your assets. To compare fixed annuity rate offers to the risk-free Treasury rate at the same maturity, check government bond rates at `ustreas.gov`.

Shopping at online annuity supermarkets

After reading this chapter, you may feel empowered to start shopping for a fixed annuity on your own. For instance, you can shop on the Internet by visiting the Web sites of insurance companies, mutual fund companies like Vanguard and Fidelity, and online annuity distributors.

You can also surf over to `annuityadvantage.com`, click on Fixed Annuities or CD-Type, and start scrolling through a list of specific annuity products. (The products are usually grouped by length of surrender period.) Another site, `annuityfyi.com`, screens the entire universe of available fixed annuities and makes specific product recommendations.

These sites offer toll-free telephone numbers that lead you to a licensed insurance agent or customer service representative. A licensed insurance agent may be able to handle the entire sale over the phone, but a customer service representative will likely refer you to an agent in your area.

I don't recommend buying a fixed annuity online unless you have a strong grasp of fixed annuities and a clear understanding of your financial needs. Nevertheless, the information at these annuity sites can help prepare you for your encounters with agents and brokers.

Buying direct by Internet and phone

If you're the do-it-yourself type, you can buy your fixed annuity directly from a financial services company like Fidelity Investments (www.fidelity.com) or The Vanguard Group (www.vanguard.com). Follow the links to the annuity section to find out more about their products. If you like what you see, you can download an enrollment kit from the Web site or call the toll-free customer service number and ask the representative to mail you the kit.

Vanguard sells a five-year fixed annuity called the *Single 5* that's issued by Jefferson Pilot Life Insurance Company. Fidelity offers a variety of fixed annuities with surrender periods ranging from three to ten years from well-known insurers like Principal Financial, MetLife, Genworth Financial, and John Hancock. Their rates may be slightly higher than the rates from an insurance agent because you're buying directly from the insurer.

Unlike a CD, whose value is backed by the FDIC, a fixed annuity is only as safe as the insurance company that offers it. So, choose a company that has an A rating from the major insurance rating agencies such as A.M. Best, Standard & Poor's, and Fitch. The more A's and plus marks you see in the rating, the stronger the insurance company — and the more easily you'll sleep at night.

Some online annuity supermarkets feature one or two B+s among their listings or recommendations. (A B+ means a slight risk that the carrier won't be able to meet its obligations.) Should you shun a fixed annuity from a carrier with a B+ rating? Not necessarily, but don't go lower. And don't take the added risk unless you're getting a higher return. (For more about ratings, check Appendix A at the back of the book.)

Locking in your rate

Fixed annuity rates, like mortgage rates, may change between the time you choose your annuity and the day your money arrives at the insurance company (or, in the case of Fidelity and Vanguard, at the mutual fund company). Your rate is not "locked in" until then.

Naming an annuitant and beneficiary

When you buy any annuity, you — the contract owner — must name an *annuitant* and a *beneficiary*. The annuitant's life expectancy is used to calculate the size of your income payments if you convert your fixed annuity to an income stream. (For more on annuitants, see Chapter 3.) The beneficiaries will receive the cash payment of your fixed annuity's current value if you die while the money is still invested.

Paying for your fixed annuity

You can pay for your fixed annuity in several ways:

- ✔ **A check or electronic transfer:** Simply attach a check to your application form and hand them both to your insurance agent: You can also mail them to the post office box of a direct marketer.

- ✔ **A transfer of mutual fund assets:** If you already have mutual funds at Vanguard or Fidelity, you can buy one of their fixed annuities with a transfer of mutual fund assets. On the annuity application, simply indicate the mutual funds you want to sell.

- ✔ **IRA assets:** As a rule, don't buy an annuity with money from an IRA or an employer-sponsored retirement plan because it means you're putting a tax-deferred investment in a tax-deferred account.

  Exceptions to the rule do occur. For example, if you're retired and have moved your employer-plan savings into a rollover IRA (an individual retirement account that you set up specifically to receive your employer-plan savings), you may use a portion of those savings to buy a fixed annuity, with the expectation that you will eventually convert the annuity to an income stream.

- ✔ **A 1035 exchange:** If you own a deferred annuity (that is, an annuity that you haven't converted to an income stream), you can transfer the assets into a new annuity with a 1035 exchange.

  Before you initiate a 1035 exchange, call your current insurance company to find out whether you'll incur a surrender charge or market value-adjustment on the withdrawal. If the answer is "Yes," reconsider the transfer. (For more on 1035 exchanges, see Chapter 13.)

- ✔ **The proceeds of a cash-value life insurance policy:** If you have a life insurance policy that you no longer need, you can convert it to a fixed annuity.

Managing Your Fixed Annuity

Fixed annuities, especially multi-year guarantee products, are low-maintenance investments. Aside from checking your quarterly statements, you can buy them and forget them until they mature (that is, when the surrender period ends).

The few fixed annuity contracts that allow you to divide your investment among different types of bonds may also allow you to shift money from one type to another periodically.

A floating-rate annuity may allow you to decide as often as every month whether to cash out of your contract or not. If you bought your annuity at Fidelity or Vanguard, you can go to your online account and watch your money grow slightly from day to day.

Getting your money out scot-free

Most contracts let you take out 10 percent of your assets every year without a surrender charge or market value-adjustment. Some allow you to take out only the interest your money earned in the prior year. Many contracts also allow you to take out all or most of your money if you become seriously ill or must enter a nursing home. You can usually request a withdrawal by phone or by mail. You may also be able to set up automatic transfers from your annuity to your bank account.

Renewing your contract (optional)

When the term of your three-, five-, seven-, or ten-year contract ends, you don't automatically receive your original interest rate when you renew. You'll need to choose one of the following options:

✔ Take your money out.

  If you do this before you're 59½ years old, you'll owe income tax on the interest you've earned and a 10-percent penalty.

✔ Leave your money where it is and let it earn whatever one-year interest rate the insurance company offers you.

✔ Roll it into a new multi-year contract at the rates the insurer offers.

As you scan a list of fixed annuities at an online annuity supermarket, the contracts with bonuses may catch your eye. But what's a bonus really worth? Consider these two contracts with 10-year rate guarantees:

✔ Annuity A pays a 5.35-percent bonus rate the first year and a 4.60-percent base rate for the next nine years.

✔ Annuity B pays a flat 4.65 percent for ten years.

Which contract is worth more? They're basically worth the same. My online compound interest calculator (moneychimp.com) tells me:

✔ Contract A will grow to $10,535 in the first year and compound to $15,791 over the next nine years.

✔ Contract B will compound at 4.65 percent to $15,754 over the full ten years.

In short, the bonus is worth only $37 per year more and at a rate only 0.03 percent higher. The bonus annuity grows at 4.68 percent over ten years, compared to the flat-rate annuity's 4.65-percent growth rate.

The moral of this story? Beware of bonuses. They're a terrific marketing tool (who can resist a bonus?), but they don't necessarily add value.

Be wary of contracts where the first-year surrender charge is higher than the length of the surrender period or where the surrender period lasts longer than the guaranteed period. (For instance, a contract may have a seven-year surrender period where the first-year penalty is 10 percent. Or a contract that guarantees a specific rate for seven years may have a ten-year surrender period.) Unless these contracts offer a higher interest rate or some other distinct advantage, don't accept the added restrictions.

When buying any financial product:

- Never take uncompensated risks.
- Never make unrewarded concessions.

Chapter 7

Experimenting with Index Annuities

*I*f everyone followed the cardinal rule of personal finance, *"Never invest in something you don't understand,"* virtually no one would invest in index annuities. Few of the insurance agents who sell index annuities — and even fewer of the people who own them — truly understand how they work. Yet tens of thousands of Americans have put tens of billions of dollars into these products since 1995.

Index annuities — also called *equity indexed* annuities (EIAs) and *fixed indexed* annuities (FIAs) — are actually a type of fixed annuity (see Chapter 6).

As such, they protect you from losing your investment and guarantee a minimum return. But they also offer you a chance to earn additional interest when the stock market goes up.

In this chapter, I explain the principles of index annuities and offer a glimpse of their infinite variety. You can decide whether or not they deliver the "best of both worlds": the safety of a bond plus the growth potential of stocks. You may just as easily conclude that they offer the *least* of both worlds: a lower guaranteed return than bonds and a smaller potential return than stocks.

Throughout this book, I refer to annuities as *contracts* or as *investments*. That's because annuities can be both. To the extent that the insurance company that sells you an annuity offers you a guarantee — a guarantee against loss of principal, a guaranteed interest rate return, or a guaranteed income —

annuities are contracts. To the extent that risk is involved — a variable annuity and an index annuity both involve a risk that the stock market will go up or down — annuities act like investments. Index annuities coyly straddle the line between the two.

Defining Index Annuities

Index annuities are as new to the investment world as digital cellphones are to the telecommunications world. They were created in 1996, when investors were shifting their attention from bond-based investments like fixed annuities to stock-based investments, including mutual funds and variable annuities. (The greatest stock market rally in the history of the universe was well underway by then.)

To capitalize on the excitement over stocks, some insurance carriers started marketing a new kind of fixed annuity, called an *equity-indexed annuity*, or EIA. Like other fixed annuities, the EIA offered protection against loss of your initial investment, a payout to your beneficiaries if you died, the ability to defer taxes on interest earned, and the option to convert your money to retirement income.

But a couple of new twists were added. If stock prices rose during a specific time period, EIA owners received an interest rate based on the rise in stocks. If stocks fell, EIA owners earned a minimum interest rate. EIAs were sold as the perfect investment for anyone who wanted the benefit of stock market gains without the risk of investing in the stock market.

Sales of EIAs languished during the late 1990s. Between 2001 and 2003, many investors avoided bonds because they paid too little interest. (Low rates were great for mortgage buyers, but not for investors!) At the same time, investors were still in shock from the stock market crash of 2000, and avoided stocks. Insurers promoted EIAs as the perfect solution: an investment that grew when the stock market went up but stayed the same (more or less) if the stock market went down. Sales of EIAs jumped from $5.5 billion in 2000 to $25 billion in 2006.

Since 2006, EIAs have undergone several changes, including a name change. Insurers began calling these products FIAs (*fixed indexed annuities*) instead of EIAs, in order to avoid suggestions (and avert any accusations) that EIA contract owners were investing their money in stocks (also known as *equities*). Many investment professionals simply called them "index annuities." That's how I refer to them in this chapter and elsewhere in this book.

Seeing How Index Annuities Work

The issuer of an index annuity contract (an insurance company) guarantees that, as long as you own the contract and abide by its rules, you can't lose money. When the stock market goes down, you lose nothing. When the stock market goes up, you reap about half the gains. Sounds reasonable. But how does it work?

What are your (index) options?

When you hand over a chunk of money — at least $2,000 or so — to the insurance company that issues your index annuity, the carrier uses your money for three purposes:

- ✔ It puts most of the money in bonds, which earn interest.
- ✔ It deducts a small amount for its own expenses.
- ✔ It uses the rest of the money to buy *index options.*

Index options are the genie at the heart of index annuities. But what is an index? And what are options?

A market *index* is a scale that reflects the average price of a particular group of stocks or bonds. The Dow Jones Industrial Average, the oldest and most famous market index, is based on an average of the prices of 30 of the largest U.S. companies. Other indexes represent the average prices of European stocks, Asian stocks, oil company stocks, and so on. The index most widely used by investors is the Standard & Poor's 500 Index, an average of the prices of the 500 largest U.S. companies.

Options are the right (but not the obligation) to buy or sell something. Originally they served as a form of insurance. For example, a bus company might buy an option to purchase 10,000 gallons of gasoline next year for a specific price as a way to protect itself from a much higher increase in prices. Or an investor might buy similar options simply to make a profit.

Suppose you pay $500 for the option to buy 10,000 gallons of gas next year at $2.50 per gallon. (Options are bought and sold every day, just like stocks.) If the price of gas rises to $3 per gallon, your $500 option will be worth $5,000, and you could sell it for that amount. That's because you own the right to buy 10,000 gallons of gas for $25,000 (at $2.50 per gallon) and sell it for $30,000. If you sell the option, your profit will be $4,500 ($5,000 minus the $500 you pay for the option).

When insurance companies buy index options, they do virtually the same thing as the person who bought gasoline options. But instead of profiting from a rise in the price of gasoline, they profit from an increase in the average prices of a certain group of stocks, as measured by a market index — usually the S&P 500 Index. Like the buyer of gasoline options who multiplied his investment ninefold when the price of gas went up, the buyers of index options can multiply their investment many times when the index goes up. If the S&P 500 Index drops, they let their option expire unused.

In short, the insurance company makes money when the index goes up and loses very little when the index goes down. This allows it to keep its promise to you: to pay you a portion of the index gain in years when the index goes up and nothing in years when it goes down. If the index never goes up during the entire life of the index annuity contract, you won't lose anything and you'll still earn a guaranteed minimum interest rate of 2 or 3 percent.

Note that the carrier never invests your money directly in stocks. Instead, it invests in options to buy all the stocks in a particular market index. Many people get confused and think that index annuities involve investments in stocks. They do not.

Buying a (hypothetical) index annuity

Here's an example of an index annuity in action. Assume that you inherited $10,000 and you want to put the money into savings for about ten years. You've considered investing in bonds, bond mutual funds (baskets of bonds), fixed annuities, and certificates of deposit, but you'd like to earn a higher interest rate than they currently pay. On the other hand, you can't afford to risk losing any of the money. So your insurance agent introduces you to index annuities.

Out of the dozens of types of index annuities on the market, the agent asks you to consider one with an *annual reset*, a 55 percent *participation rate*, a nine-year *surrender period*, and a *guaranteed minimum interest rate* of 3 percent on 90 percent of your premium, or initial contribution. He explains what each of those terms means:

- ✔ **Annual:** The word *annual* here means that every year on the anniversary of the day you bought your annuity, the insurance company will measure how far the S&P 500 Index rose or fell in the past 365 days.

- ✔ **Participation rate:** This term expresses your share of the rise of the index. In this example, your participation rate is 55 percent. If the S&P 500 Index goes up 20 percent, your account will grow by 55 percent of 20 percent, or 11 percent. If the S&P 500 didn't rise or if it fell, the value of your account stays at $10,000.

✔ **Reset:** When used in the phrase *annual reset*, this term means that your annual gains will be locked in as you earn them. If your $10,000 account grew by 11 percent, to $11,100 in the past, then it can't fall below $11,100 (unless you withdraw money from your account).

✔ **Surrender period:** The agent suggested an index annuity with a surrender period of nine years. If you withdraw more than 10 percent of your money in any given year during that time, you will pay a surrender charge on the excess amount withdrawn — not on the entire withdrawal. The charge will be 9 percent in the first year, 8 percent in the second year, 7 percent in the third year, and so on until it shrinks to zero by the end of the term. (The charge will be waived if you die or go into a nursing home.)

✔ **Guaranteed minimum interest rate:** This number tells you the absolute minimum amount that your account will be worth at the end of the nine-year surrender period. In this contract, the guaranteed rate is 3 percent of 90 percent. In other words, the insurance company guarantees the final value will be (Get out your compounding calculator!) $9,000 (90 percent of $10,000) compounded at 3 percent for nine years, or $11,742.

Why only 90 percent? According to the Insurance Information Institute, recent state laws, called *nonforfeiture* regulations, dictate that the guaranteed minimum value of an index annuity must be at least 87.5 percent of the premium paid, accumulated at an interest rate of 1 percent to 3 percent.

After hearing the agent's description, you decide to commit $10,000 to the purchase of the index annuity. Suppose that the day of purchase is May 15, 2008. Suppose further that by May 15, 2009, the first anniversary of your contract, the S&P 500 Index has risen 20 percent in value, from 13,000 to 15,600. In that case, the insurance company credits 11 percent interest (55 percent of 20 percent) to your account, pushing its value up to $11,100.

The process repeats itself each year. If by May 15, 2010, the stock market falls 20 percent, you account value stays at $11,100. Note that it doesn't lose 20 percent of its value ($2,220), as it would if it had been invested directly in stocks. If, a year later, on May 15, 2011, the S&P 500 rises another 20 percent, your account will grow by 11 percent, to $13,320. The process goes on for nine years, when the term of the contract expires and you can withdraw all of your money.

If by chance the stock market falls for nine consecutive years — a worst-case scenario that has never occurred — your contract will be worth the $11,742 previously noted.

You've heard of calendar years — they start on January 1 and end on December 31. And you've heard of fiscal years — they often start on July 1 and end on June 30. With annuities, you have *contract years*. They start on the day you buy your contract and end on every anniversary of that date. Comparing your contract's performance to the performance of any other investment is tough, because each contract lives in its own particular time zone.

Comparing Types of Index Annuities

There are two main types of index annuities, which differ in the time period over which they measure changes in the market index used in the contract. (As I mention, that's usually, but not always, the S&P 500.) These are the *annual reset* (used in my earlier example in this chapter) and the *point-to-point* contract, also known as the *term end point* contract.

Within each of these index annuity types, variations abound. Insurance companies use many different methods to calculate the percentage change in the index they credit to your account. These calculations are known as *adjustments*. The 55 percent participation rate in the example that I use in the preceding section was an adjustment to the index gain.

Adjustment methods are critical elements in index annuities. In any index annuity, your account never grows by as much as the index grows. If the index goes up 10 percent in one year, you might receive a 5.5 percent gain. If the index goes up 80 percent over the entire life of the contract, you might receive only 42 percent.

Why can't the insurance company give you the entire change in the index? Remember that the insurance company only invests a small portion of your money in index options. It invests most of your money in bonds. The profit the carrier earns from trading options can't possibly match the change in stock prices — only a portion of it. By investing in bonds, the insurance company can guarantee you a minimum return. By investing in index options, the carrier can offer gains that are linked to but not equal to stock market growth.

Annual reset (ratchet)

An annual reset index annuity can be compared to a climber scaling the face of a mountain. She climbs 25 yards and hammers a steel piton into a crevice in the rock. She then sets out to climb another 25 yards. If she loses her grip, she can fall no farther than the last piton.

An annual reset annuity works much the same way, except that it conserves progress in increments of years rather than yards. On every anniversary of the day you bought your contract, your account value resets either at the same value or a higher value, but never at a lower value. This type of crediting method is also known as a *ratchet* because, like a ratchet gear, it only allows movement in one direction.

There are many annual reset annuities, which differ according to their method of calculating your share of the change in the index. Different elements of these methods may be combined with each other, to produce an almost infinite variety of hybridized index annuities with deepening levels of complexity. Here are a few examples:

- ✔ **Annual reset with averaging:** In this method, the carrier notes the level of the market index every 30 days after you buy your contract. At the end of the year, the carrier averages the twelve monthly levels and compares that to the level at the beginning of the year. If the index starts the year at 1,100 and then averages 1,200 over the next 12 months, your gain will be 100 (1,200 – 1,100) divided by 1,100, or about 9.1 percent. This method of adjustment protects you from losing gains early in the year to a slump at the end.

- ✔ **Annual reset with monthly point to point:** This method is also called *additive serial point-to-point*. It calculates the gain or loss in the index every month, and then adds them up at the end of the year to arrive at your gain. This may be the only adjustment method where your returns can be hurt by a sharp, temporary decline in the index. A large loss in a single month can negate several months of modest gains.

- ✔ **Annual reset with a cap:** A *cap* places an upper limit on the amount of interest the insurance company will pay you in a month or year. A *monthly cap* might allow you to gain no more than 3.5 percent per month. An *annual cap* might prevent you from earning more than 12 percent in a year. Some caps (index caps) might prevent you from benefiting from more than a specific increase in the market index. For instance, the index might go up 18 percent in one year, but 15 percent might be the most that you can use in calculating your share of the return.

- ✔ **Annual reset with a participation rate:** To adjust your returns, the insurance company might combine a participation rate with a cap. For instance, a contract might offer a 100 percent participation rate, up to 8 percent per year (in other words, an 8 percent cap), rather than a participation rate of 55 percent with no cap. One hundred percent just sounds better.

- ✔ **Annual reset with a yield spread, margin, or asset fee:** Another way that insurance companies adjust the index gain is simply by taking a fee off the top. These fees are also known as *spreads* or *margins*. Suppose the market index rises 10 percent one year, and your contract has a 3 percent spread. Your account will rise in value by 7 percent.

These adjustments — caps, yields, spreads, and participation rates — are often called the *moving parts* of an index annuity. On any given contract, one of them is likely to change from year to year. That's right. You can lock yourself into a multiyear index annuity and discover after one year that the insurance company intends to lower the cap, widen its spread, or shrink your participation rate.

If all of this sounds like madness to you, don't worry — there is method in it. When you buy an index annuity, the insurance company guarantees you a return based on a specific formula. The financial markets, however, can change in ways (it can become too erratic, for instance) that would make it too expensive for the insurance company to fulfill its guarantee to you. In that case, the insurance company may decide to make its guarantee less generous — that is, it would raise prices — by lowering the cap, widening its spread, or shrinking your participation rate.

Point-to-point (term end point)

When you own a point-to-point index annuity, the insurance company waits until the end of the entire surrender period — as opposed to the end of every year — to measure the progress of the index. The carrier then credits the percentage gain or loss in the index and credits you with a percentage of the gain, if any has occurred.

The point-to-point method can leave you guessing almost right up until the end of the term — from 3 to 12 years or more — exactly what how much you'll gain over that period, if anything. In a worst-case scenario, you could watch the index rise for years, and then lose your early gains to a steep decline in the level of the market index during the last year or two of the contract.

Because most people shy away from such a stark risk, many point-to-point index annuities include a provision that protects investors against a catastrophic decline in the market index during the final years of the contract, two of which are:

- ✔ **Point-to-final average:** Under this often-used method, the starting point is the value of the index when you buy your contract. The end point may be an average of the monthly index values during the last year of the surrender period. By averaging the final year, the contract reduces the potential impact of a bear market at the end of the term.

- ✔ **High-water mark:** This is another way to protect your gains from being negated by a sharp decline in the final year of a point-to-point EIA. The insurer looks at the index values on all the anniversaries of the day you bought your contract — not the highest value ever achieved by the index — and picks the highest one. If this high-water mark is higher than the value at the end of the contract, your gain is based on the value of the index at the high-water mark, not the value at the end of the contract.

If you're a glutton for more details about crediting and adjustment methods, I recommend Jack Marrion's definitive book, *Index Annuities: Power & Protection* (Advantage Compendium, 2004).

Looking at the Pros of Index Annuities — and Avoiding the Cons

Depending on your age, your needs, your tolerance for risk, and the interest rate when you go to buy your annuity, index annuities can be either a great investment or a lousy investment. In this section I outline the pros and cons for you, and then I tell you what to do to avoid the cons.

For some people under certain market conditions, some index annuities offer "the best of both worlds." That is, they provide the safety of bonds with the potential for stock-market-like returns. For other people at other times, they might offer the worst of both worlds — a lower return than bonds and a lower return than stocks. In short, they represent a compromise.

Here are some of the reasons you might consider buying an index annuity:

- **Protection from loss:** The great attraction of index annuities is that you don't lose money when the stock market goes down. When stocks lost a third of their value in 2000 and 2001, people who owned index annuities lost nothing. When stock prices began climbing in 2003, they earned money right away. They didn't have to spend two or three years merely recovering their earlier losses.

- **Guaranteed minimum return:** If the stock market were to decline in every year that you owned your index annuity, you would still earn a minimum return. A typical index annuity offers a guaranteed return of 3 percent per year on 90 percent of your initial investment. That's the equivalent of a growth rate of about 2 percent per year.

- **Higher potential returns than bonds, bond funds, certificates of deposits, or conventional fixed annuities:** The returns on index annuities are indirectly linked to the average prices of stocks, which have more growth potential than bonds. Generally, index annuities are said to provide a rate of return somewhere between those of stocks and bonds.

- **Protection from sequence-of-returns risk:** A steep investment loss within five years before or after you retire can put you in a financial hole that you can't dig out of. This vulnerability is called *sequence of returns risk*. By keeping your money in an indexed annuity during that period, you can protect it from this risk while still benefiting from an increase in stock prices.

- **Tax deferral:** You pay no tax on interest that your index annuity earns until you withdraw it from your account. When you defer taxes, more money stays in your account, where it contributes to the snowball effect known as compounding. Tax deferral also allows you to pay taxes on your investment returns when it suits you, not when it suits Uncle Sam.

✔ **Lifetime income option:** Like almost all other annuities, index annuities give you the option to convert the value of your account to a guaranteed income that will last for a specific number of years or for as long as you live (or for as long as either you or your spouse is living).

✔ **Flexibility:** Most index annuities link their interest rates to changes in the S&P 500 Index, which reflects the prices of the stocks of the 500 largest U.S. corporations. But some contracts allow you to link your gains to other indexes, which may represent stocks of mid-size companies, small companies, foreign stocks, and so on. Some contracts allow you to diversify your premium (your investment) among several different indexes. Diversification is good: It can bring more consistent returns.

Now, here are the cons:

✔ **Complexity:** As I note at the beginning of this chapter, few people truly understands index annuities. You might grasp the general principle behind them — it's not quite rocket science — but you'll have a heck of a time understanding or evaluating the many different formulas they use to calculate your return.

✔ **Unpredictability:** Index annuities don't give you the steady, reliable returns that you expect from a fixed annuity. Stock prices move up and down. Insurance companies change adjustment factors from year to year, and don't ordinarily publish a record of their past adjustments. If you're looking for predictability, you won't necessarily find it here.

✔ **High commissions:** Insurance companies pay salesmen commissions as high as 9 percent on the sale of index annuities. In other words, when you pay the insurance company $100,000, the carrier pays the salesman $9,000. Because the carrier obviously doesn't plan to lose money on the transaction, the $9,000 must eventually come from you in the form of lower returns.

✔ **Sold mainly by insurance agents:** Virtually all index annuities, like other fixed annuities, are insurance products that can be sold by insurance agents. Such agents are, by and large, fine people, but they do not have any fiduciary responsibility toward you. Unlike financial advisers, they aren't required to provide objective, disinterested financial advice or make recommendations that have your welfare in mind, not theirs.

✔ **Lack of liquidity:** When people complain about index annuities, they rarely if ever complain about the returns. Instead, they complain about the fact that they can't access their money when they need it. Apparently, they didn't read the fine print. Index annuities, by nature, lock up your money for at least five years. If you think you'll need more than 10 percent of your money in any given year, annuities aren't the right investment for you.

✔ **No dividends to reinvest:** One of the advantages of investing directly in stock mutual funds is that many stocks issue dividends, which mutual fund companies will automatically reinvest for you. It's estimated that up to 20 percent of your returns from investing in stock mutual funds comes from reinvested dividends. But index annuities don't buy stocks, and therefore don't collect dividends.

✔ **Short track record:** Index annuities were invented in 1996. They haven't been around long enough for anyone to be sure of their long-term value.

✔ **Federal penalty for withdrawals before age 59½:** Unless you qualify for one of the hardship-related exceptions, the Internal Revenue Service will charge a 10 percent penalty for any earnings you take out of any annuity before age 59½. If a 35-year-old put $20,000 into a five-year index annuity and withdrew $22,000 two years later, he'd owe income tax on his $2,000 profit and a $200 (10 percent of $2,000) penalty.

In the next four sections, I tell you what you can do to head off some of the nastier cons.

When comparing index annuities, bear in mind that all the factors in the various crediting methods — the participation rates, caps, lengths of surrender periods, and bonuses — play a zero-sum game with each other. If one product offers a more generous participation rate than another, you can bet that it will offer a less generous cap, or a wider yield, or a longer surrender period. As one annuity seller said, "There are only so many pennies in a dollar."

Bogus bonuses

Bonuses are one of the world's most effective selling techniques. If a salesman offers four of anything for the price of three, he's bound to sell a lot of them. The top-selling index annuity in America as of this writing, the MasterDex 10 from Allianz Life Insurance Company of North America, offers a 10 percent bonus when you buy the contract. If you purchase a MasterDex 10 contract for $100,000, Allianz Life credits an extra $10,000 to your account.

But bonuses can be bogus. Generally, the greater the bonus, the longer your money will be tied up in a surrender period. Check the fine print. You may discover that you forfeit the bonus if you take any money out during the surrender period. You may also forfeit the bonus if you don't convert your entire annuity to a lifetime income stream (the conversion known as annuitization).

If you already own an annuity — any kind of annuity — an agent may propose that you transfer it to a new and possibly better annuity through a 1035 exchange (see Chapter 13). In such a situation, the agent might suggest that the bonus paid by the new annuity will offset any surrender charge you might be assessed for leaving your original annuity too early. Don't take the bait! The surrender charge you pay when you leave the other annuity is real money. The bonus, on the other hand, will only belong to you under certain conditions.

Two-tiered contracts can lead to tears

As a rule, you should avoid *two-tier* index annuities.

Most index annuities are *single-tier* products. When the surrender period — the period during which you can be hit with a penalty for withdrawing more than 10 percent of your money — is over, you can take all of your money out, interest and penalty free. Or, if you choose, you can give your money to the insurance company in return for a guaranteed lifetime income at that point.

Two-tiered index annuities, however, *require* you to convert the value of your contract to a guaranteed income during retirement. You can *never* take all of your money out at once. Two-tiered contracts often offer a more appealing crediting method — that is, you may earn more during the period before the conversion — but they may take it all back by giving you a skimpier monthly payment after the conversion.

Debunking "100 percent participation" claims

Would you rather have 100 percent of 55 percent than 55 percent of 100 percent? Many people would choose the former over the latter. That's why so many index annuity contracts offer 100 percent participation in index returns. It suggests that if the index goes up 10 percent, your money will grow by 10 percent. You will inevitably discover, however, that the contract gives you 100 percent of a portion of the change in the index. The moral of this story: Beware of crediting methods that appear to give you the entire gain in the index. No index annuity can do that.

Skirting the "monthly point-to-point with a cap" method

One very popular index annuity offered a crediting method called "monthly point-to-point with a 3 percent cap." The brochures suggested that you could earn up to 36 percent a year with this method, because if the index went up 3 percent per month for a year, it would add up to 36 percent.

The salesman probably won't tell you that, although your potential monthly gain is capped at 3 percent, there is no limit to your potential monthly loss. If the index fell by 10 percent in a month, it would wipe out more than three months of 3 percent gains. The index would have to rise 10 percent just to get you back to your previous level.

Tracking Index Annuity Performance

Although index annuity enthusiasts say that these contracts produce returns that are roughly halfway between the returns of stocks and bonds, it's not easy to find data that proves it.

Independent analysts have taken a variety of index annuity crediting methods and tested them under actual historical market conditions, hoping to find clues to how they might perform under various market conditions in the future. These efforts, which I describe in the next section, raised just as many questions as they answered, however.

It turns out that different crediting methods offer widely different patterns of returns. Depending on the market conditions, some crediting methods apparently perform better than others. You have no way of knowing which will serve you best. Still, a couple of rules of thumb seem to have emerged from what little research has been done.

Top performing index annuities (hypothetically)

Premium Producers Group (PPG), owner and distributor of MCP Premium software, (Mcppremium.com) decided to compare the hypothetical performance of 15 index annuities to the actual performance of an S&P 500 Index mutual fund (a fund whose share price moves up and down with the S&P 500 Index) under market conditions that occurred from August 1996 to August 2006.

Over that stretch of time, a $100,000 investment in an S&P Index fund would have grown to $313,123, a gain of more than 200 percent. By comparison, the 15 different index annuities in the analysis would have grown to between $158,030 and $212,528, for a gain of between 58 percent and 112 percent. In other words, the best-performing index annuities produced what their designers intended them to produce: a little over half the stock market return.

The top sellers of EIAs in the U.S., 2006

The life insurance companies listed below are the largest sellers of EIAs in the United States. They account for about 85 percent of all EIAs sold in the country. All of them have a strong or superior rating for financial strength.

- ✔ Allianz Life
- ✔ American Equity
- ✔ AmerUs Group (AVIVA)

- ✔ EquiTrust
- ✔ ING
- ✔ Jackson National Life
- ✔ Jefferson-Pilot
- ✔ Midland National
- ✔ Old Mutual
- ✔ Sun Life

Five year index annuity returns (November 2006)

One of the few sources of real-time data on index annuities is Jack Marrion of Advantage Compendium (`indexannuity.com`). He collects performance data from several of the insurance companies that sell index annuities and periodically reports his findings on his Web site. According to Marrion, during the five years from November 2001 to November 2006, index annuities (those whose returns were reported) returned between 2.25 percent and 6.25 percent per year, or roughly 4.25 percent, on average.

All things considered, that's not bad. Prices of large company stocks, as measured by the S&P 500 Index, rose by only about 5 percent per year (28 percent in total) during that time. The average stock mutual fund returned 8.35 percent per year, the average taxable bond fund (as distinguished from tax-free, municipal bond funds) yielded 5 percent per year, and the average certificate of deposit (a bond-like savings instrument sold by banks) yielded 2.3 percent per year. Index annuities, on average, delivered about half the return of the average stock fund while providing complete protection against loss. Still, with returns as low as 2.25 percent, some index annuities didn't guarantee much more than safety.

If you're looking for an investment that combines the features of both stocks and bonds, consider a balanced mutual fund instead of an index annuity. Balanced funds invest part of their assets in bonds and part in stocks, and provide a strong, relatively stable return without the restrictions on withdrawals imposed by an index annuity contract. Most mutual fund companies offer a wide range of balanced funds. If you buy your balanced fund from Fidelity Investments, Vanguard, or T.Rowe Price, you'll pay next to nothing in fees.

Product Review: Midland National Life Paragon

Let's take a stroll through Midland National Life Insurance's Paragon EIA, which appeared in 2006 as an addition to the company's Veridian and Legacy lines of EIAs. (Midland National is one of more than 30 companies that offer EIAs in the United States. This example is not intended to be a recommendation or endorsement of any Midland National Life annuity.)

Industry ratings

The company has received *very strong, excellent,* and *superior* ratings of financial strength from the major ratings agencies, such as A.M. Best, Fitch, and Standard & Poor's.

Surrender periods

Contract owners can choose among three different surrender periods, at the end of which they can withdraw all of their money with no penalty, including all index-related credits. There are 7-year, 10-year, and 14-year options.

Indexes

You can divide your premium among any combination of seven index options (S&P 500, S&P MidCap 400, the Dow Jones Industrial Average, the Nasdaq 100, the Russell 2000, the Dow Jones EURO STOXX 50, the Lehman Brothers U.S. Aggregate bond index), and a fixed account that pays a rate that may fluctuate but will never fall below the guaranteed minimum established when you buy the contract.

Crediting methods

You can also divide your premium among any of three different annual-reset crediting methods: an annual point-to-point with a participation rate; a monthly averaging with participation rate; and a monthly point-to-point with a cap. You can also put a portion of your money in the insurance carrier's general fund, where it will earn at least the minimum guaranteed interest.

The participation rate can change from year to year, but Paragon guarantees that you'll always get at least 10 percent of the percentage gain in the index. That is, if the index goes up 10 percent, you get a credit of at least 1 percent. The monthly averaging method takes an average of the index values at the end of each of the preceding 12 months and compares it with the index value at the start of the year.

Withdrawal restrictions

As for getting access to your money, Midland National lets you take out 10 percent each year penalty free after the first year. Any excess is subject to a surrender fee, plus a possible adjustment of the surrender value to reflect any rise or fall in interest rates since you bought the contract.

Suppose you invest $100,000 initially and withdraw $20,000 in the second year. Of that, only $10,000 is penalty free. The other $10,000 is subject to a 9 percent surrender fee, or $900. (If you're under age 591/2, any earnings you withdraw are subject to a 10 percent federal tax penalty.) The insurer waives the surrender charge on money taken out to satisfy federal Required Minimum Distributions after age 70½

Midland National also lets you take out 20 percent per year penalty free if you're confined to a nursing home for at least 90 days in a row, as long as you bought the contract before you reached age 75 and have owned the contract at least a year.

Converting your annuity to an income

You may have reached an age where you'd like to turn your EIA savings into a monthly income for life. Under the Paragon contract, you can do that as early as one year after you buy the contract.

(continued)

(continued)

The income options are fairly flexible. For instance, you can arrange to receive a specific income for as long as it lasts, or you can receive income for a specific number of years (between 5 and 20). You can provide an income for yourself, or for you and your spouse.

Paragon offers incentives to convert your savings to an income. Under the seven-year option, you receive a 1 percent bonus for annuitizing after the eighth year of ownership. Under the ten-year option, you receive a 1 percent bonus after the tenth year. Under the 14-year option, you receive a 2 percent bonus after the 14th year.

Why You Should Consider Waiting

As of this writing, index annuities are a legal cloud. The number of consumer complaints about them has risen, and so has the number of lawsuits against insurance companies who provide them. The annuity industry itself is partly to blame. Too many independent insurance agents, tempted by high commissions and acting with little, if any, supervision, have sold index annuities to elderly people who didn't understand that they'd suffer a surrender fee if they took too much money out of their annuity too soon.

Because of these alleged abuses, the sales of index annuities are coming under greater scrutiny. In the summer of 2005, the Financial Industry Regulatory Authority (FINRA, formerly the National Association of Securities Dealers, or NASD) announced that independent agents who are also licensed to sell securities — such as mutual funds — should henceforth submit their prospective sales of index annuities for review and approval to the same supervisors who routinely review and approve their sales of mutual funds. The index annuity industry has railed against this change. Rather than submitting to additional regulation, many independent agents (who account for more than 90 percent of all index annuity sales) have simply stopped selling index annuities.

Until the dust from this controversy settles, you might consider waiting to purchase your next index annuity. (In September 2007, Allianz Life, the largest seller of index annuities in the U.S., settled a suit filed against it by the state of Minnesota by agreeing to refund up to $325 million in index annuity premiums to as many as 7,000 Minnesotans.)

At the very least, as I suggested in the title of this chapter, you should regard a venture into index annuities as a financial experiment, at least until the next generation of index annuities is developed. Given the benefit of greater scrutiny, the index annuities of tomorrow are likely to be less complex, less expensive, less restrictive, and more rewarding than the index annuities available today.

Chapter 8

Meeting the New Generation of Variable Annuities (VAs)

In This Chapter

▶ Seeing what VAs have to offer

▶ Weighing the pros and cons of VAs

▶ Understanding guaranteed lifetime benefits

*V*ariable annuities (VAs) were once routinely described in the media as "mutual funds in an insurance wrapper." To me, this metaphor suggested a candy bar wrapped in cellophane. But, although the comparison was vivid and concise, it still didn't help me understand VAs.

As my education progressed, the candy bar metaphor gradually made more sense. VAs are simply clusters of mutual funds with insurance features. Those features usually include a full refund if you die, the right to convert your money to a lifelong income, and the right to defer taxes on your investment gains.

Tax deferral used to be the principal reason to buy a VA. After 1986, VAs were one of the few remaining tax shelters for wealthy Americans. Although most VAs were pricey, the benefit of tax deferral could eventually — after 10 or 15 years — outweigh the effect of high fees.

Today, people buy VAs for their *guaranteed living benefits* (GLB) "riders" (that's insurance jargon for "optional features"). The latest is the *guaranteed lifetime withdrawal benefit*, or GLWB. It offers guaranteed income for life — no matter how long you live — while letting you withdraw your money whenever you want. If you die before all the money in your account is paid out, your beneficiaries get what's left.

In this chapter, I define variable annuities and give you a quick tour of the alphabet soup of guaranteed living benefits. In the process, you may find a product that gives you just the right balance between protection from retirement risks (see Chapter 2) and control over your money.

Defining VAs

VAs are mutual fund investments that have certain insurance-related guarantees, such as living benefits and death benefits. (Mutual funds are bundles of stocks or bonds or a mixture of both. They make it easy for small investors to diversify their holdings and invest with less risk. See *Mutual Funds for Dummies*, 5th Edition, by Eric Tyson [Wiley].) The features of VAs include the following:

- ✔ **Minimum initial premium:** You can purchase an individual VA contract for as little as $5,000 ($2,000 in an IRA, or in installments as low as $50 in an employer-sponsored retirement plan). For certain contracts, the minimum may be as high as $50,000. "Flexible premium" contracts allow regular or sporadic contributions.

- ✔ **Surrender period:** The typical VA contract — one that is sold by a commission-earning broker or agent — has a surrender period during which you'll be penalized if you withdraw more than an allotted amount.

- ✔ **Investment options:** By definition, deferred VAs allow you to invest your premiums in subaccounts similar to mutual funds.

- ✔ **Death benefit options:** All VAs offer death benefits. If you die before or without annuitizing your contract — that is, without converting it irrevocably to a guaranteed income stream — your beneficiaries will receive a certain minimum payout.

- ✔ **Living benefit riders:** These options, available for a fee, can protect you from investment risks. In most cases, the option must be elected at the time of purchase and paid for each year, whether exercised or not.

- ✔ **The option to annuitize:** As with fixed deferred annuities, you have the option to convert the value of your VA investments to a guaranteed income stream in retirement that lasts for as long as you (or either you or your spouse) live, or for a specific number of years.

Pros and Cons of VAs

There are several pros and cons of VA ownership. Weigh them carefully before you proceed. The pros include:

- ✔ **Tax deferral on earnings until they are withdrawn:** When you invest in mutual funds, your earnings are taxed each year, even if you reinvest them. Earnings on the investments in your VA subaccounts (which resemble mutual funds) stay in the subaccounts, helping them grow.

✔ **Lifetime income options, including annuitization and guaranteed minimum withdrawal benefits (GMWBs):** The latest generation of VAs include options that offer the best of both worlds: income you can't outlive and access to your principal at any time.

✔ **A death benefit that protects heirs from market losses:** Your beneficiaries collect a benefit if you die. It's not a big selling point.

✔ **The freedom to manage your own investments and benefit from owning stocks:** Variable annuities were created in 1952 to give retirement plan participants the power to invest, not just save.

✔ **No limit on the contribution of after-tax money:** If you've already maxed out your contributions to other tax-favored retirement accounts, you can put your extra savings in a variable annuity.

✔ **No required minimum distributions (RMDs) at age 7½:** You, rather than Uncle Sam, decide when you'll pay taxes on your tax-deferred savings.

The cons of VA ownership include:

✔ **Higher fees than no-load mutual funds, especially if sold by commissioned brokers or agents.**

The total annual fees for a VA contract can range from less than 1 percent to more than 4 percent, depending on whom you buy it from, what investments you selected, and what riders you purchased. Fees can dramatically reduce your long-term returns.

✔ **When withdrawn, earnings are taxed as income rather than as capital gains.** As you know by now, there's a downside to saving in a tax-deferred account. Withdrawals are taxed more heavily than withdrawals from an ordinary taxable account. Also, your heirs won't get the tax benefits of inheriting after-tax assets.

✔ **Withdrawals before age 59½ may be subject to a 10 percent federal penalty, in addition to income tax.** This is a great reason not to buy a variable annuity (unless it's an offering inside an employer-sponsored retirement plan) when you're in your 20s or 30s. Uncle Sam doesn't want you to spend your VA savings until you're at or near retirement age.

✔ **You can lose money.** Your investment returns aren't guaranteed. If you want guaranteed returns, you want a fixed deferred annuity.

✔ **Surrender periods.** Depending on how you buy your variable annuity contract, you may be penalized for withdrawing too much of your money during the first four to seven years of the contract. For more on surrender periods, see Chapter 3.

A brief history of VAs

Although annuities have been used since Roman times, the first VA was offered in 1952 as an investment option in qualified (tax-deferred) retirement plans for college and university employees. In 1959, the Supreme Court ruled that VAs, unlike fixed annuities, are subject to regulation by the Securities and Exchange Commission (SEC).

The VA Life Insurance Company (VALIC) marketed the first nonqualified VA (for investments of after-tax money) in 1960. Between 1977 and 1980, the IRS ruled that annuity owners can't manage individual stocks in their contracts, that those who inherit annuity assets (unlike beneficiaries of appreciated stocks or mutual funds) must pay income tax on the contract's gains, and that you can't hold certificates of deposit (CDs) in VAs.

In 1982, new federal legislation required that VA owners take taxable earnings first, before tax-free principal, when withdrawing money from their contracts. Four years later, the Tax Reform Act of 1986 eliminated most tax-sheltered investments other than VAs. In 1991, the National Association of Variable Annuities, or NAVA (now called NAVA, the Association for Insured Retirement Solutions) was formed.

Sales of VAs soared in the late 1990s, along with sales of stocks and mutual funds, as a result of the unprecedented bull market. Between 1996 and 2004, insurance companies introduced the first living benefits, including the guaranteed minimum income benefit (GMIB), the guaranteed minimum withdrawal benefit (GMWB), the guaranteed minimum account balance (GMAB), and, in 2004, the guaranteed lifetime withdrawal benefit (GLWB). More recently, issuers have added the opportunity to step up the guaranteed minimum to the current market value at regular intervals. You can also buy a contract that combines a GMAB with a GLWB.

In 2006, Americans held about $1.3 trillion in VA contracts — a fraction of what they hold in mutual funds. VA sales for 2006 amounted to some $130 billion, of which about 60 percent was in tax-deferred retirement plans or IRAs. Only about 20 percent of the $130 billion in new 2006 sales, however, represented first-time purchases of VAs. Most sales were the result of tax-free "replacements" (1035 exchanges) from one brand of VA to another.

Top Selling VA Contracts of 2006

Contract	Issuer
Retirement Annuity	TIAA-CREF
Venture III[1]	John Hancock Life
Portfolio Director Plus[1]*	AIG/VALIC
Perspective II[1]	Jackson National Life
Retirement Advisor Advantage Plus[1]*	IDS Life
Innovations Select[1]	Pacific Life

Accumulator Elite 2004[1]	AXA Equitable Life
Value[1]*	Pacific Life
Accumulator Plus 2004[1]*	AXA Equitable Life
Leaders	Hartford Life

[1]These contracts feature a guaranteed withdrawal and/or lifetime income option.
*A bonus is added to the initial contribution.

Getting to Know GLBs

Guaranteed living benefits (GLBs), an umbrella term for several different options that have been added to VA contracts in recent years, have gradually transformed VAs from a marginally useful tax-management tool for wealthy investors into a robust but complicated retirement income planning tool for baby boomers.

Table 8-1 gives you a breakdown of the various GLB options and what they can do for you. In the following section, I go into the various options in more detail so you can determine which ones may be right for you.

Table 8-1	Breaking Down Guaranteed Lifetime Benefits
GMIB (Guaranteed Minimum Income Benefit) Main feature: Annuitization of no less than principal.	This option guarantees that you can annuitize (convert to a regular income) whichever is greater: the market value of your investments or a guaranteed minimum amount based on your principal plus a minimum guaranteed annual growth rate.
GMWB (Guaranteed Minimum Withdrawal Benefit) Main feature: Return of no less than principal in annual installments.	This option protects your principal and guarantees that you will receive it in equal installments (for example, 7 percent of the principal amount per year for 14.3 years). If your investments perform well, there will be an excess amount in the policy at the end of the withdrawal period.

GLWB(Guaranteed Lifetime Withdrawal Benefit-For Life) Main feature: Lifetime payments without annuitization.	This option guarantees that a certain percentage (usually 5 percent) of the amount invested can be withdrawn each year for as long as the contract owner is living. The latest GLWBs also include guarantees that the amount invested will grow at a specified rate (such as 5 percent a year) if no withdrawals are taken for the first 10 years of the contract.
GMAB(Guaranteed Minimum Accumulation Benefit) Main feature: Principal guarantee after waiting period.	This option guarantees that, after a seven- to ten-year investment period, you will receive whichever is more: your account balance or your principal.
GAV (Guaranteed Account Value) Main feature: Guarantee of principal and frequent step-ups.	This option guarantees your principal over the course of a specific investment period, and may automatically lock in any gains at the end of each quarter or year.
GPAF(Guaranteed Payout Annuity Floor) Main feature: Guarantee of value of monthly variable annuity payment	This option guarantees that the monthly payment from a life annuity with a variable payout will never fall below a certain percentage of the first payment.

Guaranteed minimum income benefit (GMIB)

This is the GLB that you're least likely to use, because you must annuitize your contract in order to receive the benefit. But most of the principles involved in GMIBs are used for other living benefits.

A GMIB guarantees that you won't lose your principal and that you'll receive a decent return on your initial premium right up until the time you annuitize. In some contracts, you'll be able to take modest withdrawals during the surrender period. But GMIBs traditionally offer less liquidity than other GLB options. To receive the benefit, you must leave all or most of your money in the account for at least ten years, after which you have the option to convert it to an income.

Example: You put $100,000 into the contract at age 55, and allocate the money to stock and bond subaccounts. Over the next ten years, the cash value of those subaccounts — your account value — fluctuates. Meanwhile, another number — your "guaranteed income base" — starts at $100,000 and grows by a guaranteed 6 percent a year. At age 65, you annuitize whichever is more: the guaranteed income base (now grown to $180,000) or the account value. Either way, you'll annuitize at least $180,000.

New twists have been added to the plain vanilla GMIB. The latest contracts allow you to withdraw your guaranteed interest every year as income. In other words, in the example above, you could spend $6,000 each year for ten years and still annuitize $100,000 at the end of that time. With each withdrawal, your current account value would either shrink by the same percentage as your withdrawal, or by the number of dollars you withdrew, or by a combination of the two.)

For an additional fee, you may be able lock in your gains periodically. If, by the fifth anniversary of your contract, your subaccounts are worth $160,000, you may be able to "reset" your guaranteed base to $160,000. From then on, you can take out almost $10,000 a year and annuitize $160,000 after at least ten years. Alternately, you can make no withdrawals and let your guaranteed base grow by 6 percent a year. The fee for this benefit may start at a modest level — say, 0.50 percent — but may rise to more than 1 percent if you exercise the step-up option.

At some point before you reach age 80, you will have to convert your money (the highest of your account value, your original guaranteed income base, the maximum value on any anniversary of the contract, or the account value when you annuitize) to monthly annuity payments. Annuitization isn't necessarily bad. In fact, it can be the most efficient way to convert savings to income. But with a GMIB, the formula used to calculate the monthly payment might be an especially stingy one.

Here's how it works. If you had $180,000 in a VA without a GMIB and annuitized it, you might receive $6 per month per thousand, or $1,080. If you had a guaranteed income basis of $180,000 in a VA with a GMIB option, and you exercised the option, you might only get, say, $5.70 per month per thousand, or $1,026. In short, the same company could be paying two different rates on the same basis, depending on what kind of contract you bought. A low annuitization factor is a largely hidden but predictable cost of a GMIB VA. Some companies are kind enough to offer you whichever of the two rates is higher.

Guaranteed minimum withdrawal benefit (GMWB)

A GMWB Rider on your VA will ensure that, even if the market dives during your retirement, you'll never lose your initial premium. After you start taking payments (typically 5 percent to 10 percent of your premium per year), you're guaranteed that you'll get back at least what you originally put in — and potentially much more. In a traditional GMWB, you could run out of money before you die.

Example: Suppose that at age 65 you put $100,000 in a VA with a GMWB that permitted a maximum annual withdrawal of 7 percent. If the money in your subaccounts didn't grow at all or lost value, you'd still receive $7,000 each year for about 14.3 years (14.3 × $7,000 = $100,000), when you are age 79. If your subaccounts appreciate, however, you can typically receive much more.

For instance, if you retire at the start of a bull market and the value of your subaccounts skyrockets to, say, $180,000 by the time you reach age 70, you may step up your guaranteed withdrawal basis to $180,000, and begin receiving $12,600 a year (7 percent × $180,000 = $12,600). The payments continue until you have received $180,000 in all.

In short, a GMWB simply returns your own money back to you. The insurance company assumes the risk that your underlying investments will lose value. In return, it deducts annual fees from your account value. Without a step-up, a GMWB would not be an exciting VA option. Without the step-up, however, it becomes more interesting. Remember, however, that contract fees are an ever-present drag on the growth of your account value.

When comparing VAs with different GMWBs, pay close attention to the maximum withdrawal percentage. It can vary from as little as 5 percent to as much as 12 percent. (At 12 percent, you'll get more money per year but you'll run through your money faster.)

Be sure to read the rules governing the step-up option, and ask these questions: How early and how often can you step up your guaranteed value to your account value? If the step-up isn't automatic, when can you choose it? Only within 30 days after the date you become eligible for the step-up? Or at any time after the step-up date? Will your costs increase if you opt for the step-up?

Guaranteed lifetime withdrawal benefit (GLWB)

The latest generation of VAs has taken the GMWB VA and extended it so that you receive not only a principal guarantee, a guaranteed growth rate, and the opportunity for step-ups, but also a guaranteed lifetime income — even if a stock market crash were to zero out the value of your account. These new income riders are sometimes called guaranteed lifetime withdrawal benefits, or GLWBs. As safety nets go, they're generous, and insurance companies are making them more attractive all the time.

One insurance company's GLWB promises that if you take no withdrawals for the first ten years of your contract, your initial premium is guaranteed to grow by 5 percent and, at age 65, you can begin taking out 5 percent of what you've automatically accumulated every year for the rest of your life.

If you take withdrawals in a given year, you will lose the 5 percent annual bonus and lower your principal. You also have opportunities on the 3rd, 6th, and 9th anniversaries of your contract to step up your guaranteed principal to match your account value — the real money, sitting in the equivalent of mutual funds — if the account value is higher than your guaranteed base. If you take withdrawals before or after you begin receiving income, however, you'll lower your guaranteed principal or your income payments, respectively.

Example: At age 55, say you put $200,000 into the VA contract and began paying the rider fee — 0.65 percent, plus about 3 percent in the usual contract costs. Your guaranteed balance is $200,000. For ten years, you get a bonus of $10,000 in every year you don't take a withdrawal, and every three years you can step up your guaranteed balance to match your real account value. Suppose that by age 65, your guaranteed value is now $400,000.

At that point, you begin taking income. If your account value is more than $400,000, you can ignore the rider and write off the fee (at least $13,000 over ten years, and perhaps double that). But if the account value is less than $400,000, you exercise your right to an income of $20,000 a year (5 percent of $400,000) for as long as either your or your spouse is living.

Another insurer's LIB VA also promises a five percent minimum growth rate and a 5 percent minimum annual income for life. Moreover, they are certain to double their money in ten years. For example, if you invested $100,000 in the contract and signed up for the LIB rider at purchase, after ten years, your lifetime annual income would be at least $20,000, assuming that you took no withdrawals.

Guaranteed minimum accumulation benefit (GMAB)

Another optional feature is the guaranteed minimum accumulation benefit, which, generally for a smaller fee than the other GLB's fee, protects your principal against losses. For example, you could retire at age 65, put $100,000 into a VA with a GMAB that costs about 0.20 percent per year, and if the market fell during the next several years — a worst-case scenario for a new retiree — your principal would be guaranteed.

In most cases, you don't have to annuitize a GMAB contract. You may make withdrawals, but they will reduce your guaranteed amount on a pro-rata or dollar-for-dollar basis. You may be restricted from putting your money in high-risk investments, such as subaccounts that invest in international equities or junk bonds. You won't be able to gamble recklessly and still be assured that the insurance company will make you whole if you lose.

Most GMAB contracts do more than guarantee your principal. If your subaccounts appreciate, you can usually, at certain times, lock in the higher account value so that it becomes your new guaranteed accumulation amount. You can only opt for these "step-ups" at certain times, and each step-up may trigger the start of a new guaranteed period. In other words, you may have to wait to be eligible for the stepped-up amount.

Example: Suppose that at age 65 you put $100,000 into a GMAB VA with a seven-year guarantee period. If, at the end of that time, your investments were worth $90,000, you'd still be good for $100,000. If your investments were worth $150,000 after five years, you could choose to lock in a new guaranteed amount of $150,000 and start a new seven-year guaranteed period. If your account value later shrank to $120,000, you'd still be eligible to take out $150,000 — but not until year 12.

Guaranteed account value (GAV)

Another VA option is the guaranteed account value benefit, or GAV. It protects your original investment while allowing you to benefit from market growth.

Example: Suppose that you wanted to save for your 11-year-old's college tuition. So you put $100,000 (your guaranteed withdrawal amount) into a VA with a GAV. Seven years later, you can withdraw whichever is larger, your account balance or the $100,000. If your investments grow, the contract may let you lock in the market value at quarterly or annual intervals so that, if the final year of the contract is a bear market, you still get the locked-in value. But the least you'll get back is your principal.

GAVs are sometimes touted as alternatives to indexed annuities, also known as equity indexed annuities, or EIAs (see Chapter 7). Unlike EIAs, GAV contracts don't have complex crediting caps that involve a confusing mix of participation rates, caps, and spreads. You also get a broader choice of investments and you receive stock dividends, which EIAs don't capture. Like all VAs, however, GAVs have significant fees that can reduce your effective returns.

Guaranteed payout annuity floor (GPAF)

One recent innovation in lifetime benefits is the guaranteed payout annuity floor. This benefit only applies to contract owners who annuitize their contracts and opt for a variable monthly payment for life. The GPAF ensures that the monthly payment will never be less than a certain percentage — from 85 percent to 100 percent — of the first payment. In other words, it protects you from a protracted bear market later in life. Some versions of this benefit allow you to lock in investment gains so that you have an ever-rising safety net below you.

Dollar for dollar versus pro rata withdrawals

Certain GLB riders let you draw off a guaranteed percentage each year of your guaranteed principal. For instance, the contract might let you take out 6 percent each year. If your guaranteed principal was $100,000, you could start taking out $6,000 a year.

Some VA contracts use the "pro rata" method to account for this type of "guaranteed withdrawal amount." Others use the "dollar for dollar" method. Not knowing the difference can cost you.

Suppose you withdrew your allotted 6 percent ($6,000) from the contract described above. And suppose that your account value — the real money, not the $100,000 that's guaranteed — had grown to $120,000 by the time of the withdrawal. Under a pro rata system, your $120,000 would go down by 6 percent, or $7,200. Under a dollar for dollar system, your $120,000 would go down by only $6,000.

Note that, in this instance, the dollar for dollar method would help you, to the tune of $1,200.

Under the pro rata method, your $6,000 withdrawal would have cost you $7,200.

Of course, if your account balance had fallen to $80,000 instead of rising to $120,000, the advantage would be reversed. A pro rata policy would give you $6,000 but reduce your $80,000 by only $4,800 (6 percent of $80,000). A dollar for dollar policy would reduce it by $6,000 (6 percent of $100,000).

Some VA policies apply a bi-level formula. One policy, for instance, uses the dollar for dollar method up to the guaranteed withdrawal limit, and pro rata for anything in excess of that.

For example, if you withdrew $10,000 (10 percent of the guaranteed base) from the preceding contract in a single year — $4,000 over the limit — your account balance would take a $6,000 haircut and would then be reduced 4 percent. In a bull market, when your account value would most likely be higher than the guaranteed base, such a formula would tend to penalize big withdrawals.

Chapter 9

Financing Your Retirement with an Income Annuity

*I*f you're a teacher, a postal worker, or a manager in a Fortune 500 company, you may still be in line for a lifetime pension when you retire. But most of us will retire with no pension — just the savings in our 401(k) or 403(b) accounts.

If you aren't eligible for a pension but wish you were, income annuities may be the cushion you need. When you buy an income annuity with a chunk of your savings, you create what people are calling a "do-it-yourself pension."

Pioneered by the ancient Romans, income annuities may be on the verge of a renaissance. Thanks to the Pension Protection Act of 2006 and to innovations in product design, income annuities are becoming both more accessible and more appealing.

In this chapter, I explain how and why to use income annuities, which are utterly different from the *deferred* annuities that I describe in Chapters 6 and 7. The act of buying and customizing an income annuity requires some homework. But, if you don't have a real pension, it's the next best thing.

Income annuities allow you to convert a large sum of cash into an immediate monthly, quarterly, or annual paycheck. You give the money to a reputable insurance company, and the insurer agrees to pay you (or you and your spouse, or a third party) an income for a certain length of time. You begin receiving payments within less than a year, which is why these products are often called "immediate annuities" or "single premium immediate annuities" (SPIAs). An income annuity is an efficient way to turn savings into retirement income, and it's the only product, aside from pensions and Social Security, that can guarantee you an income for life.

Generating Income with an Annuity

You can think of income annuities as life insurance in reverse. With life insurance, you make monthly, semiannual or yearly installment payments to an insurer, and eventually your beneficiary receives a large lump sum (if you die while the policy is in effect).

With an income annuity, you do the reverse; you pay a single premium and immediately begin receiving installment payments until you die (or until both you and your spouse die, or until the end of a specific period — I get to those options later in this chapter).

You can customize your contract to receive payments that never vary in amount, payments that fluctuate with the stock markets, or payments that are automatically increased to keep up with inflation.

Why choose income annuities?

Income annuities are attractive to retirees for two basic reasons:

✔ They extract more income from a given amount of money than you can get from a comparably safe investment in United States government bonds.

✔ They provide a steady income for life, no matter how long you live.

In 2006, a 65-year-old man could purchase a high-quality long-term bond that pays close to 5 percent a year. On a $100,000 investment, he can earn about $5,000 a year for 20 years. (Yes, a low-quality "junk bond" would pay more, but it would involve more credit risk.)

But if he puts $100,000 into a life-only income annuity, he can receive a guaranteed income of about $8,100 per year for as long as he lives. To generate that much income with high-quality long-term bonds (again at 5 percent), he'd need to lock away at least $162,000.

The return from the annuity is higher because

✔ Each annuity payment returns a small chunk of the man's $100,000 premium along with a piece of the interest that the initial premium earns.

✔ As other same-age owners of the same annuity die, their assets remain in the pool shared by the surviving annuity owners. In academic jargon, the surviving owners earn *survivorship credits* (also called *mortality credits*) from those who die. (For more on that, see Chapter 4.)

Note: These credits do not literally pass to the survivors, and the survivors' payments do not change when other contract owners die. The carrier establishes the size of the payments in advance, using mortality tables that predict exactly how many contract owners will be alive in each successive year.

In the example above, the annuity owner chose a single-life annuity, which means that the contract provided income only to him and payments ceased at his death. He could customize the contract to include income for his wife (if she outlives him) or a partial refund to his children when he dies. But those extra benefits wouldn't be free. To pay for them, he would have to increase the initial premium or accept a reduction in monthly payments. (See Table 9-1 in this chapter for a comparison of various options and payout rates.)

Reducing risks with income annuities

Everyone experiences risks, but people vary in their sensitivity to them. My wife, for instance, couldn't sleep at night without knowing that our house is insured against termite-inflicted damage. I personally don't worry about termites; I don't feel a need for insurance against them, and I don't lose sleep thinking about the harm they might do to our joists. Faced with the same risk, one person might address it while another equally rational person might choose to ignore it. (By the way, we bought termite insurance.)

Three of the most important risks are *sequence-of-returns risk*, *investment risk*, and *longevity risk*. (I define them in Chapter 2, where I discuss the risks that all retirees face.) These risks exist for almost everyone, but not everyone chooses to acknowledge them — and even fewer choose to insure against them. Annuities are for people who choose not to ignore

- ✔ **Investment risk:** The possibility that your portfolio won't earn enough to support you in retirement.

- ✔ **Sequence-of-returns risk:** The chance that, just before or after you start drawing down your savings, a sharp market downturn will take a huge bite out of your portfolio and greatly increase your chance of running out of money too soon.

- ✔ **Longevity risk:** The chance that you'll outlive your financial resources.

An income annuity, like any other form of insurance, transfers these risks from you to an insurance company. In return for your purchase payment, you receive an income (monthly, quarterly, or annual) that's immune to bond defaults, resistant to stock market crashes, and capable of lasting as long as you live.

Why people don't buy income annuities

Relatively few Americans buy income annuities. And even though they have $1.3 trillion invested in variable annuities — a fraction of the amount they invest in mutual funds — Americans rarely *annuitize* those contracts (turn them into income). Here are the most common reasons why they don't:

✔ They underestimate the value of survivorship credits.

✔ They underestimate their chance of living past the average life expectancy.

✔ They've never heard of income annuities and never intended to convert the value of their variable annuity to an income stream.

✔ They don't believe that income annuities offer good value.

✔ They don't want to give up access to their savings.

✔ They're afraid that the insurance company will get their money if they die too soon.

A life annuity *guarantees* that you'll receive an income as long as you live (or as long as either you or your spouse is living). But this guarantee assumes that the insurance company will remain financially strong enough to meet its obligations for the next 30 years or more. If the insurer fails, your payments can be in jeopardy, and you may have to fall back on your state insurance guaranty program for help. That's why you should buy your annuity from a gilt-edged, A-rated company. See more about company ratings in Appendix A.

Buying and Paying for an Income Annuity

Decisions, decisions. Before you buy an income annuity, you face some important tactical choices. In this section, I review your options with regard to when you buy your contract and how you pay for it.

Deciding when to buy your annuity

When you buy an annuity depends on *how* you intend to use it. An income annuity does double duty — it's a tool for efficiently turning savings into a do-it-yourself pension, and it's insurance against longevity risk (see the previous section). Consider these guidelines for buying:

✔ If you're using an income annuity as a do-it-yourself pension, you can buy it as soon as you need monthly income.

Poor health is no reason to shun income annuities

Just as a person in a high-risk job may have to pay higher life insurance premiums for a given amount of coverage, a person with a high-risk illness (heart disease, diabetes, and so on) can pay a *lower* annuity premium or, conversely, receive *higher* monthly payments than someone who doesn't suffer from a life-shortening illness. The adjustment is called *medical underwriting* or a *substandard annuity*. (For more on medical underwriting, see Chapter 15.)

✔ If you're highly risk-averse, and you're afraid you might lose your savings if you keep it in the markets, you should buy an income annuity sooner rather than later.

✔ If you're using an income annuity as insurance against living too long, and if you're highly risk-tolerant, don't buy the annuity until you're older. It may make more sense to keep your money invested in stocks and bonds until you reach age 75 or even 80.

Here's a rule of thumb that I've heard from annuity researchers: When you reach age 60, you should replace the bonds in your portfolio with income annuities. At age 75, you should replace the stocks in your portfolio with income annuities.

Just as life insurance is less expensive when you're young, income annuities are less expensive as you get older. Actuaries have calculated that they become a better investment than bonds by the time you hit age 60, and better than stocks when you hit age 75. Why? Because survivorship credits get bigger as you get older.

Deciding how to pay for your annuity

If you make the decision to buy an income annuity, you have to come up with the cash — typically $100,000 or more — to pay to the broker, agent, or financial advisor, who in turn sends it to the issuing insurance company.

People generally pay for annuities

✔ With savings or investments in taxable accounts

✔ With savings or investments in tax-deferred accounts

✔ By rolling over the value of an annuity they already own (like a deferred variable annuity) into an income annuity through a *1035 exchange*

After-tax money

If you have after-tax cash savings (money in certificates of deposits or money market accounts at mutual fund companies, for example), you can use it to purchase your income annuity. You can also use

- ✔ Proceeds from the sale of mutual funds in taxable accounts, most of whose gains have already been taxed
- ✔ Any tax-free money you may have received as the beneficiary of a life insurance policy

The taxable portion of your annuity income will be lowest if you bought your annuity with after-tax money, higher if you bought it with a mix of after-tax and pretax money, and highest if you bought it with pretax money. For more on taxation of annuity income, see Chapter 14.

Pre-tax money

If most of your savings is in a qualified retirement plan (for example, a 401(k), a 403(b), or a traditional or rollover IRA), you can buy an income annuity with that money. This move has pluses and minuses:

- ✔ The bad news, from a tax standpoint, is that your entire annuity income is then subject to federal income tax.
- ✔ The good news is that the annuity allows you to spread your huge backlog of deferred taxes over 10 years, 20 years, or your entire lifespan.

Each year after you reach age 70½, you have to move a certain percentage (your pretax assets divided by your life expectancy) of your tax-deferred savings into a taxable account and add it to your taxable income for that year. This step is called taking a *required minimum distribution* (RMD).

A blend of after-tax and pretax money

Suppose you paid $75,000 a few years ago for a deferred variable annuity that has since grown in value to $100,000. The $75,000 is after-tax money and the $25,000 in growth is pre-tax money. If you exchange that deferred annuity for an income annuity, a portion of each payment will come from the after-tax $75,000. You won't owe any income tax on that portion of the payment. (For more on exchanging one annuity for another, see Chapter 13.)

Deciding how much to put into an income annuity

There are three rules of thumb regarding the percentage of your savings you should commit to an income annuity:

✔ **Never put more than 30 percent of your assets in an income annuity.** This is the advice that Vanguard and Fidelity give their 30 million customers. They are conservative companies and this is a conservative recommendation. Their clients are also wealthier than the average American, and I believe this recommendation applies more to people with savings north of $500,000 than those with savings south of $500,000.

✔ **You only need to put 40 percent of your assets into an income annuity.** Respective authorities such as Morningstar, Inc., have calculated that if you follow this advice, you will reduce your chances of running out of money before you die to virtually zero.

✔ **If you need the income, put up to 100 percent of your savings into an income annuity.** David Babbel of the University of Pennsylvania's Wharton School and New York Life Insurance Company recommends that if, for instance, you need a guaranteed income of at least $3,500 a month in retirement (in addition to Social Security) and the only way to achieve it is to put 80, 90, or even 100 percent of your savings into an income annuity, then that's what you should do. Personally, I think 100 percent is too much. I'd rather stop at 80 percent and work part time selling lawn mowers or plumbing supplies at Home Depot to make up the difference.

Getting Your Money's Worth

How can you tell if buying an income annuity is the best way to generate retirement income? In this section, I show you how to evaluate an income annuity by:

✔ Assessing its MWR, or money's worth ratio

✔ Understanding its value as insurance

✔ Comparing it to the guaranteed living benefits of a variable deferred annuity

✔ Comparing it to a systematic withdrawal plan (SWP)

Understanding the annuity money's worth ratio (MWR)

When annuity experts (finance professors, actuaries, and others who like nothing better than to start each day with a bowl of crisp differential equations) want to measure whether an income annuity is a good deal for the purchaser, they examine the annuity's *money's worth ratio* (MWR).

Anybody who has shopped around for a furnace knows each brand has an efficiency rating that shows how much heat it produces compared to the potential heat in the fuel it burns. The MWR performs a similar function. It is usually the ratio of the present value of the sum of your expected annuity payments (discounted at current interest rates) to the premium the company is charging you.

Here's an example. Suppose you wanted to buy an income stream of $40,000 a year for 25 years,

and an insurance company charged a premium of $500,000. But is that a low price or a high one? To find out the rock-bottom cost of a $40,000/25-year income stream, you'd calculate its net present value (NPV), discounted at today's interest rates. If the NPV turned out to be $500,000, your MWR would be 100 on a scale of 100 ($500,000 divided by $500,000). That's excellent. If the NPV is only $400,000, your MWR would be only 80. By asking $500,000, the carrier may be overcharging you.

MWRs range anywhere from 80 to 100, according to surveys conducted in the U.S. and abroad. Insurance carriers can afford to offer better MWRs when their own profit margins are high. That usually occurs when long-term interest rates (the rates that carriers earn on their investments) are significantly higher than shorter-term interest rates (the rates that carriers pay you).

The insurance value of an annuity

To evaluate an annuity properly, you may also want to compare its cost to the cost of self-insuring against living too long. Researchers have found that, from a specific amount of savings, a retired person can enjoy a higher standard of living throughout retirement by purchasing an annuity than by not doing so.

In fact, a 2006 study, *Annuity Markets and Pension Reform* by Gordon A. MacKenzie (Cambridge University Press), shows that a new retiree *without* access to an annuity needs at least 30 percent more in savings than a retiree *with* an annuity to achieve the same level of income and the same security against running out of money. Other reports say that the person without an annuity would need 40 percent more savings.

Annuities are insurance. Homeowner's insurance pays off if a storm rips your roof off. It spares you the inefficiency of keeping enough money on hand just in case you have to buy a new roof. An income annuity pays off if you live longer than average (past age 81 for a 65-year-old man, and 84 for a 65-year-old woman). It spares you the inefficiency of keeping enough money on hand just in case you live to 85 or beyond.

Comparing annuity income to guaranteed lifetime benefits

In some respects, a variable annuity with guaranteed lifetime benefits (GLBs) offers an attractive alternative to an income annuity. For example, for an annual fee between 0.60 percent and 1.25 percent of assets per year (that's $600 to $125 per $100,000 invested), many of today's most popular variable annuity contracts offer riders that guarantee an annual retirement income stream of at least 5 percent of your accumulated assets for life. GLBs also let you dip into your principal at any time (although this reduces your income proportionately).

So why lock up money in an income annuity? The biggest reason is that variable annuities don't offer the survivorship credit (see the section "Why choose income annuities?" earlier in this chapter) that comes from pooling your mortality risk. Variable annuities with GLBs have only been available for a few years, and it's unclear why people buy them. A high percentage of the sales of GLB contracts represent exchanges from existing variable annuity contracts. Presumably, owners of GLB contracts will not exercise their income options unless their actual investment returns are poor.

Comparing annuity income to systematic withdrawals

Most retirees don't buy income annuities; they simply draw down their savings in retirement as they need it. In the investment business, this strategy is called a *systematic withdrawal plan* (SWP). If their investment returns are poor, these folks just tighten their belts and spend less of their savings.

Over the years, SWPs have developed into a near-science. One common technique, informally called the *bucket* method, keeps savings in three accounts or buckets:

- The money you expect to spend within the coming year is in cash accounts.
- The money you expect to need within three to five years is in short-term bonds.
- The rest of your money is in stocks.

A systematic withdrawal plan is labor intensive, and requires some financial expertise. Each year, you must move a block of assets from your stock bucket to your bond bucket, and replenish your cash bucket by selling bonds. If you're accustomed to doing your own taxes, you can probably handle SWPs. Otherwise, consider calling an adviser.

SWPs work fine in bull markets, and they give you the illusion of control over your assets. I say *illusion* because SWPs can leave you vulnerable to market risk. Unlike annuity-based strategies, they don't reduce the risk that you or your spouse may live to age 95 (longevity risk) or the risk that circumstances may force you to keep spending your savings even in years when the stock market tanks, as it did in 1987 and 2001 (sequence-of-returns risk). The combination of withdrawals and losses can put a double whammy on your remaining nest egg.

Customizing Your Income Annuity

If you're convinced of the value of an income annuity, you're ready to consider the next step: designing your income annuity to suit your needs. You've got lots of options. For example, you can

- ✔ Decide whether to receive fixed or variable income payments.
- ✔ Decide who will receive income.
- ✔ Decide how long payments will last.
- ✔ Arrange for (limited) access to your money.
- ✔ Protect your income from inflation.

People who tend to be wary of income annuities often think, "If I die, the insurance company will get my money." This is an understandable but irrational fear.

Buying an income annuity doesn't necessarily mean losing control over all of your money or even over the money in your annuity. Most issuers of income annuities offer options that allow you to tailor the annuity to your own needs and comfort level. In any case, the insurance company doesn't get your money. Your money, if you choose a life-only annuity, remains in a pool that is shared by all the surviving annuity owners in your age group.

Choosing fixed or variable payments

Most income annuities allow you to receive fixed payments, variable payments, or a combination of the two:

- ✔ **Fixed payments:** Your money goes into the insurance company's general fund and each payment is guaranteed to have the same value — today, tomorrow, and 30 years from now, if you live that long.

✔ **Variable payments:** Your money goes into a separate account rather than into the insurer's general fund. You can direct the insurer to invest this money in stock, bond, or money market subaccounts. You can move money from one subaccount to another as you want. (For a discussion of the difference between variable annuity subaccounts and conventional mutual fund accounts, see Chapter 8.)

✔ **Combination payments:** Most annuity contracts allow you to receive a payment that's partially fixed and partially subject to the ups and downs of the markets.

The amount of money you allocate to each type of payment depends on your appetite or tolerance for risk, which may depend on whether you have other sources of income to fall back on.

 If you're naturally conservative but don't want to miss out on the next bull market, consider putting part of your initial premium into variable subaccounts. Some contracts let you move money from the variable option to the fixed option after payments begin.

Coming up for AIR (Assumed interest rate)

To calculate your first annuity payment, an insurance company needs to know the growth rate of the portion of your premium that's not yet paid out as benefits. That's easy with a fixed income annuity, because the insurance carrier decides what to offer you. But with a variable income annuity, your money will be invested in subaccounts (similar to mutual funds), and no one knows how they will perform. So the carrier uses an "assumed interest rate" (AIR) to calculate the starting payment for a variable income annuity.

Typically, the carrier will give you a choice of AIRs, such as 3.5 percent and 5 percent. But how to choose? If you choose 3.5 percent, you'll start with a lower monthly payment (Let's say, $592 on a premium of $100,000) but you'll receive more annuity units. If you choose 5 percent, your first monthly payment will be higher (say, $683) but you'll receive fewer annuity units. (The number of annuity units you receive when you buy a variable income annuity is based on your age, the size of your premium, and the AIR. The

number of units is guaranteed to remain the same for the term of the contract.)

Every month, the insurance carrier performs a set of calculations to determine the value of your annuity units, based on the change in the value of your investments. Then it multiplies the annuity unit value by the number of annuity units you own to arrive at your monthly payment. The math is complex but the result is simple: Your payment will rise if your investments grow at an annual rate that's greater than your AIR, and will fall if investments grow at an annual rate that's less than your AIR. If your investment grows at exactly the AIR rate, your payment won't change.

In the long run, you'll receive the same amount of money, regardless of the AIR you choose. Pick the higher AIR if you want your payments to start higher and grow slowly. Pick the lower one if you want your payments to start lower and grow faster. If you want your payments to grow fast enough to maintain your spending power in the face of inflation, pick the lower one.

You can lose money by opting for variable payments. When you buy a variable income annuity, the insurance company assigns you a guaranteed number of "annuity units" every month. The value of each unit fluctuates with the value of your investments. So your monthly payment can rise or fall. If you want the same payment every month, buy a fixed income annuity.

Deciding who will receive income

You can buy a life annuity for yourself (single life) or for two people (joint and survivor) such as yourself and your spouse:

- **Single-life annuity:** If you purchase a single-life annuity for yourself, you receive payments for as long as you live. Generally, payments under the single-life option are larger than those under the joint and survivor option.

- **Joint and survivor annuity:** If you purchase a life annuity for yourself and your spouse, the payments continue for as long as either of you is living. (Guys, this option is very popular with the wives!)

    Under most contracts, you can decide in advance whether the surviving spouse should receive 100 percent, 75 percent, of 67 percent of the original payment. To maximize the income while both spouses are living, choose the lowest survivor benefit percentage.

Deciding how long payments will last

Life-only annuities offer the highest monthly payments because the contract owners who die prematurely leave the undistributed balance of their premiums in the pool, instead of reserving it for their beneficiaries.

But for a somewhat lower monthly payment, you can add an option to your annuity contract that makes sure that your heirs will get something, even if you die early. Here are some of them of those options:

- **Single life with a guaranteed period:** You can stipulate that your payments will last for life or for a guaranteed number of years, whichever is longer. If you die before the end of the guaranteed period (usually between 5 and 20 years), your beneficiaries will receive your payments until the period ends.

- **Joint and survivor with a guaranteed period:** If both you and your spouse die before the period ends, your beneficiaries will receive your payments until the period ends.

- **Guaranteed number of years only:** Under some annuity contracts, you can receive payments that end with the guaranteed period, even if you live longer. If you die before the period ends, your beneficiaries receive the remaining payments.

If you buy a life annuity, you should add the ten-year period certain. It won't cost much (that is, it won't reduce your monthly payments much) and you'll feel a lot more secure. One insurance company is so sure you'll want the ten-year period certain that the option comes "standard" with its income annuity.

Accessing your money after you buy the contract

Although you should look at an annuity as an irrevocable decision (in other words, don't convert money you think you may need sooner rather than later), some options give you flexibility:

- ✔ **Single life with cash or installment refund:** If you choose a single-life annuity with fixed income payments, you can usually select either a full cash or installment refund. If you die before receiving payments equal to your original premium, your beneficiaries will receive the remaining premium in a lump sum or installments.

- ✔ **Withdrawal of assets:** A few annuity contracts let you withdraw part of your annuity assets, but usually you must choose variable payments with a guaranteed period to qualify, and each withdrawal may trigger a fee.

  A withdrawal generally reduces the size of your remaining income payments and/or shortens the length of the guaranteed period.

Protecting your purchasing power from inflation

If you're old enough to remember when gasoline cost 33¢ a gallon or when $4,600 could cover a year's tuition, room, and board at a private college, then you understand how much the purchasing power of a fixed annuity payment may shrink over the next two to three decades. This information is dealt with at greater length in Chapter 15.

You have several ways to tame the inflation beast:

- ✔ **Look for an annuity with an inflation adjustment option.** Several insurers offer them, but there's no magic. You simply receive lower payments in the early years and gradually increasing payments in subsequent years.

- ✔ **Choose the variable or combination payment option and put some of your money into stock subaccounts.** Investing in stocks is traditionally the best way to keep pace with inflation, and it's as true for annuities as it is for mutual funds.

- ✔ **Buy a *ladder* of fixed payment annuities with increasingly higher monthly payments**. I discuss this option in Chapter 15.

- ✔ **Choose the higher assumed interest rate (AIR) if you buy a variable income annuity.** As I mention previously in this chapter, your monthly payments will grow fastest if you choose the lowest AIR.

Getting and comparing SPIA quotes

After you decide on a few different payment options, you can find out how much you'll have to pay for a particular income stream or how much income you'll get for a particular premium.

To compare these different payouts, go to a Web site like Vanguard's (www.vanguard.com) that offers a *wizard (*annuity quote calculator). Plug your choices into the calculator and see what numbers come up. Table 9-1 has some sample options and payments.

Table 9-1	A Comparison of Monthly Payouts under Different Options*			
I. Compare Male, Female	**Life Only**	**Life + 10-yr Certain**	**5-year Medical Adjustment**	**10-year Medical Adjustment**
Male, age 65, life only, fixed	$666/mo	$583	$763	$902
Female, age 65, life only, fixed	$613	$599	$692	$815
II. Compare Couples and Payment Calculation	**100%**	**75%**	**50%**	**100% with 2% Annual Inflation Increase**
Couple, age 65, J&S, fixed	$548	$573	$601	$362
Couple, age 65, J&S, variable, 3.5% AIR	$476	$500	$528	n/a
Couple, age 65, J&S, variable, 5% AIR	$562	$588	$617	n/a
III. Compare Start Ages	**60**	**65**	**70**	**75**
Male, single life, fixed	$597	$666	$763	$902
Female, single life, fixed	$557	$613	$692	$815

*The Vanguard Group

There are two kinds of income annuity quotes that you can get from insurance carriers. You can ask, "How much monthly income can I get per $100,000 of premium?" In that case, go with the carrier that offers the highest quote. Or you can ask, "How much premium will you charge me per $1,000 in monthly income?" In that case, go with the carrier that offers the lowest quote.

When looking for annuity calculators on the Web, avoid sites that ask for your name, address, phone number, and e-mail address. The sponsors of the site may simply be phishing for sales leads, and you may receive an unwanted phone call from a telemarketer or insurance agent.

New and noteworthy SPIA products

One drawback of a fixed SPIA is that a policyholder is locked into a payment and can't raise it to adjust for inflation or to capture the benefit of rising interest rates. A mortgage holder can refinance if rates go down, but the owner of a fixed SPIA can't ordinarily refinance if rates go up.

In 2006, New York Life introduced several options to overcome this drawback. Its Income Enhancement rider offers a one-time step-up in monthly benefits if long-term bond yields rise to a certain threshold by a certain date.

For instance, a 65-year-old opting for this rider may pay $76,829 for a monthly payment of $500. After five years, if the benchmark rate for ten-year Treasury bonds rises 2 percentage points or more, his payment will increase to $590. This step-up means about $16,200 in added income over the next 15 years.

The Income Enhancement isn't free. Annuity riders never are.

The price of the Income Enhancement rider is equal to 3.5 percent of the initial premium and is spread evenly over the life of the contract. In the previous example, the contract with the option pays out $18 less each month than a contract without the option. In other words, the owner is betting $18 a month that his payments will permanently jump from $500 to $590 after five years.

If Treasury rates fail to go up two points or more in that time, he loses that $18 a month. Hmm. *Note:* The cost of a $500 monthly income from New York Life *without* the Income Enhancement is $74,231 (that's $2,598 *less* than with the rider). What would you do? The annuity-buying process is fraught with such trade-offs. Other New York Life riders allow SPIA policyholders to change the size of their payment up or down after three years, to raise their payments by 3 to 5 percent per year to keep up with inflation, or to draw down six months' worth of payments at once, two times during the life of the contract.

Chapter 10

Aging Gracefully with an ALDA

· ·

In This Chapter

▶ Keeping those later years golden

▶ Understanding the nuts and bolts, highs and lows of ALDAs

▶ Checking out some sources

· ·

*O*ver lunch not long ago, I was talking with some 50-something friends about new ways to ensure financial security in old age. Would you buy an insurance policy today, I said, that would cost you about one-fifth of your savings and pay you a guaranteed lifetime income starting at age 80 or so?

"If you died before age 80, you'd lose your original premium," I quickly added. "But if you lived to age 85 or 90, you'd eventually get back much more than you paid up front."

Their reaction was swift and unanimous. "No way," they all said, shaking their heads. "That's a terrible investment."

What I described to them was an advanced life deferred annuity, or ALDA. And they were right: An ALDA is a terrible investment. Because it's not an investment at all. Instead, it's insurance against the risk that you'll live longer than you can afford to. Indeed, actuaries and economists call it *longevity* insurance.

You've probably never heard of ALDAs. So far, only a few insurance companies sell them. But they're worth considering. In addition to removing your fear of running out of money in retirement, they can make retirement planning easier. They can even make spending money in retirement more fun.

Married couples in good health are prime candidates for ALDAs. That's because one spouse or the other is likely to live to age 90 or beyond. ALDAs are popular among public policy experts because, like car insurance, they promote the general welfare. And the science of ALDAs is advancing. At the end of this chapter, you find examples of the enhancements with which a few pioneering insurance carriers are making ALDAs more attractive to a broader audience.

Insuring Your Old Age: What ALDAs Do

The other types of annuities I cover in this book tend to be multifunctional insurance/investment/income gadgets. They slice, they dice, and so on. Here's a quick review:

- ✔ Deferred fixed annuities help you save conservatively, and give you an income option.

- ✔ Index annuities give you the safety of a bond along with the potential for higher returns. They also offer an income option.

- ✔ Deferred variable annuities help you invest in mutual funds on a tax-deferred basis and provide an option for lifelong income.

- ✔ Single-premium immediate annuities (SPIAs) are a savings distribution tool that also provides lifelong income and protects against sequence-of-returns risk.

But an ALDA is more like pure insurance. It's akin to fire, car, or term life insurance. In its purest form, it has no cash value. It only pays out if you live past a trigger date of 80, 85, or 90 — whichever you choose. If you don't live past that date, it doesn't pay. And it's relatively cheap — much cheaper than supporting yourself from, say, age 85 to 90.

Moshe Milevsky, finance professor at Toronto's York University, compares ALDAs to SPIAs with big deductibles. A SPIA typically pays a lifetime income when you're age 65. An ALDA doesn't pay out until you're 85. Your "deductible" is those first 20 years, when you provide the income. The later the income start date (what I'm calling the trigger date), the bigger the deductible, and the less you pay for the ALDA.

How ALDAs Work

In an unadulterated ALDA, you give a portion of your retirement savings — 10 to 25 percent — to an insurance company in return for a guaranteed specific monthly income starting at whatever age you choose — 75, 80, or 85 years.

The earlier you pay for the contract, the better, because your premium will have time to earn in the carrier's coffers and buy you more income later. The later you start receiving payments, the more income you'll get each year, simply because you'll collect your benefits for fewer years.

One basic example: A married couple, ages 60 and 58

Suppose you and your spouse are ages 60 and 58, respectively, and want to receive about $2,000 each month starting at age 85. Suppose you and your spouse have also accumulated $480,000 in savings over the past 30 years. (I'll assume that your money is *after-tax*, not assets in a rollover IRA or 401(k) plan. As I show later, it's easier that way.)

You and your spouse seek out an insurance company that sells ALDAs and plunk down 10 percent of your savings, $48,000. The carrier promises you $2,000 a month starting in 25 years and lasting for as long as either of you is alive. After you pay for the contract, you have $432,000 to spend over the next 25 years. Thanks to the ALDA, you don't have to worry about keeping any of that money in reserve in case you live longer than expected.

But what happens to the $48,000 during those 25 years? Can you get access to it in an emergency? What happens to it if you die without reaching age 85?

The cheapest type of ALDA has no cash value. If you and your spouse die before payments begin, you forfeit the $48,000. Insurance carriers know that most people will balk at those terms, however, so they are likely to offer one or more of the following features:

- **Cash refund:** If and your spouse both die before collecting the amount of your initial payment, the insurance company refunds your beneficiaries any unpaid premium.

    In the previous example, if you die at 83 and your spouse dies at age 86 after receiving 12 payments ($24,000), then the beneficiaries you named on your ALDA contract will receive the balance ($24,000).

- **Death benefit:** If you die before you receive any income, your beneficiaries may receive a death benefit.

    One company offers a death benefit equal to your initial payment, growing at a compound interest rate of 3 percent. For example, if you pay $20,000 for your ALDA at age 60 and die at age 81, your beneficiaries will receive $37,206.

How ALDAs save you money

What ALDAs lack in cash value, they make up for in insurance value. You can guarantee yourself much more income at age 80 or 85 by buying an ALDA than by self-insuring — that is, by under-spending or setting up a rainy-day fund that you can use "just in case" you live longer than you expect.

Here's a comparison of the two strategies:

- ✔ **With self-insuring**, you might set aside your own personal old age fund at age 60.

  For instance, if you put $23,700 in reserve at age 60 and invested it in bonds paying 5 percent per year, you'd have about $80,000 by age 85. You could then buy an annuity that paid $1,000 a month for life. If you died before age 85, your heirs would get the entire reserve.

- ✔ **With an ALDA**, you'd pay only about $16,000 (according to one company's quote) at age 60 for a lifetime income of $1,000 starting at age 85. That's a savings of $7,700 ($23,700 – $16,000).

Why is the ALDA cheaper than self-insuring? For the same reason that homeowner's insurance is cheaper than paying for damage to your home: because most homeowners never file a claim, and their premiums are used to reimburse the few who do. Similarly, the premiums of the ALDA owners who don't reach age 85 — and never file a "claim" — go to pay for the ones who do. (See the discussion of *survivorship credits* in Chapter 1.)

Pros and Cons of ALDAs

Before I tally up the advantages and drawbacks of ALDAs, let me mention that most people can't see the need for them. Generally — and studies bear this out — the average person expects to die by age 80 or so. Most people underestimate their lifespan by about five years.

The truth is that half of all 65-year-old American men will live past age 81 and half of all 65-year-old American women will live past age 84. You might be one of the survivors. And if you can't live with your children or grandchildren when you're frail, you might benefit from an ALDA.

Examining the pros

Insurance is an appropriate tool, it's been said, when you face an expensive event that may not happen. That truism applies to ALDAs.

- ✔ **An ALDA is the most efficient way to address longevity risk.** If you're 60 and want to eliminate the risk of being broke between the ages of 85 and 90, ALDAs are the way to go. And like life insurance benefits for the young, annuity income for the very old is cheap.

- ✔ **The income is guaranteed.** Instead of buying an ALDA, you can take the money, invest it in the stock market, and hope it'll finance your twilight years. But the investment can't be guaranteed so it can't provide as much peace of mind as an ALDA. (See the earlier section "How ALDAs save you money.")

✔ **An ALDA gives you more bang for your buck than a single premium immediate annuity (SPIA).** The folks at Financial Engines, founded by Nobel Prize winning economist William F. Sharpe, claim that the less money you're thinking of putting into a SPIA (see Chapter 8), the more you should consider buying an ALDA instead.

For instance, suppose you're a man with $400,000 and want to spend 25 percent on a SPIA at age 60. You can pay $100,000 and receive about $655 per month for life (according to the Vanguard Lifetime Income Program, as of September 2007). Social Security and earnings from your remaining $296,000 can supplement your income.

Alternately, you can spend $104,000 on an ALDA at age 60 and begin receiving $2,000 a month for life starting at age 75. (See "The Hartford Income Security" later in this chapter.) You can use the remaining $296,000 plus Social Security to finance the intervening 15 years.

Note: If you have $800,000 in savings, these figures all double; you can spend $208,000 on the ALDA and receive $4,000 a month at age 75.

✔ **An ALDA makes financial planning in retirement much easier.** In the previous example, you have a choice between rationing your $400,000 over an indeterminate number of years, or spreading $296,000 over the 15 years between age 60 and age 75. The latter strategy is arguably simpler.

✔ **An ALDA allows you to spend more during retirement.** This sounds counterintuitive, but it's true. Suppose you retire at age 60 with $400,000 in invested assets. Financial advisers often say that, to ensure that your money lasts your entire life, you may have to limit your annual withdrawals to 4 percent. In this case, that's $16,000 per year.

In contrast, if you buy an ALDA with $104,000 of your savings, you can look forward to $2,000 a month for life starting at age 75. The remaining $296,000 has to last only 15 years. Even if that $296,000 didn't appreciate in value, which is unlikely, you could spend almost $20,000 a year ($296,000 ÷ 15 = $19,733). That's $4,000 more per year and almost $60,000 more over 15 years.

In the first strategy, you can dip into your $400,000 if you have to, but you have to increase your withdrawals to more than 4 percent in order to keep receiving $1,333 a month. If you do that, you should be aware that you increase your chance of running out of money.

Research by Fidelity Investments has shown that older retirees often regret being "too cautious" and "not enjoying the early years more fully" because they intentionally *under-spent.* They were afraid that extreme longevity and poor market returns would impoverish them in old age, so they hoarded their money. When you have an ALDA, you have less fear of old age and less reason to under-spend before then. You can spend more.

At the same time, financial planning becomes much easier with an ALDA. Retirement planning is difficult mainly because you don't know exactly how long you'll have to finance your life or your spouse's life. When you buy an ALDA, you can create a realistic budget. You know exactly how long your money has to last — until the ALDA starts making payments.

✔ **ALDAs are becoming more flexible.** Some insurance companies have added cash-refund or death-benefit options to their ALDAs so that, if you die before reaching the trigger age, your beneficiaries will receive a benefit. Carriers know that most people won't buy an all-or-nothing product, and they're tweaking their ALDAs accordingly.

✔ **An ALDA may be the only insurance you can look forward to collecting on.** When you buy life, car, or fire insurance, you don't look forward to collecting benefits. No one gets in a crash in order to cash in on his or her collision insurance. But with an ALDA, you win both ways. You live longer and you get the money.

ALDAs and long-term care

An annuity expert once said your biggest financial risk in retirement won't be that you'll live too long but that you'll "die too expensively." He believed that you're more likely to spend the last of your savings on nursing-home care than on an octogenarian surfing safari in Maui.

Some ALDA contracts allow you to take a portion of your guaranteed income early if illness forces you into a nursing home before you reach the trigger age. An ALDA is no substitute for real long-term care (LTC) insurance, however.

Income from the ALDA isn't tax free, and you may have to endure a waiting period or pay a deductible before money becomes available. But if you're buying an ALDA anyway, you should look for an ALDA contract that offers this small but important bit of flexibility.

Examining the cons

The biggest drawback of an ALDA is that it's insurance, and you won't necessarily get to file a claim.

✔ **You relinquish access to a large sum of money.** In plain English, you may never recoup the money that you've paid for your ALDA. Even if your contract includes a death benefit or cash refund, your heirs receive the money, not you.

✔ **The stock market may boom.** You have to consider the opportunity cost of buying an ALDA. That is, would you be better off using the money to buy real estate or stocks? Sure, but you'll only know that in hindsight. In retirement, you want security more than opportunity. An ALDA provides security.

✔ **The insurance company may go out of business.** Annuities provide guaranteed income, but the guarantee is only as strong as the insurance carrier that offers it. If the company fails (a rare event, fortunately) and isn't absorbed by another carrier, you can lose your money. That's why buying an annuity from a company with high ratings for financial strength is so important.

✔ **ALDAs are subject to inflation too.** Ah, inflation — the invisible worm that eats at the heart of your retirement. With an annual inflation rate of only 2 percent, the bottle of spring water that costs $1.00 in 2007 will cost $2.50 in 2032. And your grandchild's *first* year at a private college? Well over $100,000.

If you're buying an ALDA, keep in mind the purchasing power of your future income. In 20 years, $1 will buy less than 40 cents buys today. In other words, you may have to sink more into your ALDA than you first thought.

Longevity Risk: The Reason for ALDAs

"I should *live* so long!" was my grandmother's usual response to warnings of calamities that the distant future might or might not bring. And she in fact enjoyed an eventful and kreplach-filled life. But when she did live *so long* — to 100 — she saw old age from a new perspective. "*Enough* already," she told us at the end.

Extreme longevity is a blessing, surely, but it can be a financial catastrophe for those who don't plan for it. And most people underestimate their longevity risk. Few retirees expect to live past the average age of death (about 83 years) even though half of them inevitably will. Surveys show that you'll live, on average, about five years longer than you expect to.

Because you have a better than 50-50 chance of living into your late 80s, you should consider insuring yourself against it.

Table 10-1, based on National Vital Statistics Reports (updated in 2007), shows that the older you get, the longer you're likely to have lived.

Table 10-1	The Half-Lives of the Average American Retiree
Half of All Americans Who Reach Age . . .	*Will Also Reach Age . . .*
65	83.4
70	84.8
75	86.7
80	88.9
85	91.6
90	94.8

These statistics apply to the United States population as a whole. Some groups tend to live longer than others. For example:

- At age 65, the average woman can expect to live about 18 months longer than the average man.

- The average Caucasian can expect to live about 18 months longer than the average African American.

- People with higher incomes tend to live longer than those with lower incomes. As Ben Franklin suggested long ago, health and wealth tend to go together.

Table 10-2 looks at life expectancy from another angle — your odds of living from age 65 to subsequent age milestones. Notice that for more than half of all married couples, one member will reach age 90.

Table 10-2	Probability of Survival at Age 65*		
To Age	*Female*	*Male*	*One of a Couple*
70	93.9	92.2	99.5
75	85.0	81.3	97.2
80	72.3	65.9	90.6
85	55.8	45.5	75.9
90	34.8	23.7	50.3
95	15.6	7.7	22.1
100	5.0	1.4	

*Society of Actuaries

Paying for an ALDA

If you reach retirement and want to buy an ALDA, you have to decide which of your buckets of savings (mutual funds, retirement accounts, the proceeds of a reverse mortgage) you'll take the money from.

Qualified (Pretax) or nonqualified (After-tax) money

The best way to pay for an ALDA is with after-tax money — not the money in your deductible IRA, qualified employer-sponsored plan, or rollover IRA. That will allow you to set the trigger age as late as age 85. It also means that your guaranteed income will be partially taxable. Your insurance carrier will tell you how much of your payment you can exclude from taxation.

In theory, you could buy your ALDA with pre-tax money, but I don't recommend it. You'd have to start taking benefits at age 701/2, and that's too early for an ALDA to start. Why 701/2? That's when the IRS requires you to begin taking so-called required minimum distributions (RMDs) from all of your pre-tax accounts.

Single- or multi-premium?

Like other annuities, ALDAs can be paid for with a lump sum or in installments. As you see in the following section, various contracts allow you to pay for an ALDA all at once, a little at a time, or with deductions from the money in a variable annuity contract.

Shopping for an ALDA

As I mention earlier, only a handful of insurance companies offer ALDAs to individuals. Here are brief descriptions of ALDA products from MetLife, The Hartford, and New York Life.

MetLife Personal Income Builder

The MetLife Personal Income Builder allows you to buy future income in installments as little as $2,500 (first payment) and $500 (each additional payment). MetLife offers three variations: one for nonqualified money, one for qualified money, and a more specialized version called *Retirement Income Insurance.*

Standard version, nonqualified

The standard, nonqualified variation of the Income Builder has the following guidelines:

- ✔ You can make deposits as early as age 21.
- ✔ You can start receiving guaranteed income for life as early as age 50.
- ✔ You must receive your first income payment by age 85.

When you make a contribution, you must pick a date to begin receiving income. MetLife then calculates how much future income your contribution will buy.

As with any income annuity, you decide whether you want to receive guaranteed income

- ✔ For as long as you live.
- ✔ For as long as you or your spouse lives.
- ✔ For a guaranteed number of years or life, whichever is longer.

You can't change your income start date after you purchase the ALDA, but the company gives you a 60-day grace period during which you can withdraw any or all of your money.

If you die before receiving income, your beneficiaries receive the money you contributed plus 3-percent interest from the date you sent the money to MetLife.

Standard version, qualified money

This version is a bit more restrictive than the nonqualified version, because of the need to take RMDs. In this version:

- ✔ You can't make your first contribution until age 50 (or until at least two years after the purchase date if you're past 50).
- ✔ You have to start taking income at age 70.

In all other respects, the two versions are identical.

Retirement Income Insurance version

The MetLife retirement income insurance product is a pure ALDA. These are the guidelines:

✔ You can only purchase it with nonqualified money.

✔ You can't buy it until age 55.

✔ You can't receive your first payment until you reach age 85.

✔ You don't have a *period certain* option. That is, you can't receive your first payment at age 85 *and* get payments for a guaranteed five or ten years.

✔ The product has no withdrawal option and no death benefit if you die before you reach age 85.

The Hartford Income Security

The Hartford Income Security is a deferred income annuity you can buy only with after-tax money, not money from your rollover IRA or 401(k). Other guidelines include the following:

✔ You can buy your contract anytime from age 40 to age 83.

✔ You (or you and your spouse) can start receiving payments at any time up to age 85.

✔ Payments begin no sooner than 13 months after your last installment contribution.

✔ You can contribute as little as $1,000 at once, but you must contribute at least $10,000 within 10 years in order to receive income payments.

This product has an option that guarantees that your future income will keep pace with the rising cost of living. You can arrange for each year's income to go up by 1, 2, 3, 4, or 5 percent. So, instead of getting a uniform income throughout retirement, your payments will start small and get bigger.

The Income Security is also good for people who want an ALDA to help them handle the cost of nursing-home care. With this option:

✔ If you enter a nursing home ten or more years after you buy your contract, you can receive supplemental income from your annuity.

✔ The supplements don't start until you've been in the facility 180 days.

You can't withdraw any of your money after you buy your contract. However, by paying a little extra, you can get a cash refund death benefit; if you (or you and your spouse if you have a joint contract) die before receiving payments, your beneficiary receives an amount equal to your initial premium.

Table 10-3 shows how much a 60-year-old man, woman, and married couple would pay in 2007 to begin receiving $1,000 a month for life from a Hartford Income Security at ages 75, 80, and 85. The price includes a cash-refund death benefit for beneficiaries.

Table 10-3	Payouts from the Hartford Income Security*		
Contract Owner	Cost at Age 60 for a $1,000-Per-Month Lifetime Income if Payments		
	Begin at Age 75	Begin at Age 80	Begin at Age 85
Male	$54,000	$31,000	$16,000
Female	$61,000	$37,000	$19,000
Couple	$70,000	$44,000	$24,000

New York Life LifeStages Longevity Benefit Variable Annuity

The New York Life LifeStages Longevity Benefit Variable Annuity combines a deferred variable annuity with an ALDA. It allows you to buy retirement income gradually, by paying just 1 percent of the money in your variable annuity each year. The catch? Actually it has two:

- It has a high minimum initial contribution.
- You can only use nonqualified money.

The typical purchaser is a pre-retiree between the ages of 40 and 65 who can buy the policy with an initial purchase premium of $50,000 or more, which is then divided among stock or bond subaccounts (mutual funds).

The following are two major differences between this product and other ALDAs:

- Each year, the insurance company uses 1 percent of the contract's value to purchase monthly income that can begin at age 75, 80, or 85.

- The carrier charges a 1.35 percent annual mortality and expense fee (see Chapter 3) on the account value as well as investment management fees. These fees are fairly typical of deferred variable annuities.

The owner of the contract has two products in one. He owns the variable deferred annuity, whose assets will presumably grow in value over the years. Separately, when he reaches the trigger age (75, 80, or 85) for the longevity insurance, he'll begin receiving benefits from that.

For example, a 50-year-old woman might invest $100,000 in the New York Life product. By age 67, her variable annuity might be worth about $315,000 (if it compounded at 7 percent a year). Starting at age 85, the ALDA portion of her contract will pay her $2,151 per month for life, according to New York Life estimates.

This product represents an interesting twist. Over the years, you probably won't even miss the extra 1 percent that gets deducted from your account value to pay for your ALDA. It's painless — just as the payroll deductions that pay for your Social Security benefits are fairly painless.

As Moshe Milevsky puts it, "This might be the ultimate behavioral trick. Get people to pay for something they need, but would never have purchased on their own, by confusing them into thinking that they aren't paying anything up front." Sometimes we have to fool ourselves for our own good.

Part III

Making the Most of Your Annuity

The 5th Wave   By Rich Tennant

"We've got several hollow tree options to consider. How many nuts were you looking to invest at this time?"

In this part . . .

Think of this part as *Zen and the Art of Annuity Maintenance.* Here you find out how to choose, optimize, and maintain various types of annuity contracts. Of course, you can always let your broker or adviser make the big decisions for you. But, as an owner, you'll be much happier — and less likely to meet with unpleasant surprises — if you know all the options, opportunities, and restrictions that an owner faces.

Chapter 11

Structuring Your Annuity Correctly

In This Chapter
▶ Building a proper structure
▶ Avoiding trouble before it starts
▶ Designating beneficiaries

Deferred annuities have some odd rules about what happens to the money if the owner or the annuitant (the person whose age is used to calculate annuity payments if the owner annuitizes) dies. When misunderstood, these rules can cause lasting pain.

For instance: A husband and wife invest in a deferred variable annuity, eventually worth $300,000. But when the man dies unexpectedly, the money goes not to his widow — as he intended — but to his son from a previous marriage. The widow ends up with nothing, zilch, nada.

That tragedy wouldn't have occurred if the family had understood how to properly *structure* a deferred annuity. Structuring an annuity means more than just naming the owner, the annuitant, and their beneficiaries. It means understanding the rules about who gets what when an owner or annuitant die.

In this chapter, I show you how to avoid potential disaster by explaining how to structure a deferred annuity properly. Structuring is not a big deal — unless you do it wrong. Much of my advice boils down to a simple prescription: Make sure the owner and annuitant are the same person.

Building a Proper Structure

When you buy an annuity contract, you need to name all the players and their respective roles in the contract. As the owner, you can change these designations later if necessary. But, as I said, if you or the annuitant dies unexpectedly, a mistake in the structure can come back to haunt you. In this section, I show you how to create a safe structure.

Getting free advice

If you need advice on structuring your contract, your broker can help. And having earned a sizable commission from the insurance carrier for selling you your contract, the broker should feel obligated to assist you.

Alternatively, if you bought a no-load deferred annuity directly from an insurance company or a mutual fund company, you can call the firm's toll-free annuity-customer service line for fairly good, free advice. (The quality will vary from firm to firm and from phone rep to phone rep.)

Don't confuse the process of *structuring a deferred annuity* with the process of *designing an annuity payout option for an income annuity,* which I discuss in Chapter 8:

- ✔ *Structuring* establishes the owner, annuitant, and beneficiaries of a *deferred* annuity.
- ✔ *Designing a payout option* means deciding what type of income stream the owner of an *income* annuity will receive.

You may recall that a deferred annuity is generally a tool for saving for retirement, while an income annuity is a tool for converting savings into retirement income.

Naming names

The first step toward structuring your deferred annuity is to name the key participants in your contract (I also describe the participants in Chapter 3.) Every participant — that usually means you and your family members — plays a specific role.

Structuring an annuity contract is almost like writing a last will and testament — there's potentially a lot of money at stake, it's all legally binding, and errors can lead to litigation. Here's a brief review of the roles:

- ✔ **Contract owner:** The owner is the alpha dog — the person who writes the check for the purchase and gets to name all the other players. There may also be a joint contract owner.
- ✔ **Annuitant:** If the contract is ever converted to income, the annuitant's age will be used to calculate the payments. (You have to name an annuitant even if you — like 98 percent of all deferred annuity owners — don't plan to convert the contract to income.) There may also be a joint annuitant.

✔ **Contract owner's beneficiary:** This person receives the *accumulated value* of the contract if the owner dies before converting the contract to income.

✔ **Annuitant's beneficiary:** This person receives the *death benefit* (which may or may not be different from the accumulated value) if the annuitant dies before the contract is converted to an income stream.

Previously, I introduced two terms: *accumulated value* and *death benefit*, which first arose in Chapter 3. Both terms refer to the assets in the contract. The accumulated value is simply what the contract is worth today — your initial premium, plus any appreciation through dividends, interest, or capital gains, minus any fees or withdrawals you may have made.

The death benefit might be the same as the accumulated value, or it might be equal to the original premium, if that's greater. Some contracts now offer optional enhanced benefits for an added fee. An enhanced death benefit might be the contract's highest value on any anniversary of the purchase of the contract.

Understanding annuitant- versus owner-driven contracts

It's important to know whether your deferred annuity contract is *owner-* or *annuitant-driven:*

✔ In an *annuitant-driven* contract, the annuitant's beneficiary receives the *death benefit* when the annuitant dies. But when the owner dies, his beneficiary receives the *contract value,* which may be less than the death benefit.

✔ In an *owner-driven* contract, the owner's beneficiary receives the death benefit when the owner dies.

Following the money (after a death)

As I mention, a structure involves rules that determine the movement of the money in the annuity after a death. By understanding the consequences and implications of the structure, you'll be able to create a structure that doesn't blow up in your face like an exploding cigar. Here's what generally happens:

If the owner dies:

✔ The owner's beneficiary must receive the accumulated value as a lump sum within five years after the owner's death, or as an income stream starting within a year after the owner's death.

✔ If the owner's spouse is the owner's beneficiary or is a joint owner, the spouse can continue the contract as if she were the original owner.

✔ If the joint owner is not the owner's spouse, the joint owner must receive the accumulated value within five years after the owner's death.

✔ If the owner was also the annuitant, his beneficiary may receive a death benefit. The exact benefit depends on the death-benefit option in effect when the annuitant dies.

If the annuitant dies:

✔ In an *owner-driven* contract, nothing happens. The owner continues the contract.

✔ In an *annuitant-driven* contract, the annuitant's beneficiary receives the death benefit (see the section "Understanding annuitant- versus owner-driven contracts").

✔ If the annuitant's beneficiary has died and no new beneficiary has been named, the death benefit reverts to the contract owner or to the annuitant's estate.

✔ If the contract has a joint annuitant, the death benefit may not be paid until both the annuitant and joint annuitant have died. (Some authorities recommend avoiding the naming of two annuitants.)

✔ If an annuitant's beneficiary was never named, the death benefit goes to the annuitant's estate.

Some owners just assume that the annuitant is the beneficiary, so they name their spouse as the annuitant. Wrong! Although an annuitant generally receives the income from an *immediate* annuity (see Chapter 8), the annuitant does *not* receive the money if the owner of a *deferred* annuity dies unless he or she is also the owner's beneficiary.

Perplexed? You're not alone. Many brokers have to reread annuity prospectuses to get this straight — and they don't always succeed. "Failure to understand the rules set out in this section can be hazardous to your career!" wrote John L. Olsen and Michael E. Kitces in *The Annuity Advisor* (The National Underwriter), their book for financial professionals.

Avoiding trouble before it starts

Here's how you can prevent structure problems. Assuming that you purchased your deferred annuity for you and your spouse, and assuming that you want the surviving spouse to control the annuity if one of you dies, you should:

✔ Name the same person as owner and annuitant.

✔ Name one spouse the owner and the other the annuitant; then name each as the other's beneficiary.

✔ Name husband and wife as joint owners or joint annuitants. (Some authorities discourage the use of this structure, however, because it can cause ambiguities and unintended consequences.)

Table 11-1 describes structures where the surviving spouse will control the assets regardless of which spouse dies first. These structures also maximize the surviving spouse's flexibility in timing taxable withdrawals, and they apply equally well to owner- and annuitant-driven contracts.

Table 11-1		Structures Where the Surviving Spouse Receives the Assets		
Owner	*Owner's Beneficiary*	*Annuitant*	*Annuitant's Beneficiary*	*Effect*
Husband	Wife	Wife	Husband	If husband dies, wife receives accumulated value or continues contract in her name. If wife dies, husband claims death benefit or continues contract.
Husband	None	Husband	Wife	If husband dies, wife continues contract or, as annuitant's beneficiary, claims death benefit. If wife dies, husband continues contract.
Husband and wife	None	Wife	Husband	If husband dies, wife continues as owner and annuitant. If wife dies, husband continues as owner or claims death benefit.
Husband	Husband and wife	None	None	If husband or wife dies, and wife wifesurviving spouse continues as owner and annuitant.

Understanding beneficiary options

The contract owner must also name beneficiaries for the owner and the annuitant. Before doing so, you should understand the beneficiaries' options after the owner or annuitant dies. Those options depend on two issues:

✔ Whose beneficiary he or she is

✔ Whether he or she is the spouse of the deceased person

Generally, a beneficiary has these four options:

✔ **Withdraw all the money in a lump sum.** The beneficiary can get a check for the contract value or death benefit (see the next section "Understanding Death Benefits") as soon as she sends a copy of a death certificate to the insurance company. That amount — minus the contract owner's after-tax contributions to the contract, if any — is taxable income for the beneficiary.

✔ **Convert the money to an income.** The beneficiary can convert the money to a regular income for life or for a specific number of years. Two restrictions apply:

  • She must make this decision within 60 days after the owner or annuitant dies.

  • Payments must begin within a year of the death.

✔ **Defer withdrawal for up to five years.** The beneficiary can simply continue the contract up to five years. In addition, she can

  • Take money out as needed or make systematic withdrawals.

  • Move money from one subaccount to another.

✔ **Assume ownership of the contract (spouse only).** If the owner's beneficiary is also the owner's spouse, he or she can choose to become the new owner and simply continue the account.

If your beneficiary receives the annuity assets as a lump sum or in occasional withdrawals over five years, he or she will owe income tax on the withdrawals until only the original after-tax premium remains. The rest of the money can be withdrawn tax free.

For example, if you purchased a contract for $100,000 with money outside a tax-qualified retirement plan and it's worth $150,000 today, the first $50,000 you withdraw will be taxed as income. You can then withdraw the rest tax free. *Note:* If the beneficiary converts the assets to a lifelong income stream, then she pays tax on a fraction — determined by the *exclusion ratio* or the *exclusion amount* — of each regular payment. For a discussion of the exclusion ratio, see Chapter 14.

As the owner, be sure to name beneficiaries on your contract. If you don't, the value of your contract may end up in your estate when you die. Your intended beneficiaries may receive the money eventually, but it'll take longer.

Also, talk to a certified financial planner or tax specialist before you name a trust as the owner or beneficiary of a deferred annuity. (An annuitant, by definition, has to be a living person with a life expectancy.) Some people put annuities in living trusts, hoping for a tax advantage. But the tax laws are ambiguous about annuities and trusts; financial planners discourage mixing the two.

Understanding Death Benefits

In the famous Broadway musical *Fiddler on the Roof,* a farmer spurns a beggar with the excuse that he (the farmer) "had a bad week." The beggar says, "Why should I suffer just because you had a bad week?"

With a death benefit, your beneficiaries won't suffer just because your investments were having a bad year when you died.

Its grim name notwithstanding, the death benefit is a standard insurance feature of deferred annuities. A beneficiary who receives a death benefit is guaranteed to receive the premium or the current value of the contract, whichever is more, minus withdrawals and fees.

The death benefit isn't a major selling point of a deferred annuity. In fact, Fidelity Investments dropped the death benefit from its latest variable annuity product. But other insurance companies have created new death benefits that do more than just guarantee the premium. These new death benefits

✔ Are optional

✔ Carry slightly higher fees than the standard feature

✔ May have age restrictions; typically they aren't sold to people over a certain age (like 69 or 75) because of the investors' shorter life expectancies

Here are a few examples of the types of death benefits that annuity contracts offer:

✔ **Standard death benefit:** The least-generous death benefit is generally available at no cost above the contract's mortality and expense risk fee. It offers your beneficiary the current value of the contract, which:

  • May be fixed on the day the insurance company receives proof of the owner's or annuitant's death

  • May fluctuate until a beneficiary files a claim if the assets were invested in stocks

✔ **Return of premium death benefit:** Some contracts offer the beneficiary one of the following (whichever is greater) at no additional charge:

- The contract's current market value

- The sum of all contributions minus any withdrawals and fees

Other contracts offer this benefit for about 0.05 percent a year ($50 per $100,000).

✔ **Stepped-up death benefit rider:** For an additional fee (about 0.20 percent per year), the insurance company records your contract's balance on every anniversary of the purchase date. Your beneficiary then receives the highest of those anniversary values, adjusted for your withdrawals and additional contributions.

✔ **Enhanced death benefits:** For an additional fee, some carriers enhance the death benefit with bonuses. The method of calculating the bonus may vary from carrier to carrier. The prospectus will explain it in detail.

Death benefits, like living benefits, may be subject to *proportionate* withdrawals. So if you withdraw money from the contract at a time when the death benefit is worth more than the contract value (this can happen when a bear market follows a bull market), you'll reduce the death benefit by the same *percentage* (not the same *dollar amount*) that you reduced the contract value.

For example, if your $1,000 contract drops to $800, then a $200 withdrawal (25 percent of $800) reduces the death benefit by $250 (25 percent of $1,000). Under a *dollar-for-dollar* withdrawal method, the death benefit would only go down by $200.

Annuities aren't designed for the purpose of passing assets from one generation to the next. In fact, for tax reasons, they are very poor vehicles for leaving money to anyone. That's because the person who inherits your annuity also inherits your obligation to pay income tax on the difference between what you paid for your annuity and what it's worth when you die.

If you reach a lofty age and know you won't need the money in your variable annuity for living expenses or long-term care, consider cashing out of the contract, paying the income tax, and using the remainder to buy life insurance on yourself. Life insurance payouts are tax free. (For more on the feasibility of converting an annuity to life insurance, see Chapter 13.)

Chapter 12

Optimizing Your Variable Annuity (VA) Investments

- -

In This Chapter

▶ Choosing subaccount investments

▶ Finding your spot on the risk/return spectrum

▶ Managing your subaccounts for maximum performance

- -

As investors, we're all a bit like Dorothy in The Wizard of Oz. At first, we think our fortune lies in the hands of an all-knowing wizard (read: financial guru). Later, we discover the secret right in our own back yard; if we build a simple, diversified portfolio out of low-cost mutual funds, we can sleep soundly through the worst financial tornado.

When you buy a variable annuity contract — either deferred or immediate — you divvy up your purchase premium among the contract's subaccounts (which resemble mutual funds). In this chapter, I cover basic principles that help you choose and manage subaccounts. (You won't need advice about investing in fixed annuities, because you don't manage your investments).

Investing in variable annuity subaccounts is the same as investing in mutual funds inside an IRA or retirement plan — although guaranteed living benefits change the rules of the game a bit (see Chapter 8). If you're an experienced investor, you can skip certain parts of this chapter — but skip to the sidebar at the end of this chapter, "Lessons from the land of Oz," if you want to find out the real meaning of The Wizard of Oz.

Choosing Investments for Your VA

When VAs were first introduced a half-century ago, they represented a quantum improvement over fixed annuities: For the first time, annuity owners could manage their own money as they saw fit and, just as significantly, they could invest in stocks by purchasing subaccounts, which are similar to mutual funds.

When shopping for a VA, you should look in the prospectus, like the one shown in Figure 12-1, to see which investments are offered. Sometimes the insurance company offers investments under its own brand. It may also offer investments from a variety of mutual fund companies. You (solo or with the help of a financial adviser or broker) manage these investments just as you would manage the mutual funds in an IRA or an employer-sponsored retirement plan.

Figure 12-1a:
The Penn Mutual Funds Prospectus gives you an overview of their variable annuity products.

PROSPECTUS — MAY 1, 2007

PENN SERIES FUNDS, INC.

600 Dresher Road, Horsham, PA 19044 - Telephone 800-523-0650

MONEY MARKET FUND

LIMITED MATURITY BOND FUND

QUALITY BOND FUND

HIGH YIELD BOND FUND

FLEXIBLY MANAGED FUND

GROWTH STOCK FUND

LARGE CAP VALUE FUND

LARGE CAP GROWTH FUND

INDEX 500 FUND

MID CAP GROWTH FUND

MID CAP VALUE FUND

STRATEGIC VALUE FUND

SMALL CAP GROWTH FUND

SMALL CAP VALUE FUND

INTERNATIONAL EQUITY FUND

REIT FUND

The Securities and Exchange Commission has not approved or disapproved these securities or passed upon the adequacy of this Prospectus. Any representation to the contrary is a criminal offense.

Figure 12-1b: The opening page of the prospectus shows the types of funds available.

Subaccounts versus mutual funds

In a VA, the mutual fund investments are called *subaccounts* (and sometimes *portfolios*) and the difference between mutual funds and subaccounts is not merely semantic. It involves a difference in the way they're taxed. Subaccounts grow tax-deferred. Mutual funds (unless they're inside a retirement plan) do not.

The manager of a mutual fund regularly distributes taxable earnings, dividends, and capital gains to shareholders. Even if you reinvest your distributions (using them to buy more mutual fund shares), they're still distributed and reported to the IRS. This holds true even if your funds are in an IRA or employer-sponsored retirement plan.

But managers of annuity subaccounts don't make or report taxable distributions. The dividends, interest, and capital gains are still there. But they're all retained in the account, serving to bulk up the value of shares, rather than being distributed and reinvested through the purchase of more shares.

Because of this difference in accounting, the value of a subaccount share is called its accumulation unit value, or AUV. The value of a mutual fund share is known as its net asset value, or NAV. Like NAVs, AUVs are reported online (at the insurance company's Web site) or in financial periodicals. You can track their progress just as you'd follow the price of a stock or your favorite baseball player's batting average.

Finding a match between you and your subaccounts

Some contracts offer scores of investment options from many different mutual fund companies. Others may offer only a dozen mutual funds from a single mutual fund company. (Fidelity's new low-cost VA with a lifetime income guarantee, called Fidelity Growth and Guaranteed Income, offers just two.)

When considering a contract, make sure that you'll have enough investment choices to adequately diversify your holdings. Diversification (in other words, not "keeping all your eggs in one basket") lowers the overall risk of your investments and it can be accomplished through an almost unlimited number of subaccount combinations.

You can diversify by buying a single "balanced" subaccount or a selection of broadly based stock index subaccounts. You can also diversify by holding a mix of three or four stock and bond subaccounts or by holding a diverse mixture of specialized funds.

The philosophy of the insurance company will help determine the character of the subaccounts it offers. For instance, a conservative company might offer subaccounts whose managers purposely shoot for average returns. A more aggressive-minded company might offer subaccounts where the managers take huge risks in seeking astonishing returns.

When you're leafing through a VA's marketing literature or listening to a broker's spiel about a VA, you might ask some of the following questions about the contract's investment options:

- ✔ **Do well-established, well-trusted mutual fund companies offer the funds?** Is the company known for conservative management (that is, managers adhere to a specific style, such as value investing) or aggressive management (that is, managers can invest in anything they think will boost returns)?

- ✔ **Do the offerings seem to match your investment style?** If you're a so-called passive investor, are there index subaccounts? If you're a big risk taker, does the contract offer junk bond funds, small-cap funds, foreign equity funds, and so on?

- ✔ **Do the subaccounts have a history of strong performance, when compared with similar subaccounts?** Do they charge reasonably low fees? In general, index funds are cheap to own because they aren't very labor intensive. Actively managed funds, whose managers have to look high and low for bargains, are often more expensive because they may require lots of research.

Reviewing types of VA subaccounts

The three basic categories of subaccounts (as in the case of mutual funds) are equity, fixed income, and balanced subaccounts, each of which can be broken into subcategories. In this section, you find out more about them. If you're not familiar with mutual funds, the information here may be new to you.

Equity subaccounts

An equity subaccount invests in a basket of dozens, hundreds, or even thousands of individual stocks. (*Equity* is financial jargon for stocks.) Here are a few of the types of equity subaccounts:

- ✔ **Growth or value:** In growth subaccounts, the managers buy stocks of recognized, fast-growing companies whose stock prices are rising and are expected to keep rising. In value subaccounts, managers look for bargains. They buy stocks that they consider to be undervalued by the other investors. The prices of value stocks tend to be less volatile than the prices of growth stocks.

- ✔ **Domestic or international:** Domestic subaccounts hold the securities of U.S. companies. International subaccounts hold the securities of foreign companies, especially European or Japanese companies. *Emerging market* funds hold the securities of companies in less developed but often rapidly growing countries, such as China. They offer opportunities for higher returns but carry higher risk.

> ✔ **Small-cap, mid-cap, large-cap:** These terms refer to the capitalization of a company, which is equal to the number of stocks it has outstanding times the current share price. Exxon Mobil is the ultimate large-cap stock. Generally, the smaller the company, the smaller the capitalization, and the greater the volatility of its share price.
>
> ✔ **Leveraged:** Some VAs offer subaccounts that attempt to double the returns that other subaccounts produce by investing borrowed money in stocks. By borrowing in an attempt to achieve higher returns, they take on substantial risk.

Fixed income subaccounts

There are several types of subaccounts that invest in fixed income securities otherwise known as bonds. Here are a few of the different kinds of bonds they invest in:

> ✔ **Government:** These are bonds issued by the U.S. Treasury or government agencies. They vary in maturity, from 6 months to 30 years, and represent virtually no risk of default.
>
> ✔ **Corporate:** These are bonds issued by U.S. corporations. The strength of each borrower — that is, the issuing company's risk of not paying its debts — is graded by rating agencies. The higher the rating, the lower the risk. The highest bond rating is AAA by Standard & Poor's and Aaa by Moody's.
>
> ✔ **Mortgage-backed:** These bonds are backed by loans on real estate. (During the summer of 2007, the market for these bonds temporarily collapsed, after investors realized that some of them were much riskier than they at first appeared.)
>
> ✔ **High-yield (junk):** These are bonds that carry substantially higher risk than government or high-rate corporate bonds, and tend to pay higher interest rates than those bonds.

Balanced subaccounts

These are subaccounts that hold a mixture of stocks and bonds, enabling investors to hold both asset classes in a single convenient investment.

> ✔ **Balanced:** This type of balanced subaccount tends to hold an unchanging proportion of stocks and bonds, such as 60 percent stocks and 40 percent bonds, at all times.
>
> ✔ **Asset Allocation:** In this type of balanced subaccount, the manager may have discretion to change the proportions of stocks and bonds, depending on whether he expects the prices of one or the other to rise or fall in the near future.

✔ **Life-stage subaccounts:** Life-stage subaccounts are similar to life-stage mutual funds. These increasingly popular balanced subaccounts usually offer blends of stocks and bonds to investors of a certain age or who plan to retire in a certain year. Typically, the balance will automatically become more conservative as the investor ages, which means that it begins holding more bonds than stocks.

Finding investments that match your risk-and-return preferences

In Table 12-1, you find the names of the most common VA subaccounts. They are arranged from left to right, starting with the ones that present the lowest potential risk (chance of loss) and lowest expected returns and proceeding to those that present the highest risk and highest expected returns. Like items on a Chinese restaurant's takeout menu, you can combine them in many different ways.

Table 12-1		Risk-and-Return Spectrum for Subaccounts		
Lowest Risk-and-Return Ratio *Bond Investments*		*Highest Risk-and-Return Ratio* *Stock Investments*		
Money market subaccounts Short-term bond subaccounts	Corporate bond subaccounts Bond index subaccounts Intermediate-term bond subaccounts	Total stock market index subaccounts Value stock subaccounts Large-cap stock subaccounts	Mid-cap stock subaccounts Growth stock subaccounts	Small-cap stock subaccounts Real Estate Investment Trusts(REITs) International stock subaccounts Sector stock subaccounts
	Balanced subaccounts that hold both stocks and bonds			

While reviewing Table 12-1, keep the following in mind:

✔ **Value subaccounts** invest in stocks considered underpriced by the market.

✔ **Growth** subaccounts invest in stocks whose prices are rising and are expected to keep rising.

✔ **REITs** invest in stocks of publicly owned companies that manage investments in real estate.

The most popular variable annuity subaccounts

What types of subaccounts do most variable annuity contract owners choose? The safe ones. The following table from *SourceMedia*, December 2006, shows that the five most-popular subaccounts have conservative risks and rewards. Of these, the two most-popular subaccounts invest in large, reliable United States corporations or in a fund that pays safe fixed returns.

✔ Large blend (growth and value stocks)	23.4 percent of industry assets
✔ Fixed	19.0
✔ Balanced (stocks and bonds)	9.3
✔ Large value	7.3
✔ Intermediate-term bond	3.7
✔ World stock	3.2
✔ Foreign large blend	2.7
✔ Mid-cap growth	2.3
✔ Real Estate InvestmentTrust (REIT)	1.9
✔ Mid-cap value	1.5

✔ **International or emerging market** subaccounts invest in stocks of companies headquartered outside the United States.

✔ **Sector** subaccounts invest only in stocks of companies in a certain industry sector, such as utilities, energy, pharmaceuticals, or information technology.

✔ **Large-cap**, **mid-cap**, **and small-cap** subaccounts invest in companies the value of whose publicly held stock is either more than $5 billion, between $1 billion and $5 billion, or under $1 billion, respectively.

How GLBs affect your investment choices

Depending on your variable annuity contract and its living benefit options, you may be limited in your choice of investments, even within the contract's narrow range. For instance, if you choose a rider that promises guaranteed growth over a specific number of years, you may have to choose a fund from only four or five moderate-risk groupings.

Why the restriction? The insurance company can't afford to insure you against big investment losses at the same time you take risks that may produce big losses. In some contracts, the insurance company also reserves the right to move your money into a safe, fixed income account when stock prices are expected to fall significantly.

You can't have the guarantees without the investment restrictions — any more than you can buy low life insurance rates and still be a sky diver, a chain smoker, or work as a salmon fisherman in the choppy, frigid waters of the Bering Sea. That's the trade-off. But the restrictions generally prohibit you only from taking huge risks — like putting all your money in subaccounts that invest in small foreign companies — that you probably wouldn't take anyway.

Although the insurance company doesn't want to you to take big risks, it doesn't want you to invest so conservatively that you'll end up with less money in your account than the GLB safety net promises you.

Even as they place "speed limits" on investment choices in GLB contracts, insurance companies say that they want the presence of the GLB safety nets to encourage overly timid investors to start taking at least moderate risks with their money. They want the slow drivers to pick up the pace and start driving at the speed limit, so to speak.

I've heard GLBs described as investment *guardrails*. If you're driving at night across a bridge with no guardrails, insurers say, you'll probably drive about 30 mph. But if guardrails line the bridge, you'll be confident enough to drive 55 mph.

Why is it so important for slow investors to pick up the pace? Because safe investments like bond subaccounts appreciate too slowly. Their tortoise-like returns may not be big enough to help you finance a long retirement and keep up with inflation.

But GLBs are not the only element of VA contracts that may affect your investment choices. The high fees of many VA contracts almost compel you to put more of your premium into stock subaccounts — just to compensate for the return-reducing effect of the fees.

For example, if the GLB contract's annual expenses are 3.5 percent, your subaccounts have to earn 3.5 percent just to break even each year. If the contract guarantees that your benefit base will grow by at least 6 percent each year, your subaccounts will have to earn 9.5 percent just to match the minimum guaranteed return. To beat the 9.5 percent goal year after year, you'll have no choice but to invest in stock subaccounts.

When investing in a VA with guaranteed living benefits, you may want to work closely with a knowledgeable adviser or trustworthy broker. Many trade-offs will be involved, and there will be few easy answers to the questions that arise.

Managing Your Accounts for Optimum Results

You should expect the same account management services from your VA provider that you expect from a mutual fund company. You should be able to go to the provider's Web site and transfer money from one subaccount to another tax free, to practice dollar-cost-averaging, and to keep track of the daily performance of your subaccounts.

Either by phone or through the Web site of the carrier or mutual fund company that sold you your contract, you should be able to

- Track the growth of your annuity assets.
- Periodically exchange money from one subaccount to another.
- Set up an automatic rebalancing program.
- Set up automatic contributions to your annuity.
- Set up automatic transfers from your annuity to your checking or savings account.

Tracking the growth of your annuity

Just as the share prices of stocks and mutual funds change a bit every day, so do the accumulation unit values or AUVs (which are comparable to fund share prices) of variable annuities subaccounts. You can usually check your unit prices, the value of each subaccount you own, and your contract's account balance online or by telephone.

Exchanging between subaccounts

As the owner of the variable annuity contract, you can make exchanges among the portfolios in your contract. Because the contract grows tax-deferred, you have no tax consequences or fees when you sell shares in one portfolio for a profit and buy shares in another with the proceeds.

As with mutual funds, you must submit requests for exchange before 4 p.m. eastern time to get the same day's closing prices. The issuer of your annuity might set a minimum amount of money you can move with each exchange.

Note: Some investors and financial advisers like to use tax-deferred accounts such as variable annuities to rapidly trade into and out of subaccounts. They don't have to worry about generating a tax bill every time they make a profitable exchange.

A few variable annuity contracts are marketed to investors and advisers for that very purpose. Such contracts may include dozens of subaccounts, including some that take huge risks by investing borrowed money in attempts to double the returns of a market index. Don't go there.

Most contracts, however, discourage frequent trading, so they restrict (or retain the right to restrict) the number of exchanges you can make in a month or year. Generally, investors who create *and* stick with a sensible portfolio receive much better long-term returns than investors who jump from subaccount to subaccount.

Making regular contributions

If your variable annuity is a *flexible premium* contract, then you can add money on a somewhat regular basis. When you purchase your contract, you

- ✔ Set up automatic monthly or quarterly transfers from another source, such as your checking or savings account at a bank.
- ✔ Indicate which subaccounts should receive the new money.

Obviously, your account grows much faster over time if you make regular contributions. Keep this in mind: Contributions to the contract are not tax deductible.

Dollar cost averaging

Sometimes, when something you like goes on sale, you buy two of them, right? The same principle applies to the world of investing. With the practice of *dollar cost averaging,* you invest the same amount in a given subaccount at regular intervals instead of buying the same number of shares. The result is that you buy more shares when they're cheaper and fewer shares when they're expensive. Over the long term, dollar cost averaging produces better returns.

To practice dollar cost averaging, you can write a check for the same amount each month or quarter or, for greater convenience, set up automatic transfers of fixed amounts from your bank to your subaccounts.

Rebalancing your portfolio

Because asset allocations are built on the shifting sands of the financial markets, they can get out of alignment in just six months or a year. For example, if you start out with a portfolio of 60 percent stocks and the stock market goes up 15 percent, you soon see the stock portion of your portfolio rise to 70 percent or so. As a result, your portfolio is now riskier than you intended, and you should consider resetting it to its original allocation.

The Securities and Exchange Commission's Web site, www.sec.gov, has a section that advises beginning investors. Go to the Investor Information section of the home page and click on "For Seniors." Under "Asset Allocation and Rebalancing" you'll find three ways to rebalance your portfolio:

✔ Sell off investments from over-weighted asset categories and use the proceeds to purchase investments for under-weighted asset categories. In other words, if you have too many stocks, sell some.

✔ Purchase new investments for under-weighted asset categories. If your bond allocation has dropped, add new money to your account and restore your original bond allocation by buying bonds.

✔ If you're regularly contributing to the portfolio, alter your contributions so more go to under-weighted asset categories until your portfolio is back into balance.

For example, if you're consistently putting 60 percent into stocks and 40 percent into bonds, change the blend of your contributions until you gradually restore your original asset allocation.

After you retire, you can reverse this practice to generate retirement income each year. Every January, look at your accounts and take your annual income from the asset class or portfolios that have appreciated the most during the year.

Lessons from the Land of Oz

At the beginning of this chapter, I mention Dorothy, the Wizard, and the Land of Oz. It may seem odd to refer to a 107-year-old children's story in a book on annuities, but L. Frank Baum's original book, *The Wonderful Wizard of Oz,* was actually an elaborate financial allegory — or so some people believe.

According to several credible interpretations, the author built a detailed fable littered with symbols of the late 19th century political debate over the Populism movement, the Gold Standard on which the U.S. dollar was based until August 14, 1971, and the so-called Free Silver movement. Baum himself was a Populist, and although he denied any intention of writing an allegory, the evidence says otherwise.

In this interpretation,

- Oz is the abbreviation for ounce, as in ounces of gold and silver.

- Dorothy, whose slippers were originally silver, not "ruby" as in the film, is said to be based on a real-life heroine of the Free Silver movement, Leslie Kelsey, whose nickname was "the Kansas Tornado."

- The Tin Man represents the neglected American miner and/or factory worker.

- The Scarecrow is the destitute American farmer, hurt by low commodity prices.

- The Cowardly Lion represents the Populist Party or William Jennings Bryan, the failed Populist candidate for president in 1896.

- The Emerald City (green for money) represents Washington, D.C.

The story symbolizes the epic (but now largely forgotten) conflict between bankers on Wall Street and in London, who favored a strict gold standard and tight money, and Western farmers and miners who advocated the unlimited minting of silver dollars to expand the U.S. money supply and raise commodity prices.

The journey to Emerald City represents the Populists' unsuccessful assault, led by Bryan, on Washington, D.C., in the 1896 election. This chapter of American history ended with the start of the Spanish-American War.

This account appeared in The History of Money, by Jack Weatherford (Three Rivers Press) and in Economics, 5th Edition, by Roger A. Arnold (South-Western College Publishing), which cited the Journal of American Culture, Winter 1993, and American Quarterly, 1964. Also see "Political Interpretations of the Wizard of Oz" at wikipedia.com.

Chapter 13

Accessing, Escaping from, or Converting Your Annuity

An annuity, as I mention in Chapter 1, is a contract, not an investment. Like an automobile lease, a three-picture movie deal, a mortgage, or a marriage, annuities usually entail binding agreements that are difficult and expensive to break.

And that's not necessarily a bad thing. Without its stickiness, so to speak, an annuity contract couldn't deliver on the guarantees that made it desirable in the first place. If you didn't agree to leave your money in a fixed deferred annuity for a specific number of years, for instance, an insurance carrier couldn't offer you a guaranteed rate of return.

Contracts sometimes have to broken, however. Your circumstances may change, and when the proverbial wolf is at your door, you may need to take a hammer to that piggy bank known as an annuity. In this chapter, I talk about some of the ways you can get to your cash if you absolutely must.

With a bit of compromising, you can enjoy the benefits of an annuity and still keep your money within reach for yourself or your beneficiaries. But don't forget that annuities, like traditional IRAs and employer-sponsored retirement plans, involve a serious commitment of both money and time.

Knowing Where the Exits Are

When it comes to getting your money out, annuities are not as inflexible as you may have been led to believe. Most deferred annuities allow you to take out at least some of your money each year. Many contracts allow you to apply the money in your annuity to nursing-home costs. If you really dislike your annuity, you can swap it for a new one or even sell it.

Taking free withdrawals during the surrender period

Keep this fact well in mind: Even deferred annuities with surrender periods allow you to withdraw part of your money every year after the first year with no surrender penalty. Most of these contracts allow 10-percent free withdrawals (not counting the 10-percent penalty for withdrawals before age 59½), but some variable annuities allow up to 15 percent per year after the first year.

The annuity horror stories you read on the Internet — about the elderly who put $100,000 into an annuity and are charged a $15,000 fee just to touch their money — rarely (if ever) mention the 10-percent free withdrawals. Those stories are alarming but usually misleading. They prefer to reference only unusually complicated products with unusually long, 15-year surrender periods.

Here's a more common scenario: Suppose you're a 70-year-old who invests $100,000 in a deferred variable annuity that has a 7-percent surrender charge in the second year. If you withdraw $20,000 from the contract that year, the first $10,000 is penalty free and the second $10,000 is subject to a 7-percent surrender charge, a $700 penalty.

My point is *not* that surrender periods are good or that salesmen don't try to hoodwink senior citizens. My point is this: The threat about annuity surrender periods has been exaggerated. Annuities are long-term savings tools. If you're not in for at least ten years, don't mess with them!

Liquidity (access to your money) problems generally don't crop up if you put no more than half of your investable assets into an annuity and avoid putting money into an annuity too early in life.

Surrender periods and no-load variable annuities

Do you want an annuity that gives you total access to your funds? Buy a no-load contract that has no surrender period. (A surrender period, is the multi-year period after you buy a deferred annuity when you may be penalized for withdrawing more than is permitted. See Chapter 3.)

The main goal of surrender periods and fees is to make sure you pay the insurance company at least enough to cover its sales commission to your agent or broker. Generally, the higher the commission, the longer the surrender period (also known as the *contingent deferred sales charge period*).

But, if you buy a no-load annuity without assistance from a salesman, then there's no commission, no surrender charge, and low annual fees. A variety of companies (American Skandia, Peoples Benefit Life through Vanguard, Pacific Life, T. Rowe Price, and Fidelity) offer these products.

The downside to these annuities is that you have to buy the annuity directly from the manufacturer to eliminate the middleman. The average investor may not have the confidence to do that. As a result, less than 10 percent of variable annuities are sold direct.

No-load annuities typically don't offer all the fancy living benefits that conventional, loaded contracts now offer. But you don't need those benefits until you're nearing retirement. When you approach that age and you want living benefits, use a tax-free *1035 exchange* to move your money to an annuity that offers them. For more on this policy, see "Swapping One Annuity for Another (1035 Exchange)," later in this chapter.

Using nursing-home waivers

If you're concerned that you may need money for medical emergencies, you can easily find a deferred annuity that waives the surrender charge for a contract owner who goes into a nursing home, is disabled, or is diagnosed with a fatal illness. Read the prospectus and the contract closely to find out what conditions must be met.

In some contracts, the restrictions limit your rights to medically related withdrawals. For example, you may have to

- ✔ Be younger than 75.
- ✔ Be confined in a nursing home for at least 90 days.
- ✔ Have a serious illness that's usually fatal within two years or has an 80-percent mortality rate.

Typically, the money isn't available for a spouse who becomes ill, and only the first $500,000 of your money may be available for penalty-free withdrawal.

If you're over age 75 and think you may need the money for family medical expenses, don't buy an annuity with a surrender period.

Using the "period certain" of an income annuity

If you're reluctant to buy an income annuity (a contract that lets you convert a lump sum of money into guaranteed income; see Chapter 8) because the insurance company keeps any unpaid premium when you die, there's an easy remedy. Just add a "period certain" or a "joint-and-survivor" option to your contract.

A period certain option lets you specify that your annuity payments must last for a certain period — typically ten years — and that if you die during those first ten years, your beneficiaries (such as your children) will receive the remaining payments. The joint-and-survivor option ensures that if you or your spouse dies, the surviving spouse continues to receive annuity payments until he or she dies.

These options let you avoid the scary sense of finality that comes when you buy a "single-life only" income annuity, where annuity payments end at your death. For instance, if you die two years after paying, say, $200,000 for a single-life only annuity that pays $16,000 a year, you lose all the unpaid premium. In this example, that's $168,000.

Choosing a lifetime benefit over annuitization

If you're looking for liquidity, try a guaranteed minimum withdrawal benefits (GMWB) option. The latest deferred variable annuity contracts let you have your cake and eat it, too; they guarantee you a lifetime income *and* give you access to all of your money in an emergency. See Chapter 7 for a discussion of these or Guaranteed Lifetime Withdrawal Benefits (GLWBs).

Note: You get more guaranteed income from a SPIA than from the GMWB. Consider these two scenarios with a $100,000 purchase:

- ✔ Given a joint-and-survivor SPIA with full payments to the survivor, a man may receive $602 a month ($7,200 a year).
- ✔ At age 65, a GMWB rider may offer a guaranteed 5 percent per year for life, or $5,000 a year.

Under the GMWB:

- ✔ You have access to your $100,000 (you can't enjoy that type of liquidity with a SPIA).

✔ Your beneficiaries will receive your unspent savings.

✔ Any withdrawals in excess of a permitted annual amount (like 5 percent) reduce the guaranteed income.

Eluding the federal penalty — legally

The United States government levies a 10-percent federal penalty (excise tax) on the taxable portion of withdrawals from those accounts to people under age 59½. Tax-favored accounts include annuities, along with traditional IRAs and employer-sponsored retirement plans.

However, the tax code offers a few exemptions to the penalty. If you meet certain hardship provisions before age 59½ or convert your money to an income stream, then you can take money out penalty free. Generally, the exemptions include:

✔ **Withdrawals taken as an annuity.** The rule defines *annuity withdrawals* as "early withdrawals that are part of a series of substantially equal periodic payments (not less frequently than annually) made for the life or life expectancy of the taxpayer or the joint lives or life expectancies of the taxpayer and a beneficiary."

✔ **Distributions forced by the death of the owner or annuitant.**

✔ **Withdrawals taken as a consequence of total, permanent disability.**

Be careful about interpreting these rules without the help of a tax expert. According to *National Underwriter's Tax Facts on Insurance and Employee Benefits, 2007,* the income from an immediate annuity may not qualify for the exception if it was purchased through an exchange with a pre-existing deferred annuity.

Swapping One Annuity for Another (1035 Exchange)

Every year, millions of people transfer their money from one deferred annuity to another in a process known as a tax-free *1035 exchange*. These exchanges now account for roughly 80 percent of the total sales of deferred variable annuities.

Certain rules govern these swaps, however:

- ✔ You *can* exchange any kind of deferred annuity for any other kind. For instance, you can exchange a fixed deferred annuity for a variable deferred and a deferred annuity for an immediate annuity.
- ✔ You *can't* exchange an immediate annuity or any annuity that's been converted to an income stream into a deferred annuity.
- ✔ You *can* exchange a cash-value life insurance policy into an annuity, but you *can't* exchange an annuity into life insurance.

Whew! Got all that?

Reasons to trade

People swap annuities for several good reasons. For example, by exchanging a high-cost contract for a Vanguard variable annuity, the owner can save at least 1 percent per year in costs. If the annuity has a $500,000 value, that's $5,000 a year.

People also exchange annuities for the same reason they trade cars — they want the latest features. Since about 2004, many people have traded up to annuities that offer the latest guaranteed minimum withdrawal benefits.

A new surrender period starts when you exchange an existing annuity contract for a new contract.

Unfortunately, many people exchange annuities because a salesman talks them into it. The salesman's motive is clear: to earn a commission. But the swap isn't always good for the customer, who may have to pay surrender charges on the old annuity and then start a whole new one with the new contract.

Most odiously, some salesmen tempt people to swap by offering new contracts with bonuses that supposedly offset the surrender charges. But the bonuses may be contingent on certain events such as converting the assets to an irrevocable income stream. Bottom line? The bonuses may never materialize in their customers' wallets.

Death benefits (the promise that your beneficiaries will receive at least what you originally paid for the contract) aren't transferable from contract to contract. If you decide to swap annuities, you give up whatever death benefit you had and choose a new one. Unfortunately, the new contract's death benefit options may or may not be as generous as the first annuity's were.

Questions to ask before you execute a 1035 exchange

The Financial Industry Regulatory Authority (FINRA; it was known as NASD before June 2007), the watchdog group by which the securities industry polices itself advises consumers to quiz any broker or agent who tries to sell them on swapping one annuity for another through a 1035 exchange. Important questions are:

✔ What is my total cost for this exchange?

✔ What does the change in the surrender period or other terms mean for me?

✔ What are the new features? Why do I need or want those features?

✔ Are those features worth the increased cost?

✔ Will you be paid a commission for the exchange, and if so, how much is it?

Despite the potential for exploitive brokers and new surrender charges, the 1035 exchange process is your escape hatch from a bad annuity. The money you can save on annual fees by switching from a high-cost annuity to a low-cost annuity may make that surrender charge worth your while. You can move on and chalk it up to experience.

If a broker advises you to swap one annuity contract for another, you will need to fill out a "suitability form" before completing the application for an exchange. The form will include questions designed to investigate whether you're gaining or losing anything by making the swap.

Eventually, an officer at a brokerage firm will review your suitability form and your application to make sure you're doing the right thing. It's possible that your application for a 1035 exchange will be rejected on the grounds that you simply don't have much to gain from one.

Web-ifying the 1035 process

Don't expect to complete a 1035 exchange overnight. The exchange process can last for several weeks because it requires much paperwork between your previous and new annuity issuer. The previous issuer may, in fact, drag out the process just to hold onto your interest-bearing money for a little longer.

In 2007, the annuity industry and the Depository Trust and Clearing Corporation (DTCC) in New York launched a program to conduct 1035 exchanges over the Internet rather than via surface mail or overnight delivery, but that route on the information highway isn't expected to be fully functional for several years.

Selling an Annuity

What happens when you're already receiving an income stream from an income annuity but you've changed your mind and want to turn the contract back into a wad of cash? Answer: A number of companies will buy some or all of your future monthly payments. These firms borrow money on Wall Street, buy lots of income annuities, and then use the ongoing monthly payments to pay off the money they borrowed. In the process, they make a healthy profit.

Here's an example: A 59-year-old woman receives $1,900 a month from an income annuity that her late husband bought in March 2004 for $400,000. The annuity has a 30-year period certain — that is, it makes exactly 360 monthly payments. But her circumstances have changed and she needs some of the money to pay college tuition for her sons.

She decides to sell the 120 payments that are due to her from March 2009 to March 2019, which add up to $228,000. But the present *value* of those payments (what a $1,900 per month, ten-year income stream might cost today) may be $180,000 or so before taxes. She found a firm that would pay her $145,000 for her income stream, and she took it. The woman would resume receiving payments of $1,900 a month between 2019 and 2024.

Obviously, you'll pay a big fee when you sell an annuity. Notice that the woman sold an income stream worth $180,000 for $145,000. The difference represents the purchasing firm's fee. Out of that fee, the purchasing firm might pay an 8 percent commission to the salesman who brokered the transaction. The rest goes to the firm's costs and profits.

Note: Not all annuities can be sold this way. The contracts have to be non-qualified (purchased with after-tax money, not with transfers from an employer-sponsored retirement plan). Also, the income annuity must have a period certain option. It can't be a "life only" annuity.

Be careful when you sell an annuity for cash. Transactions (which require complex calculations to determine an accurate present value) are fertile ground for scams. It will be hard for you to tell whether you're getting a fair price for your annuity or not. If a stranger approaches you and suggests that you sell or replace your annuity, call your state insurance commission.

Such a sale also has tax implications. If you retain ownership of the annuity after a finance company buys part of your income stream, the IRS will hold you responsible for income taxes on distributions.

Converting an Annuity to Life Insurance

Some people with variable annuities may decide to leave the assets in the contract to their children rather than use it for retirement income. In this case, their financial planner may recommend that they turn the contract into life insurance. The life insurance death benefit may be higher than the annuity benefit, and it's tax free for the beneficiary.

Suppose you and your spouse are each 75 years old and have a deferred variable annuity that cost $100,000 but is now worth $200,000. You don't think you'll need the income during your lifetime, so you'd like to leave the money to your children (they're already the beneficiaries on the contract). What are your options? You can

- ✔ Do nothing and let your children receive the death benefit from the contract after you and your spouse die. They will pay income tax ($30,000) on the $100,000 gain so they'll net $170,000.

- ✔ Cash out the annuity, pay the income tax, and apply the $170,000 to a *second-to-die* variable life insurance policy that will pay your children about $250,000 after you and your spouse die. (Thanks to a woman's longer life expectancy, second-to-die insurance is much less expensive than insurance for a man or the first to die.)

- ✔ Keep the annuity, withdraw $20,000 every year, and buy a $250,000 second-to-die life insurance policy. At your death, your children will receive $250,000 plus the remainder of the variable annuity. (The first $100,000 you withdraw from the annuity is fully taxable; the second $100,000 is a tax-free return of your original investment.)

- ✔ Convert the variable annuity to a lifelong income stream and apply the payments each year to renew a $250,000 life insurance policy on you and your spouse. Only part of each payment is subject to income tax. (The *exclusion ratio* makes part of every payment from a nonqualified annuity tax free; see Chapter 14). Your children receive the tax-free $250,000 and the partially taxable death benefit of the variable annuity.

  This strategy has an advantage over the previous one because your income stream continues to pay the life insurance premiums for as long as you live. You can't exhaust your ability to pay them.

In these examples, the life insurance strategy looks like a no-brainer — as long as you and your spouse don't need the money for living expenses or self-insurance against potential nursing-home expenses.

But it's not always that clear a choice. For example, as elderly persons, you and your spouse may not qualify for affordable life insurance. And if your children are in the 15-percent tax bracket, their tax bite on the annuity death benefit (see the first bullet in the preceding choices) may not seem so scary.

No two situations are alike, and variables are limitless. Talk to an experienced tax or insurance specialist before you try this one at home.

Chapter 14

The Taxing Side of Annuities

*T*axes can be a toxic topic. Most people head for the hills — or to H&R Block — when they hear the word. Uncle Sam doesn't help much. He created income tax breaks to help Americans save for retirement, and then hid those breaks in a thicket of regulations.

The rewards for hacking through that thicket, however, can be significant. You can use a deferred annuity, for instance, to protect your savings from taxes until you retire. You can use an income annuity to spread your tax obligation over the course of your retirement.

This chapter is intended to serve as your machete, so to speak. I clarify the differences between taxes on qualified and nonqualified annuities, between the tax rules for an annuity's "accumulation" and "distribution" stages, and between the taxation of annuity and non-annuity withdrawals.

Annuity taxation is a moving target. The IRS hasn't determined, for instance, exactly how to tax the income provided by the popular new living benefits of variable annuities, such as guaranteed minimum withdrawal benefits (GMWBs). And, as I write, several bills are pending in Congress that would exempt some annuity income from taxes entirely.

Understanding Annuity Taxation: The Basics

For tax purposes, there are two kinds of annuities: qualified and nonqualified:

✔ Nonqualified annuities (either deferred or income annuities) are purchased with *after-tax money* — money that you've paid income tax on.

✔ Qualified annuities (either deferred or income annuities) are purchased with *pre-tax money* — the money you've contributed to a "qualified" employer-sponsored retirement plan or traditional IRA. (A "qualified plan" is simply a retirement plan, such as an IRA or 401(k) plan, that qualifies for certain tax breaks under IRS code.)

Nonqualified annuities and taxes

In the case of nonqualified annuities, 90 percent of what you need to know can be distilled into three simple principles:

✔ When you buy the annuity, you can't deduct the purchase amount from your taxable income.

✔ As long your money stays in the annuity, you won't pay taxes on any capital gains, interest, or dividends that your money earns.

✔ When you (or someone you choose) start withdrawing your money from the annuity, you'll have to pay ordinary income tax on those gains. Your principal will be returned to you tax free.

Qualified annuities and taxes

In the case of qualified annuities, the fundamentals are even simpler:

✔ You can deduct your contributions from your taxable income.

✔ While your money is invested, you won't pay any taxes on your gains.

✔ You'll owe ordinary income tax on whatever you withdraw.

Note: This chapter focuses on the rules that pertain to *nonqualified* annuities. That's because qualified annuities are governed mainly by the rules that govern traditional IRAs and qualified employer-sponsored retirement plans. I talk first about the tax treatment of contributions to nonqualified annuities. Then I discuss the tax rules for withdrawals.

Taxing Additions to Deferred Nonqualified Annuities

Between the time you first buy a deferred annuity and the time you begin taking regular withdrawals — generally in retirement — there's a stretch of (ideally) 10 to 20 years called the "accumulation period." It's the growth stage of your contract, when you either just let your original contribution grow or make additional contributions. The following rules apply to your contributions:

- ✔ **You can contribute virtually any amount of after-tax money to a non-qualified annuity.** How many dollars can you fit inside a nonqualified annuity? As many as you have. You can contribute virtually *any amount* of after-tax money to an annuity. (Contributions over $1 million may require the insurance company's permission.) Compare this to the limits on contributions to an IRA ($5,000 a year to an IRA for 2008; more if you're over age 50), and to employer-sponsored retirement plans (no more than about $15,000).

- ✔ **You can't deduct contributions to a deferred annuity from current income.** Although your contributions have no limit, you can't deduct a single penny of them from your taxable income. Contributions to traditional IRAs and employer-sponsored plans are limited but tax deductible.

- ✔ **You pay no taxes on the growth of your account until you take withdrawals.** This is the essence of tax deferral. It distinguishes tax-deferred accounts from taxable mutual fund accounts, where your dividends, interest, and capital gains are distributed and taxed each year. (See the sidebar "Assessing the benefits of tax deferral.")

- ✔ **You can exchange money between investment options without tax.** If you have money in several subaccounts — that is, mutual funds — in a variable deferred annuity, you can move money from one subaccount to another without piling up a bunch of profits that you'll have to pay taxes on the following year. The IRS doesn't keep track of the profits or losses you incur inside a deferred annuity when you exchange money between subaccounts.

Not that I encourage exchanges. Research shows that hyperactive investors lose in the long run (see Chapter 12). In fact, many variable annuities restrict the number of exchanges you can make.

- ✔ **The IRS restricts access to your money.** Because the purpose of tax deferral is to encourage saving for retirement, the government actively discourages premature withdrawals from tax-deferred accounts — IRAs, employer plans, and annuities.

  All withdrawals (with some exceptions for personal hardship) before age 59½ are subject to a 10 percent federal penalty. In addition, you may have to pay a "surrender charge" if you withdraw more than 10 percent of your annuity assets in a single year during the "surrender period" — that initial 3- to 15-year period after your purchase. (For a fuller discussion of surrender charges, see Chapter 3.)

Assessing the benefits of tax deferral

Just how healthy for your wealth is tax deferral? How much juice does it add to your savings? After 20 years or so, how much more can you accumulate in a tax-deferred account than in a conventional account, all other factors being equal?

The Internet has many calculators that demonstrate the effect of tax deferral. For example, ING, which issues many highly regarded annuity contracts, has a good one at

www.ing-usa.com/us/individuals/
planningtools/calculatorstools/
taxdeferral/index.htm

I tried it, plugging in numbers from a typical scenario:

✔ Initial contribution to the annuity: $10,000

✔ Number of years for it to grow: 20

✔ Anticipated return: 8 percent, based on a moderate-risk investment mix

✔ Income tax rate: 25 percent

✔ Monthly contributions: $100

The calculator indicated that this hypothetical investment, after 20 years, would grow at 8 percent to $76,471 in a taxable account but to $108,170 in a tax-deferred account, before taxes. After taxes (at 25 percent), the tax-deferred account would have been worth $87,402, or almost $9,000 more than the taxable account. By changing my inputs to the calculator, I could see that the benefit of tax-deferral increases when the contributions are higher, the return is greater, and the tax rate is higher.

When your money is in a tax-deferred annuity, you don't pay taxes on your gains each year. This benefit is especially important during retirement, when you're trying to minimize expenses. In contrast, if your money is in a taxable investment, you have to pay taxes each year on the capital gains, dividends, or interest generated by the funds.

Tax deferral is most effective when

✔ You're in a high tax bracket today.

✔ You expect to be in a lower tax bracket during retirement.

✔ You have a large sum of money to set aside.

✔ You can afford not to touch the tax-deferred money for at least ten years.

✔ Your annuity contract's fees are less than 1 percent per year.

✔ You've already contributed as much as you can to IRAs and employer-sponsored retirement plans.

Like a crock-pot cooker, tax deferral works its magic very slowly. To make the most of tax deferral, plan on keeping your money in the deferred variable annuity a long time — 15 to 20 years.

Taxing Withdrawals from Deferred Nonqualified Annuities

The second stage in the life cycle of an annuity begins when you begin taking regular withdrawals from your contract. This stage is known as the "distribution period," and it usually begins after age 59½, when your withdrawals are no longer subject to a 10-percent federal penalty. The following rules describe the tax treatment of those withdrawals:

✔ **Only part of the money withdrawn from a nonqualified annuity will be taxed.** Think of the money in your deferred annuity as a mixture of cream and skim milk. The skim milk represents the money you originally paid for your contract — that is, your premium. The cream represents the growth of the premium through market appreciation or the accumulation of interest and dividends (sometimes called the "internal buildup"). When you withdraw money from your nonqualified annuity — it can be either a deferred or an income annuity — you'll owe taxes only on the cream, not the skim.

✔ **You'll owe ordinary income tax (not capital gains tax) on the taxable portion.** The "cream" in your annuity is taxed as income. Unlike the profits you earn on the sale of investments that you held in a conventional (taxable) brokerage or mutual fund account for at least a year, which are taxed at the capital gains tax rate of 15 percent, all the profits (including dividends, interest, and capital gains) you earn on your investments in an annuity contract are eventually taxed at what are called "ordinary income" tax rates, which range as high as 35 percent.

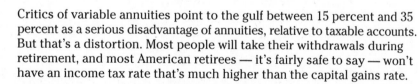

Critics of variable annuities point to the gulf between 15 percent and 35 percent as a serious disadvantage of annuities, relative to taxable accounts. But that's a distortion. Most people will take their withdrawals during retirement, and most American retirees — it's fairly safe to say — won't have an income tax rate that's much higher than the capital gains rate.

Table 14-1 shows a quick rundown of marginal tax rates. If you're married and filing jointly, your first $63,700 in taxable income (after exemptions and deductions) is taxed at a mere 15 percent. Your next $64,800 or so is taxed at 25 percent. That's an average of 20 percent on the first $128,500 in taxable income. At that income level, the difference (5 percentage points) between the income tax rate and the capital gains tax rate isn't trivial, but it's not dramatic either.

Table 14-1	Marginal Tax Rates, 2007
Ordinary Income from . . .	*Is Taxed at the Rate of . . .*
0 to $15,650	10 percent
$15,650 to $63,700	15 percent
$63,700 to $128,500	25 percent
$128,500 to $195,850	28 percent
$195,850 to $349,700	33 percent
$349,700 and over	35 percent

✔ **If you take partial withdrawals from a deferred annuity, your taxable money comes out first.** This is the so-called LIFO ("last in, first out") rule. For tax purposes, the IRS requires you to withdraw all the cream (and to pay taxes on it) before you take out any of the tax-free skim. That's not necessarily a bad thing — you'll be making tax-free withdrawals later in life. But this rule only applies to occasional withdrawals from a deferred annuity — not to the regular payments you might receive during retirement from an income annuity.

Here's an example: Suppose you put $50,000 of after-tax savings into a deferred variable annuity at age 55. Further suppose that the contract grows to $80,000 by the time you retire at age 65. Assuming that you don't convert the value to a regular income (through "annuitization"; see Chapter 3), the first $30,000 you withdraw will be fully taxable as income. You can withdraw the remaining $50,000 tax free.

✔ **If you "annuitize" a deferred annuity or buy an income annuity (or SPIA; see Chapter 8), only a portion of each payment will be taxed.** A completely different tax rule applies when you receive your annuity assets in the form of a guaranteed retirement income stream, either by converting a deferred annuity to income or buying an income annuity.

In that case, every payment consists partly of cream — please pardon the extended metaphor — and partly of skim milk. If the income annuity makes fixed payments, the ratio of skim to cream in each payment is called the *exclusion ratio*. Generally, it will be the same as the ratio of principal to earnings in your contract. If the income annuity makes variable payments, a certain dollar amount of each payment (the *exclusion amount*) will not be taxed.

The "exclusion ratio" is irrelevant if you buy your annuity with "qualified" money from a tax-deferred account. For instance, if you moved all of your 401(k) savings to a "rollover IRA" (a rollover is a transfer that lets you move money out of a 401(k) account without all your deferred taxes suddenly

Calculating the exclusion ratio or exclusion amount

Fortunately, you probably won't have to calculate your own exclusion ratio. The insurance company that sells you an income annuity or converts your deferred annuity into an income stream will do it for you. But the basic calculations for single-life fixed income and variable income annuities are described below.

The calculations for customized annuities — contracts that guarantee a certain number of payments, or that provide income for a husband and wife, or that offer a refund of any unpaid portion of your premium if you die — are somewhat more complicated. You can rely on the insurance company for that.

If you're truly interested — and your glazed eyeballs tell me that you aren't — you can look up the formulas in IRS Publication 939, "General Rule for Pensions and Annuities" (available at www.irs.gov) or in "Tax Facts on Insurance and Employee Benefits 2007," which you can order from The National Underwriter Company (www.taxfactsonline.com).

Fixed income annuity exclusion ratio: To calculate the exclusion ratio of a fixed income annuity (one that pays the same amount every month) you need several numbers: the amount of after-tax money you used to purchase your annuity (your principal), the amount of each income payment (provided by the insurer), and the number of years you are expected to live, based on IRS mortality tables.

Suppose that at age 65 you bought an immediate fixed annuity for $100,000 in after-tax money. The insurance company offered to pay you $700 a month ($8,400 a year) for the rest of your life. Your "expected return multiple" — similar to, but not

the same as your life expectancy — is 20, according to Table V of the IRS Annuity Tables. Your expected return then equals $168,000 ($8,400 × 20).

Since $100,000 is 59.52 percent of $168,000, you can exclude 59.52 percent of your annual annuity income of $8,400 from income tax. In dollars, the excludable amount would be exactly $5,000.

Formula for calculating exclusion ratio of fixed income annuity:

$$\frac{\text{Investment in the contract}}{\text{Expected payments}} = \frac{\$100,000}{\$168,000^*} = 59.52 \text{ percent exclusion ratio}$$

*($8,400/year × expected return multiple of 20 from Table V, IRS actuarial tables)

Variable income annuity exclusion amount: No one can predict the returns from a variable income annuity. The market value of the underlying stocks and bonds fluctuates from month to month. But because the carrier knows how much after-tax money you paid for your income annuity, and how many years you'll live (on average), it simply divides your contribution by the average number of expected payments to arrive at the amount of each payment that you can exclude from your taxable income.

Suppose a person is 65 years old and wants to buy a variable income annuity with $100,000 in after-tax money. The issuer of the contract offers to pay him $8,200 a year for life. Because his life expectancy is 20 years, he will be able to exclude $5,000 ($100,000 ÷ 20) from each year's income. The exclusion ratio will be 61 percent ($5,000 ÷ $8200).

coming due), and then bought an immediate income annuity with that money, you would owe income tax on your entire annuity income each year. None of it could be excluded.

✔ **If you live long enough, your entire annuity income will be taxable.** If you own an income annuity you may eventually — with luck and good health habits — reach an age (your life expectancy) when your entire principal will have been returned to you. From then on, your income payments will consist entirely of earnings or survivorship credits (the money that surviving contract owners receive, in effect, from contract owners who have died; see Chapter 8) and all of it will be subject to income tax for the year you receive it.

✔ **You don't have to take Required Minimum Distributions (RMDs) from a nonqualified deferred annuity.** When you own a nonqualified deferred annuity, you don't have to withdraw a portion — your RMD — every year, starting by April 1 of the year after the year you reach age 70½. That means your money can benefit from tax deferral for a longer time. It also means you have more control over when to pay taxes on your assets. In this respect, nonqualified annuities offer more flexibility than traditional IRAs and employer plans. Those accounts, and annuities bought with the pretax money in those accounts, are subject to RMDs.

Taxation of guaranteed lifetime withdrawal benefits

Over the past few years, many people have purchased deferred variable annuities with guaranteed lifetime benefit (GLB) income riders, such as guaranteed minimum withdrawal benefits or guaranteed lifetime withdrawal benefits (see Chapter 7). By definition, GLB riders offer a guaranteed, relatively stable annual income in retirement, while also providing liquidity — access to the money in an emergency. The question is this: Are GLB payments subject to taxation under the LIFO rule or under the exclusion ratio rule?

The answer can make a big difference. If GLBs are taxed by the LIFO method, every withdrawal is fully taxable as ordinary income until all earnings are withdrawn. Subsequent withdrawals are tax free. If they are taxed under the exclusion ratio rule, as income annuities are, the tax bill will be spread out over the entire retirement.

At least some insurance companies now operate with the assumption that GLBs will be governed by the LIFO rule. As one prospectus explains, "It is not clear whether guaranteed minimum withdrawal benefit (GMWB) payments made during the settlement or income (payout) phase may be taxed as either withdrawals or annuities. In view of this uncertainty, we intend to adopt a conservative approach and treat GMWB payments . . . as withdrawals."

Pros and Cons of Annuity Taxation: A General Overview

From a tax perspective, here are the advantages and disadvantages of non-qualified annuities. The pros are

✔ You pay no taxes on the growth of your investments until you take withdrawals.

✔ You can contribute virtually any amount of money to a deferred annuity.

✔ You don't have to begin taking taxable Required Minimum Distributions from your contract at age 70½.

✔ Your original investment is returned to you tax free.

✔ You can annuitize your contract and spread your tax burden across your retirement, taking advantage of the exclusion ratio.

The cons are

✔ The insurance fees of deferred variable annuities can negate the benefits of tax deferral.

✔ It takes at least ten years for tax deferral to produce a significant benefit.

✔ Investment gains are taxed as ordinary income, at a maximum marginal rate of 35 percent, rather than at the regular capital gain top rate of 15 percent.

✔ Withdrawals from a deferred annuity before age 59½ are subject to ordinary income tax and to a 10 percent federal penalty tax (unless certain hardship exceptions apply).

✔ Annuities, like all tax-favored retirement accounts, aren't good tools for passing money to your descendants. Beneficiaries will inherit your tax liability along with any money they receive. Unlike appreciated securities (which have risen in value since they were purchased) in taxable accounts, appreciated annuity assets don't qualify for a "step up in basis." The step up in basis exempts beneficiaries from inheriting taxable gains when they inherit appreciated securities.

Other Annuity Tax Issues

Here are brief discussions of other tax issues that affect annuities.

Taxes and annuity beneficiaries

If you die while owning or receiving income from an annuity, your beneficiary may be entitled to a payment. The payment could be a death benefit, the current market value of the investment in the contract, a refund of unpaid premium, or any remaining unpaid guaranteed payments. The exact amount will depend on several factors: whether you had already converted the assets to an income stream, whether you chose a period certain or refund option, and whether the beneficiary is your spouse. The timing of the payments can also vary: immediately after your death, over a period of five years after your death, or over the beneficiary's lifetime.

But whatever the situation, beneficiaries will be taxed the same way the owner would have been taxed. If the annuity was a nonqualified annuity, paid for with nondeductible money, the beneficiaries owe income tax on whatever they receive in excess of what the owner paid into the annuity. If the annuity was purchased through a retirement plan or with the money in a rollover IRA, the beneficiaries owe income tax on every cent they receive.

See Chapter 11 for tips on structuring your contract so that you know exactly what will happen to the money in your contract if you die. Unless you are already an expert in personal finance, I recommend that you consult a tax specialist on the potential tax ramifications of owning an annuity. If you make a mistake in this area, unintended consequences can result. Your money may not end up in the hands of the person you intended.

States that levy premium taxes

A few states charge a "premium tax" on annuities. Maine, South Dakota, and Wyoming (see Table 14-2) levy a tax on the premiums paid to fund a nonqualified annuity. California, Nevada, and West Virginia (see Table 14-3) levy a tax on the value of the contract if the annuity owner converts it to a guaranteed income stream.

Table 14-2	States with a Tax on Purchase Premiums	
State	*Qualified Contracts*	*Nonqualified Contracts*
Maine	-	2.00 percent
South Dakota	-	1.25 percent
Wyoming	-	1.00 percent

Table 14-3	States with a Tax on Accumulated Value (If Withdrawals Aren't Taken As a Lump Sum)	
State	*Qualified Contracts*	*Nonqualified Contracts*
California	0.50 percent	2.35 percent
Nevada	-	3.50 percent
West Virginia	1.00 percent	1.00 percent

1035 exchanges aren't taxed

A *1035 exchange* is the technical term for a tax-free transfer of one kind of annuity for another. If you don't like the annuity you have because its fees are too high, the subaccounts perform poorly, or it doesn't have the latest options, you can swap it for a different contract. In any case, the exchange doesn't count as a withdrawal, so you don't have to pay a tax. (For more on 1035 exchanges, see Chapter 13.)

Surrender fees are not tax deductible. If you take money out of a deferred variable annuity before the end of the surrender period (anywhere from 3 to 14 years after the purchase date, depending on the contract), you could pay a surrender charge of up to 14 percent on annual withdrawals of more than 10 percent of the value of the contract. You will owe income tax on your entire withdrawal, not your withdrawal minus the surrender fee.

The contract owner picks up the (tax) tab

Even when the owner of an annuity contract isn't the one who receives income from it, he or she is still on the hook for the tax on that income. If you buy an immediate annuity for your aunt and she receives the monthly checks, the IRS will look to you for the income tax. In most cases, however, people who buy income annuities intend the income to be paid to themselves alone or to themselves and their spouses.

Taxes on income payments can be withheld

Unless you expressly tell it not to, the insurance company will withhold federal income taxes from every withdrawal you make from your annuity.

Be skeptical if someone advises you to buy a variable deferred annuity with the money in your IRA. If you're still saving for retirement, it doesn't make much sense. The money in the IRA is growing tax-deferred. Putting it into a tax-deferred variable annuity would be redundant — like wearing a raincoat in the shower. You don't need two layers of tax deferral.

But if you're retired or about to retire, it's a different story. You're probably looking for ways to turn your IRA assets into retirement income. At that point, there's nothing wrong with buying a variable deferred annuity if you're buying it for the guaranteed living withdrawal benefits. That's a feature that IRAs don't offer.

On the Horizon: Exemptions for Annuity Income?

To encourage more people to convert their retirement savings to a guaranteed lifetime income, a number of legislators in both the U.S. Senate and House of Representatives have submitted bills that would exempt half of an individual's income from a life annuity from taxation, up to an annual exclusion of $20,000. The maximum tax savings would be $5,000 a year. The bills have broad public support, much of it channeled through an organization called Americans for a Secure Retirement (www.paycheckforlife.org). Stay tuned.

Part IV
Navigating the Annuity Superstore

The 5th Wave   By Rich Tennant

LOCALLY GROWN STOCKS
FARM FRESH CDs
FREE RANGE ANNUITIES

In this part . . .

In these three chapters — and with help from Appendix A — you discover the smart way to buy an annuity. You tour the annuity industry and meet the companies and various agents, brokers, and advisers who sell annuities. You find out how to research annuities online, where to get the best deals, and how to avoid common missteps. One thing more: You begin to realize that the process of buying annuities (like the process of buying automobiles) has evolved over the years. Thanks to the Internet, consumers have more information and more choices than ever.

Chapter 15

Getting Creative with Annuities

In some chapters in this book, I describe annuities as if they were home appliances: telling you how they work, what their features are, and so on. In this chapter I want to look at annuities the way the pros do: as tools for cutting financial risk and machinery for generating lifelong income.

As this chapter shows, you can use annuities — fixed or variable, deferred or income — to produce retirement income in a virtually unlimited number of ways. You can blend annuities with other assets, customize them, and even mix different kinds of annuities together. They're a financial version of LEGO blocks.

Building on the latest research in the field, I offer recommendations on finding the right proportion of annuities in your portfolio, on combining annuities with long-term care insurance, on inflation-proofing your retirement, on turning your home equity into an annuity, and a lot more.

Several of the ideas in this chapter are new and experimental. Some are on the academic drawing board; others are still brewing in the math labs of huge insurance companies. But they demonstrate that getting creative with annuities can go way beyond the many payout options of income annuities (Chapter 8) and deferred variable annuities (Chapter 7). But proceed with caution. Consult a financial professional before you make any irrevocable decisions about your money.

Combining Stocks, Cash, and Income Annuities

Suppose that you're 60 years old. Your financial priority is to generate retirement income and not run out of money. Your secondary goal is to leave some of your money to your children. Where should you put your money?

Two retirement income gurus, Peng Chen of Morningstar, Inc., and Moshe Milevsky of Toronto's York University, have answered this question by developing a range of specific recommendations for adding income annuities to the usual mix of stocks, bonds, and cash. Based on their own assumptions about market returns, they offered precise asset recipes — all designed for people who want to pass wealth to the next generation but who have varying degrees of tolerance for investment risk.

Matching annuity ownership to your risk tolerance

Peng Chen and Moshe Milevksy created a useful chart to depict their recommendations. A simplified version of it appears in Table 15-1, from "Merging Asset Allocation and Longevity Insurance: An Optimal Perspective on Payout Annuities" by Peng Chen, PhD, and Moshe A. Milevsky, PhD; *Journal of Financial Planning;* June 2003. To find your own place in the chart, choose the risk tolerance level you think applies to you from the column on the far left. (A risk tolerance of 1 means the stock market doesn't scare you a bit; a risk tolerance of 6 means you've never gotten over the tech crash of March 2000.) Then read across that row.

Table 15-1   Risk Tolerance and Asset Mix (Including Annuities)

Risk Tolerance (1 = Most)	% Risk-free Assets (Cash or Treasury Bills)	% Stocks	% Fixed Income Annuity	% Variable Income Annuity	Ratio of Annuity Assets/ Conventional Investments	Ratio of Stocks/ Cash or Treasury Bills
1	4	30	0	66	66/34	96/4
2	22	38	14	26	40/60	64/36

Risk Tolerance (1 = Most)	% Risk-free Assets (Cash or Treasury Bills)	% Stocks	% Fixed Income Annuity	% Variable Income Annuity	Ratio of Annuity Assets/ Conventional Investments	Ratio of Stocks/ Cash or Treasury Bills
3	42	30	16	12	28/72	42/58
4	54	24	14	8	22/78	32/68
5	60	22	14	4	18/82	26/74
6	68	18	12	2	14/86	20/80

For instance, according to the chart, the $300,000 portfolio of a 60-year-old with a risk tolerance level of 2 looks like this:

✔ Cash or short-term government bonds: $66,000 (22 × 300,000)

✔ Stock mutual funds: 114,000 (38 × 300,000)

✔ A combination fixed and variable life annuity: $120,000 (40 × 300,000) composed of:

  • Fixed income annuity: $42,000 (14 × 120,000)

  • Variable income annuity: $78,000 (26 × 120,000)

Creating an all-annuity portfolio

The previous section applies to someone who wants to leave some of her wealth to her children. But what if you took the so-called "bequest motive" out of the picture (perhaps because you set money aside separately for your children at the beginning of retirement) and settled on an amount that you wanted to use purely to generate income for yourself?

Table 15-2 shows annuity purchase strategies for people with six different levels of risk tolerance. According to this chart, if you have a risk tolerance level of 3 and $300,000 to create retirement income, you should put all the money in a life annuity: $126,000 (300,000 × .42) in variable subaccounts (stock mutual funds) and $174,000 (300,000 × .58) in a fixed subaccount. The $300,000 will generate about $2,000 every month at a 5-percent interest rate, with higher payouts if stock prices rise over time.

Table 15-2	Risk Tolerance and Suggested Ratio of Variable to Fixed Income Annuities	
Risk Tolerance	Variable Income Annuity (%)	Fixed Income Annuity (%)
1	98	2
2	64	36
3	42	58
4	32	68
5	24	76
6	20	80

Dialing down your "risk of ruin"

To determine how much an annuity can reduce a person's risk of running out of money, Peng Chen of Ibbotson also imagined a 65-year-old couple with a pre-retirement annual income of $100,000 and a $1 million investment portfolio. The couple wanted an annual income of $75,000 during retirement, including Social Security benefits, and wanted to leave money to their children.

As Table 15-3 shows, the no-annuity portfolio provided the couple with 90-percent assurance that their money would last until they reached age 84. But the portfolios that included annuities offer 90-percent protection to age 88 and age 93, respectively. The more annuity in the portfolio, the longer the money was likely to last. In this scenario, the couple earned an 8.8-percent compound return on their 60 percent stock/40 percent bond portfolio, experienced 3-percent annual inflation rate, and paid annual mutual fund fees of 1.37 percent and variable annuity fees of 2.22 percent. Their portfolio, including Social Security benefits, produced an annual income of $75,000.

Do the differences matter? Absolutely. The average 65-year-old American couple faces a 75-percent risk that one of the two will live to age 86, a 56-percent chance that one will reach age 91, and a 25-percent chance that one will reach age 96. An income annuity would insure them against those risks.

Table 15-3	How Much Can Annuities Reduce Longevity Risk?
Portfolio of 65-Year-Old Couple	*A 90% Chance the Couple's Money Will Last To:*
60% stocks, 40% bonds, no annuities*	Age 84
58% stocks, 14% bonds, 28% fixed income annuity (strong desire to leave money to heirs)	Age 88
48% stocks, 8% bonds, 8% variable income annuity, 36% fixed income annuity (moderate desire to leave money to heirs)	Age 93

Buying Guaranteed Income in Stages

According to one group of German researchers, you should buy annuities in two stages rather than all at once. This strategy serves a couple of purposes:

✔ It allows you to keep more of your money accessible during the first part of your retirement.

✔ It takes advantage of the cheaper life annuities that are available as you get older.

Table 15-4 provides the recommended proportions of stocks, bonds, and income annuities that five types of people (a man, a woman, a person in poor health, a person with a large private pension, and a person with a small pension) should hold at three different points in their lives: age 45, age 60, and age 75. This table is adapted from "Optimizing the Retirement Portfolio: Asset Allocation, Annuitization, and Risk Aversion," Michigan Retirement Research Center Working Paper WP 2006-124, by W.J.Horneff, R. Maurer, O.S. Mitchell, and I. Dus.

Note: Because at age 45 all the investors have 20 years until retirement, virtually none of them owns annuities; they can afford to keep most of their money in stocks. At age 60, all types of investors introduce some annuities into their portfolios. At age 75, they increase their income annuities.

In Table 15-4, note the people who don't need extra lifetime income — people "in poor health" or with a "large pension" — held less money into annuities. Men held more savings into annuities earlier than women because women have longer life expectancies.

The deciding factor in determining the timing of annuity purchases is the *survivorship credit* (see Chapter 4; it's the extra income that surviving annuity owners share as the pool of living annuity owners declines over time). Some actuaries believe that

✔ After age 60, the survivorship credit gives annuities a higher effective return than bonds.

✔ After age 75, the survivorship credit gives annuities a higher effective return than stocks.

Note: These age estimates do not take into consideration the impact of annuity fees. If you accounted for fees, which vary from one annuity contract to another, the recommended ages would be somewhat higher. In other words, the ideal ages for buying annuities might be 65 and 80 rather than 60 and 75.

Table 15-4	Ratios of Stocks, Bonds, and Annuities for Five Investor Types at Three Ages		
Investor Type	Age 45 (Stock/Bond/ Annuity Ratios)	Age 60 (Stock/Bond/ Annuity Ratios)	Age 75 (Stock/Bond/ Annuity Ratios)
Man	89.6/10.4/0.1	59.8/1.9/38.3	40.9/7.7/51.5
Woman	90.4/9.6/0.0	64.8/17.4/17.7	45.9/4.1/50.0
In poor health	90.3/9.7/0.0	65.2/26.6/8.2	48.6/18.5/32.9
Large pension	94.5/5.4/0.0	81.6/15.0/3.2	63.0/6.0/30.8
Small pension	86.1/13.9/0.0	53.9/11.2/35.0	37.7/3.3/59.0

Creating Inflation-Proof Income

Inflation inevitably eats away at a retiree's income. The Consumer Price Index (CPI), the standard for measuring the cost of living in the United States, doubled during the 25 years between 1982 and 2007. According to one estimate, an $8,500-a-year payout from a fixed annuity today will be worth only $4,500 in terms of purchasing power in 20 years.

You can customize an income annuity to protect your income from the impact of inflation. Many insurers now add inflation indexing, graded payments, or fixed annual increases as part of their annuity income options. So far they don't sell especially well, in part because they involve "back-loading" your income — that is, accepting smaller payments today in exchange for a higher, inflation-adjusted income down the road.

In the following sections, I describe some of the anti-inflation options available today.

Add an inflation adjustment to your fixed income annuity

A growing number of fixed income annuity contracts (also known as single-premium immediate annuities, or SPIAs) will help you offset the effects of inflation by linking your payments to the CPI or increasing your payments each year by a certain percentage (see Table 15-5, from Vanguard Lifetime Income Program; July 2007). Bear in mind, however, that this will mean taking lower payments during the first part of your retirement.

Table 15-5	Monthly SPIA Payments with Varying Adjustments for Inflation
Single-life SPIA for 65-Year-Old Man with $100,000 Premium	*Monthly Payment*
Not adjusted for inflation	$720
Increased 3% per year	$546
Indexed to the CPI	$515

Buy a combination fixed-variable income annuity

Owning stocks is a time-tested way of preventing inflation from whittling away at your purchasing power. (Although stocks do not, historically, always go up when inflation is high. When high inflation is accompanied by rising interest rates, stock prices tend to be depressed.) If you buy an immediate annuity and put all or part of your money into stock mutual funds, your income will be at least partly protected from inflation in the long run. (See the section "Being Bullish with a Variable Income Annuity" later in this chapter.)

Buy a guaranteed lifetime withdrawal benefit (GLWB) with a built-in inflation adjustment

One insurance company, Penn Mutual Life, has introduced a deferred variable annuity with a lifetime withdrawal benefit that includes an inflation adjustment. There is a trade-off, however. Whereas many deferred variable annuities with GLWBs offer an annual payout equal to 5 percent of a guaranteed benefit base (which may be more than the actual value of your account), Penn Mutual's GLWB pays 4 percent per year but payments are increased every year to match any increase in the CPI-U (the Consumer Price Index for urban dwellers).

If you buy a variable income annuity, set the "AIR" at the lowest setting

When you buy a variable income annuity, you have to choose an *assumed interest rate,* or AIR. This is a hypothetical growth rate (3.5 or 5 percent, for example) that the insurance company uses to calculate the value of your first variable annuity payment (see Chapter 7). From then on, your payments will increase only if the stock market produces a higher return (after expenses) than the AIR. By choosing a low AIR, you make your early payments lower and your late payments higher (and vice versa for the higher AIR), which gives you the higher income needed to maintain your standard of living.

Building a Ladder of Fixed Annuities

A safe and predictable way to create retirement income is to build a "ladder of annuities." You may be familiar with bond laddering — the practice of buying bonds of short, medium, and long terms so that they don't all reach maturity at once. With a ladder of fixed annuities, you own fixed deferred annuities of different terms and convert them to income as they mature.

One laddering strategy suggested by fixed-annuity specialist Jeremy Alexander (www.annuitynexus.com) enables you to generate retirement income safely as it protects you from *interest-rate* risk (the risk that interest will rise, thereby driving down the price of existing fixed income investments) and *company* risk (the risk that an insurance company will have financial problems).

Suppose you have $400,000 in savings at age 55 and want to use fixed deferred annuities to build your savings for retirement at age 65. Instead of putting all the money in one fixed deferred annuity with a maturity of ten years, a safer strategy is to

✔ Buy four $100,000 fixed deferred annuities with four different insurers at age 55. This reduces your reliance on the financial strength of one insurance carrier.

✔ Make sure those annuities have staggered maturity dates: ten years, seven years, five years, and three years.

This staggering strategy protects you from interest-rate risk. If rates are higher in three years, you have the flexibility to roll at least one of your annuities into a higher-yielding contract.

At age 65, when each annuity is worth about $180,000 (assuming a 6-percent annual return), you can

✔ Convert two of the annuities to income. To protect your heirs, you can

- Annuitize one of them with a ten-year period certain. All the money is paid out in ten years to you or (if you die) to your beneficiaries.

- Annuitize the second one for "life with a ten-year period certain" (payments continue for ten years or for as long as you live, whichever is longer).

Together, the two annuities guarantee an income of roughly $2,500 a month for at least ten years.

✔ Use the $360,000 in the other two fixed annuities to buy two new fixed annuities that have either ten-year or laddered maturities.

When you reach age 75, these annuities will be worth $644,000 (at a guaranteed rate of 6 percent). At that time, depending on your needs, you can do any of the following:

- Convert one or both annuities to five or ten more years of income.

- Convert part of the money to income and invest the rest in a ten-year fixed deferred annuity.

- Convert both to income and use half of the income to buy life insurance. (For more on buying life insurance with an income annuity, see Chapter 8.)

Using an Old-Fashioned Split Annuity

A *split annuity* is a simpler version of Alexander's plan in the preceding section, and it too should appeal to anyone who's highly averse to putting money in stocks. This version can also reduce or eliminate *sequence of returns* risk (the risk that the stock market will tank in the first few years of your retirement, putting your portfolio in a hole that it won't have time to grow out of).

Suppose you have $200,000 for retirement in taxable accounts (not tax-deferred accounts such as IRAs or employer-sponsored retirement plans). You invest in two forms of annuities:

- ✔ With $78,000 you buy a SPIA that will pay you about $800 a month for a "period certain" of ten years. Of that $800, very little will be taxable because you purchase the income with after-tax money.

- ✔ With the remaining $122,000 you buy a fixed deferred annuity that pays 5 percent and matures in ten years. At the end of the ten years of tax-deferred growth, your investment is worth about $199,000 — very close to your original nest egg.

Fans of split annuities love the elegance of this arrangement. You receive a guaranteed income of $8,400 a year for the first ten years and end with the same amount of money you started with — guaranteed. If you die during those ten years, your beneficiaries are entitled to the money in your deferred annuity. If you don't die, you repeat the process, buying a ten-year income annuity and a fixed deferred annuity that matures in ten years.

Being Bullish with a Variable Income Annuity

Within annuity circles — and across America such circles do exist, like covens of witches and wizards — variable income annuities are starting to gain favor. I think they deserve a closer look. Check out these pluses:

- ✔ You get a guaranteed income for life.

- ✔ You get the protection against inflation that comes from investing in stocks.

- ✔ You continue to manage your own investments, even if you can't take the money out.

- ✔ You can get the survivorship credits that come from relinquishing ownership over the principal.

- ✔ You can even fine-tune the stability of your income by putting part of your premium into a variable payout and part into a fixed payout.

When you buy a variable income annuity, you have to choose an *assumed interest rate* (AIR, see Chapter 8). The insurance company uses this hypothetical growth rate (3.5 or 5 percent, for example) to calculate the value of your first variable annuity payment. From then on, your payments increase only if the stock market produces a higher return (after expenses) than the AIR.

By choosing the lowest AIR setting, you ensure that your early payments are lower and your late payments are higher; this choice gives you the higher income you'll need in the future to maintain your standard of living.

For example, suppose you have $300,000 in savings at age 65. If you choose a 3.5-percent AIR, you can put $100,000 in the bank and $200,000 in a variable income annuity with payments starting at about $13,740 per year. The payments start low but will grow if your investments grow faster than the AIR.

If your portfolio averages 8-percent growth per year (the average for a portfolio consisting of stocks and bonds), your income will rise each year 4.5 percent (the growth in excess of the AIR) before expenses. If your expenses are 1.5 percent per year — a reasonable expectation — your payments might grow by 3 percent per year. At that rate, your annual annuity income would double in 24 years. In other words, your income would keep pace with inflation.

Whereas a *fixed* immediate income annuity pays you a guaranteed number of *dollars* every month for life or for a specific number of years (with optional increases or inflation adjustments), a *variable* immediate income annuity pays you a guaranteed number of *units* for life or for a specific number of years.

The option works like this. When you purchase a variable income annuity, you buy a specific number of units. The exact number depends on the *accumulation unit value* (AUV; the average current share price) of the portfolios and on your payout options (life only, joint and survivor, cash refund, and so on). In theory, the value of your units can fall. But, over the long run, this hasn't been the case.

Buying Future Income at a Discount

If you decide to use 10 to 30 percent of your savings to buy guaranteed income, as some annuity experts recommend, consider buying an *advanced life deferred annuity* (ALDA; also called *longevity insurance*), which only pays you an income after you reach age 80 or 85. (For more on this topic, see Chapter 10.)

Why? The later you buy your annuity, the less it costs and the more annual income you get for your premium. It's that survivorship credit at work again. Only about half the men who buy life annuities at age 65 live to collect benefits at age 81 (for women, it's age 84), so annuities that pay off later can sell at a steep discount. And you get another discount for prepaying your annuity by 20 years.

If you know you have enough money to last until you reach 80, you don't need to buy guaranteed income for the intervening years. Instead, buy income that begins at age 80. To rationalize this move, think of this premium the same way you thought of your term life insurance premiums when you were younger. The best part? You can safely plan your finances for the years before you turn 80 and not need a reserve in case you live too long.

Note: Very few ALDAs are on the market. Some companies are making them more attractive by including a refund or death benefit so the initial premium isn't forfeited. But those options inevitably add to the cost of the annuity and, conversely, reduce the future income.

Turning Home Equity into an Annuity

Reverse mortgages (see the following paragraph for an explanation) have emerged as a last-resort source of retirement income for baby boomers who didn't save as much as they should have but who do have a lot of equity in the empty nests they call homes. Doubters say that millions of Americans have already consumed their home equity through cash-out refinancing and lines of credit. Obviously, every family's situation is unique.

A reverse mortgage (also called a *home equity conversion mortgage*) is a loan secured by the value of your home. Because it can pay you an income for life (or until you sell your home), it's also a kind of annuity. Your income is based on

- ✔ Your life expectancy
- ✔ Current interest rates
- ✔ The appraised equity in your home (up to certain limits)

Under a reverse mortgage contract, you receive a lump sum payment, or a line of credit, or a series of monthly payments. Currently, reverse mortgages are financed by the United States Department of Housing and Urban Development (HUD), by Fannie Mae, and by the Financial Freedom Senior Funding Corporation.

The nice part is that you still own the house. Later, you can sell the house and use the proceeds to pay back everything you financed — the principal, accumulated interest, and fees. If you die, your beneficiaries can do the same.

If the house loses value, you don't have to make up the difference. But if you or your beneficiaries sell at a profit, you (or they) may have to share the appreciation with the lender. If you die and your children want the house, they can buy it by paying off the reverse mortgage lender with cash or a new mortgage.

Reverse mortgages aren't for everybody. They make sense only if you're determined to stay in your home indefinitely. Otherwise there's no justifying all the expenses involved. Before making up your mind, you should consider all possible alternatives.

Another way to capture your equity is to sell your home and use part of the proceeds to buy a smaller home or to invest the entire amount and use the interest to pay rent. A $300,000 profit from the sale of your home, invested at 5 percent, can produce $15,000 a year to apply toward rent. In this case, you also don't have the psychological burden of taking on a large debt (the reverse mortgage is a loan, after all) at such a late stage in life.

Bridging Your Way to Higher Social Security Benefits

What's the ideal age to start taking Social Security benefits? For some reason, that's one of the most emotionally charged issues in the entire field of personal finance. Some people believe in taking benefits as soon as possible, at age 62. If they don't need it, they invest it in the stock market. Others believe in the value of postponing benefits until age 70, when (thanks to the survivorship credit!) monthly payments are more than 50 percent higher.

Suppose you want to semi-retire at 62. You have modest savings and expenses, and you think you can live on Social Security from age 70 onward, thanks to the higher payout at that age. In this case, you can take your savings — let's say it's about $150,000, which many middle income people might have in their 401(k) at age 62 — and put $125,000 of it in an income annuity, leaving aside $25,000 for emergencies. Between your part-time income and your annuity income of about $18,000 a year, you may be able to hold out for the highest Social Security benefits.

Blending an Annuity with LTC Insurance

Health risk is one of the major financial risks of retirement. Nursing-home expenses can consume vast amounts of savings. *Long-term care* (LTC) *insurance* makes sense for some people, but it's expensive.

Until recently, tax laws made it difficult to combine annuities and LTC insurance into a single product. The main problem is that LTC payouts are tax free, but annuity income is at least partly taxable. (Although most companies allow generous withdrawals without penalties in the event of a serious illness, the withdrawals are still taxable.) But a provision of the Pension Protection Act of 2006 modifies the law in a way that such hybrid products will be possible after 2010.

Here's how a combination product may work. A retiree buys a variable deferred annuity for $146,000, from which 0.75 percent is deducted every year to buy LTC insurance. From then on (after a 90-day waiting period), if the contract owner needs nursing-home care, he'll pay for it with the annuity assets, at the rate of $200 a day for up to 730 days or 2 years ($200 × 730 = $146,000).

Additional care — up to four years — is covered by the LTC insurance purchased with the 0.75 percent annual fee. That's a lot of coverage for the money, and it's cheap because of the large deductible (the contract owner is basically paying for the first two years of care out of his own pocket). If the owner never needs the money for LTC expenses, he can take it out as retirement income. ***Note:*** Annuity income is taxable, but LTC benefits aren't.

The previous example is based on a hybrid between LTC insurance and a deferred annuity. LTC/immediate annuity hybrids are also possible. In one scenario, 65-year-olds buy a hybrid contract for $156,000. In return, they receive $1,000 a month for life with ten years certain. If they become disabled, they're eligible for LTC benefits up to $2,000 a month for partial disability or $3,000 a month in case of severe disability.

Actuaries have estimated that such a hybrid product costs about $5,000 less than separate policies for an income annuity and LTC insurance. The primary reason for the savings is the insurer's lower costs. People who are healthy and expect to live a long time want annuities, and people who expect to get sick want LTC insurance. In a hybrid product, the risks posed by the two populations at least partly cancel each other out, reducing the insurer's underwriting costs.

Earning a Discount for Poor Health

Conventional wisdom says that you buy a life annuity only if your parents and grandparents lived to a ripe old age. If you have a serious medical infirmity, forget about a life annuity. You'll probably die before you get your money out.

But that's changing. Some insurance carriers now offer *impaired* or *substandard* life annuities (not the most endearing terms). These annuities have lower prices and are meant for people who suffer from debilitating chronic illnesses such as diabetes, kidney disease, or heart disease and who, as a group, have shorter life expectancies than individuals without such ailments.

A physical examination is required. Based on the results, you're assigned a physical age that's higher than your chronological age, and your benefits are based on that higher age. As a result, you either:

✔ Receive higher monthly benefits for a higher premium

✔ Are charged a lower price for a lower level of monthly payments

Obviously, getting a discount on an annuity is not a huge consolation for having a serious illness. But if you're in the market for an income annuity anyway — if you think you may run out of money without one — then why not apply for a discount? It can't hurt. You could end up getting a surprising amount of income out of a modest amount of money. And you'd have the peace of mind that comes with guaranteed lifelong income.

Chapter 16

Going to Meet the (Sales) Representative

In This Chapter
▶ Checking out the variety of retail annuity sellers
▶ Benefiting from your employer's annuity plans
▶ Taking the step to buy your annuity *direct*

Most adults can shop without much hand-holding from a flesh-and-blood sales clerk. Whether people buy a DVD online, a water heater at a home improvement store, or a grandé decaf mocha cappuccino at a coffee bar, they know what they want and ask for it by name — except when it comes to annuities.

Sure, a few adventurous souls have enough confidence to call a direct marketer and order their annuities over the phone like they're ordering pepperoni pizzas. But those direct purchases represent only 7 percent of all *retail* annuities (which exclude employer programs).

Most people don't buy annuities (or other kinds of insurance, for that matter) unless a broker, banker, adviser, or insurance agent first explains how annuities work, or recommends a specific product, or — I wish it weren't so true — wheedles their client into buying one. Hence, the time-honored axiom of the annuity industry: *Annuities are sold, not purchased.*

In this chapter, I identify the types of people who sell annuities and say a few words about their training and compensation. At one end of the spectrum are the licensed phone reps who earn no commissions and work for companies like Vanguard that are direct sellers of financial services. At the other extreme are the agents who earn commissions up to 9 percent on index annuities.

Before you buy an annuity from someone, find out as much as you can about that person. His or her position (agent, banker, broker, registered investment adviser), and the way he or she gets paid (by commission, by a flat annual percentage of your total assets, by the hour, and so on) have everything to do with the types of products that person will offer you, the price you'll pay for those products, and the level of service you'll get.

Try to buy your annuity from someone who takes the time to understand your needs, who doesn't apply the hard sell, who has your best interests at heart, and who isn't wedded to any particular brand or type of product. An adviser who knows a lot about annuities and who charges by the hour might be the safest place to start.

Getting to Know the Annuity Sales Force

Insurance companies used to employ huge sales forces. These salespeople were called *career* agents or *captive* agents because they traditionally spent many years with one company and sold only that company's products. Some insurers still employ captive sales forces, but virtually every carrier distributes its annuity contracts and insurance policies through many *distribution channels*.

To grasp this process, imagine a giant national bakery. The bakery distributes thousands of buns, rolls, cakes, and loaves of bread each day to consumers via supermarkets, mom-and-pop groceries, schools, vending machines, and restaurants. When a customer eventually buys the baked goods, the seller may be a machine, a teenage sales clerk, or a veteran headwaiter.

Similarly, life insurance companies distribute annuities through insurance agencies, banks, brokerage firms, mutual fund companies, financial planners' offices, and, most recently, the Web. The person who actually takes your money may be a licensed insurance agent, a registered stockbroker, an accountant, a lawyer, an MBA, or someone with a Certified Financial Planner(r) designation.

The players in the annuity game include:

- **Captive or career agents:** These full-time employees of a single insurance company are licensed to sell insurance and/or securities (stocks, bonds, and mutual funds). They earn sales commissions.

- **Independent agents:** These agents are licensed to sell insurance in one or more states and may or may not be licensed to sell securities. They earn sales commissions.

✔ **Brokers (also known as account executives or registered representatives):** All these brokerage employees are licensed to sell stocks, bonds, and mutual funds.

Brokers may or may not be licensed to sell insurance or provide financial advice. They may receive a salary, commissions, or volume-related or product-specific incentives.

✔ **Financial advisers and investment counselors:** This is a nonofficial designation often used by advisers who have the Certified Financial Planner degree. They may not be licensed to sell insurance or securities.

✔ **Phone representatives of mutual fund companies:** These are salaried workers who are licensed to sell fixed and/or variable annuities.

✔ **Brokers at annuity Web sites:** These are licensed agents and brokers who work on commission.

✔ **Employer-sponsored plan custodians:** These financial services companies may invite specific insurance companies to offer immediate fixed annuities (which pay a fixed or inflation-adjusted monthly income in retirement) to their 401(k) plan participants.

In the following section, I give the lowdown on how to keep your dealings with annuity salespeople on the up and up.

Insurance agents — selling fixed and index annuities

Insurance agents account for about 40 percent of the *individual* annuities sold in the United States each year. (These annuities are distinct from the *group* annuities through retirement plans at not-for-profit organizations.) To sell insurance products (including fixed or index annuities), an agent must pass a formal examination and receive an insurance license from each state where she does business. *Note:* Agents can sell index annuities because, although index annuity returns are linked to performance of a stock index, these products do not involve direct investment in stocks (see Chapter 9).

When a financial product entails risk, it is a security and the seller must hold a securities license. Variable annuities, unlike fixed annuities, are securities because the premium is invested in subaccounts (similar to mutual funds), which can gain or lose value. Therefore, to sell variable annuities, mutual funds, and other securities, the agent must pass a *Series 7* exam and be registered with the Financial Industry Regulatory Authority (FINRA), the securities industry's self-regulatory organization. FINRA was known as NASD until June 2007.

Captive agents

Captive or career insurance agents sell about one of every five individual annuity contracts in the United States each year. These agents have a few obvious advantages:

- ✔ This neighborhood agent may be the same person who's been selling you home, life, and auto insurance for decades.

- ✔ Because such agents have a local reputation and long-term relationships to maintain, they're probably not looking for a drive-by sale that reaps a quick commission.

- ✔ Because they sell only one company's products, captive agents know their products inside and out. In the world of annuities, where complex new products come out every day, that's a plus.

   But specialization can be a minus. Just as a Ford dealer will show you only Fords and not Toyotas or Hondas, a captive agent will show you only one brand of annuity. It pays to shop around and look at several companies' products.

- ✔ If they sell both fixed and variable annuities, captive agents must hold both insurance and securities licenses.

- ✔ Agents at some companies now receive special training in retirement income planning, which helps them understand your needs and where an annuity might fit into the picture.

Independent agents or insurance brokers

Independent agents sell about one-fifth of all individual annuities each year. Unlike captive agents, an independent agent can sell any insurance company's products in the state where he's licensed and where the specific annuity contracts are approved for sale.

Some independent agents can now access powerful online databases that sort through hundreds of different annuity contracts to find the half dozen that match your particular needs, resources, and preferences.

The independent channel is sometimes called the *Wild West* of the annuity distribution world. Many independent agents are licensed only to sell insurance, which means

- ✔ They can only sell fixed annuities (guaranteed rates of return) or index annuities (returns based on the performance of the stock markets).

- ✔ They may not have securities licenses, so they can't sell you variable annuities.

Independent agents sell almost all the index annuities in the United States. Issuers of index annuities (Allianz Life of North America is the largest, selling about one in three) offer generous commissions (as high as 9 percent) and other incentives to encourage independent agents to sell these products.

The insurance carrier pays the agent his commission and incentives shortly after the sale and earns back the commission from you through annual fees. So, you may wonder, what's wrong with that? Aside from the fact that the agent's sales commission eventually comes out of your pocket, commissions can distort the sales process. Because commissions vary from product to product, a commission that pays the most can also bias the agent's advice.

Independent agents may not be as independent as they seem. They often receive training or recommendations about specific annuity contracts from *independent marketing organizations* (IMOs; insurance wholesalers). In fact, insurance carriers sometimes pay IMOs incentives to promote certain products to agents, who then promote them to you. Some marketing organizations are even owned by carriers, and independent agents may receive incentives directly from an insurance company. But unless you ask, you may never know about these distortions of the sales process. See Chapter 19 for more information.

Brokers or registered reps — selling securities with or without guidance

By definition, brokers (also called *stock brokers, account executives, registered representatives,* or *registered reps*) hold Series 7 securities licenses to sell stocks and bonds, are supervised by managers who review their sales, and are registered with FINRA. They also have insurance licenses to sell annuities.

In 2006, they sold about 14 percent of the individual annuities in the United States. If you've worked with a particular broker over the years, you may want to start the search for an annuity with him.

Brokers work in many different settings. For example, they can work for

- ✔ Big New York *wirehouses* (giant brokerages) like Merrill Lynch, Morgan Stanley, and UBS
- ✔ Large independent brokerages such as Raymond James or LPL
- ✔ Small regional or local brokerage firms
- ✔ Brokerage services that are subsidiaries of insurance companies or mutual fund companies

As a smart consumer, it's up to you to determine whether the broker is merely a sales representative working for commissions or whether the broker is acting as a financial adviser. A broker with only a Series 7 license can sell you a security but isn't supposed to give you advice. You'll often meet that kind of broker at a *discount* brokerage firm. Such firms, such as ETrade or TDAmeritrade, charge low prices for executing trades (usually online) and may provide few or no other services. They're not likely to try to sell you an annuity.

Some brokers hold additional licenses:

- ✔ A *Series 63* license demonstrates knowledge of the state's specific securities laws.

- ✔ A *Series 66* license allows a broker to give financial advice and recommend specific investment products and strategies.

  Note: Brokers with these licenses are more commonly found in *full service* brokerages, such as Merrill Lynch or Morgan Stanley. Unlike brokers at discount brokerages, they are supposed to give you advice and act with your best interest in mind, and they charge much higher fees than discount brokers.

  This is not the place to debate the relative merits of discount and full-service brokerages. Suffice it to say that going to a discount broker is like having your oil changed at Jiffy Lube, while going to a full-service broker is like having your oil changed at the dealership by a mechanic making $75 an hour.

A broker's earnings may be based on a variety of factors:

- ✔ The amount the customer invests

- ✔ The number of transactions in a customer's account

- ✔ Bonuses for selling her own company's products

- ✔ A *12b-1 marketing fee* by the issuer of a specific product

  In some cases, mutual fund companies use these controversial fees to pay brokers to sell their products. The fees are controversial because they provide no benefit to the shareholders (customers).

  Some mutual fund companies, such as Vanguard, don't collect or pay 12b-1 fees.

Only a few years ago, brokers were reluctant to sell variable annuities. They preferred to sell mutual funds because they could execute the sale quickly and easily and get paid promptly. In contrast, annuities traditionally require almost as much time and paperwork as an application for a mortgage.

That disadvantage is disappearing, however. Many large brokerages now enable their brokers to research and buy annuities online. The amount of time the supervisors need to review and approve sales and the time insurance companies need to process transactions are steadily shrinking. As annuity transactions get easier, brokers are more likely to recommend them.

You can find out the disciplinary or criminal history of any brokerage firm and sales representative online (www.finra.org.) via FINRA's BrokerCheck service (click on FINRABrokerCheck on the home page) or call 800-289-9999, a toll-free hotline operated by FINRA. State securities regulators can also tell you whether a sales representative is licensed in your state. (You can locate your regulator through the North American Securities Administrators Association at www.nasaa.org.

Bankers — wearing more hats than they used to

If you're like me, you don't spend much time in your bank's branch office . . . unless you hanker for a free lollipop! Instead, you simply make deposits or withdrawals at an ATM or through online electronic bank transfers. But if you do cross the threshold, you'll discover that banks now employ brokers who sell mutual funds and annuities.

In 2006, about 17 percent of all individual annuities in the United States were sold through banks. Insurance companies are steadily putting more effort into what they call the *bank channel,* and insurers are hiring more wholesalers to visit banks and educate bankers about their products. In turn, banks are hiring more people who are licensed to give people financial planning advice in addition to selling fixed and variable annuities.

Banks are nice and solid, and some bankers get excellent training about annuity products. On the other hand, banks are constantly merging, consolidating, and vanishing. Turnover among bank employees can be high. In the old days, banks, like museums and railroad terminals, were neoclassical temples with marble columns and lofty ceilings. You banked in one place for life. Not anymore. But if you're lucky enough to have a close relationship with a banker, you can probably rely on his advice on annuities.

Financial advisers — bringing a new perspective to the annuity picture

"The rich are different from you and me," said F. Scott Fitzgerald, a brilliant novelist who never had to finance a retirement because he died an alcoholic at age 44. (So much for *his* longevity risk; see Chapter 20.) But he was right; the rich are just as likely to have personal financial advisers for their wealth as they are to have personal trainers for their health.

Note: Financial advisers are also called *wealth managers, financial planners,* or *investment consultants,* but these titles have no technical or legal meaning. If someone claims to be a financial adviser, ask to see her credentials.

Some financial advisers hold *Certified Financial Planner, Certified Financial Analyst, Chartered Financial Consultant,* or *Accredited Estate Planner* designations. If they do, that's a plus. To earn those designations, the advisers undergo rigorous training and pass difficult examinations. Just as important, they take an oath of fiduciary responsibility. That is, they promise not to cheat you or sell you a product just to score a fast commission. For more information on designations, go to the FINRA Web site, at `http://apps.finra.org/datadirectory/1/prodesignations.aspx`. Advisers generally don't work for commissions. Instead, their charge is based on one of these methods:

- ✔ An hourly fee for advice
- ✔ A percentage of the amount they manage (1 to 2 percent per year, typically) if they manage your investments

Advisers don't necessarily pay the same fees for financial products and services that you would; they can go straight to an insurance company, buy a *C-class* variable annuity that has lower fees than a retail variable annuity, and pay no commission. For more on annuity share classes, see Chapter 12.

But just as neurosurgeons don't recommend psychotherapy for a brain disorder, financial advisers generally don't recommend annuities. It's not their thing. They may not even hold the licenses necessary to sell them. Most advisers pride themselves on controlling financial risks through

- ✔ **Diversification:** Holding a blend of stocks and bonds
- ✔ **Sage money management:** Selling assets high and buying low

They're not interested in your paying an insurance company to assume those risks (which is what you're doing when you buy an annuity). At the same time, people with advisers often have enough money — say, $1 million or more — not to worry about running short in old age.

Nevertheless, as more and more well-to-do baby boomers — the yuppies of yesteryear — enter the retirement zone, advisers may warm up to annuities. Here's why: With income from an annuity as the ultimate financial safety net (annuities are guaranteed for life), you and your adviser can afford to invest the rest of your money in risky, but potentially high-yield, assets like foreign stocks or junk bonds. And you can do it at age 75 or 80, when people without annuities tend to seek the shelter of bonds.

To encourage this trend, insurance companies are developing fancy computational tools that blend annuities with other investments for retirement income. Massachusetts Mutual Life Insurance (MassMutual) offers a Retirement

Management Account that shows the adviser how to help her retired clients spend down their savings efficiently by gradually converting chunks of money into guaranteed monthly income. (See more about this *annuity laddering* in Chapter 15.)

Registered investment advisers (RIAs) — finding the best, blowing whistles on the worst

In the United States, some financial advisers call themselves *registered investment advisers* (RIAs) and may work for RIA firms that manage investments for clients. The advisers have submitted necessary paperwork to the United States Securities and Exchange Commission (SEC) and typically hold a Series 66 securities license.

RIAs have legal and fiduciary obligations to their clients and must abide by the terms of the Investment Advisers Act of 1940. The publication, "What Every Investor Should Know . . . ," produced by the CFA Institute (www.cfainstitute.org), explains that RIAs must

✔ Act in the best interests of their clients.

✔ Disclose all fees associated with their services and how those fees are charged.

✔ Disclose whether the firm or its employees have an affiliation with a broker-dealer (a brokerage house) or any other securities professionals or issuers that might bias their recommendations.

✔ Disclose any facts that might cause the firm to render advice that is not *disinterested*.

✔ Complete and file with the SEC a Form ADV, which contains information about the adviser and its operations and discloses information related to disciplinary matters. This form must be made available to clients and should be reviewed before hiring a financial adviser.

Con artists and unscrupulous salesmen of all kinds frequently target retired people, who often have significant savings. In recent years, self-styled *senior specialists* or *certified senior advisers* have been the subjects of investigations in several states. There is no legitimate designation by that name. Typically, these specialists invite seniors to educational seminars or "free lunches" where they advise the seniors to sell their current investments and then buy index or variable annuities. Don't ever buy an annuity from a senior specialist offering a free meal. Instead, call your state insurance commissioner.

Be wary of any sales representative who advises you to invest more than half of your assets into an immediate annuity, especially if you've retired recently. Some experts suggest no more than 30 to 40 percent of your money should go into an annuity. Using 40 percent as the upper limit, a person with $300,000 in savings should limit her immediate annuity investment to $120,000. The remaining savings is then available for unanticipated expenses, medical emergencies, vacations, or bequests.

Buying Annuities on the Job

So far in this chapter I've talked about the retail annuity market and buying an annuity from a broker, banker, agent, or adviser. But you can also obtain an annuity at work, usually through your company's human resource department.

In this section, I cover workplace programs that offer variable annuities, guaranteed retirement incomes, and conversions of retirement savings to immediate annuities.

On-the-job annuities are expected to become a much bigger phenomenon in the future. When included in a 401(k) plan as investment options, they give participants a built-in method for converting their savings to income when they retire. They can be used to re-engineer 401(k)s into something resembling the old-fashioned lifelong pensions that only a dwindling number of Americans still enjoy.

Buying annuities on the job before you retire can be cheaper, more convenient, and more prudent than waiting until retirement to start thinking about how you'll turn your savings into income. (You're already buying Social Security benefits at work with your payroll taxes.) And it averts the temptation to blow your entire savings on a high-performance bass boat.

Turning your nest egg (presto!) into income

If you're one of the millions of American workers who, collectively, have several trillion dollars in 401(k) tax-deferred employer-sponsored retirement plans, you'll probably use some of it to replace your paychecks when you retire.

When that time comes, you may be interested in a single-premium immediate annuity (SPIA; see Chapter 8). Until very recently, the only way to turn your 401(k) savings into a SPIA took two steps: First, you moved the money to a rollover IRA, and second, you bought the SPIA on the open market. However, like health insurance, SPIAs are expensive outside a group plan.

In addition, only about one-fourth of all 401(k) plans currently offer an annuity payout. It's often a restrictive, one-size-fits-all option that forces you to convert all your 401(k) savings to an annuity.

Income Solutions from Hueler

In 2004, Minneapolis-based Hueler Investment Services devised a remedy to the rollover dilemma. Hueler created *Income Solutions,* an online service that lets people in certain 401(k) plans buy SPIAs at a group rate from any of several insurance companies. So far, participants in 401(k) plans managed by Hewitt Associates, CitiStreet Advisors, T. Rowe Price, and Wachovia can buy SPIAs from nine insurance companies: Genworth Financial, AIG, John Hancock, The Hartford, Integrity, Principal Financial, Prudential, MetLife, and Mutual of Omaha. And the program is growing.

Hueler's SPIAs are relatively cheap. People who buy them online or through a phone representative pay an estimated 3.5 to 5 percent less for their contracts than if they bought them from an agent or broker. Check out the following example.

Hueler calculates that a 59-year-old man who pays $200,000 for a life income annuity with a ten-year *period certain* (that is, the checks keep coming for at least ten years, even if the annuity owner dies before then) will receive at least $43 a month more in lifelong income ($1,274 versus $1,231) by purchasing through Income Solutions instead of paying retail. Over 20 years, the accumulated advantage will equal about $10,400.

Note: In a similar move, Fidelity Investments, the Boston-based financial services company that runs 401(k) plans for thousands of United States employers, now offers participants the opportunity to use their 401(k) savings to buy competitively priced SPIAs from several insurance companies including John Hancock, ING, Principal Financial, and The Hartford.

Inflation-protected income

Beginning in 2006, Income Solutions began offering SPIAs with inflation-protection options, where the monthly payments rise gradually over time to match the rising cost of living. At present, you must belong to a 401(k) plan in Hueler's network in order to purchase their SPIAs, but that network is constantly growing. The participating insurance companies pay Hueler a fee (1 to 2 percent of each annuity's investment) and gradually recover that fee by subtracting a few dollars from your monthly income checks.

Contributing to a group annuity

A few 401(k) plans allow you to apply your biweekly payroll deductions to a group annuity instead of investing them in mutual funds. Although you pay higher fees for a group variable annuity than for mutual fund investments, this annuity probably costs a lot less than a deferred variable annuity through a bank or brokerage. Unfortunately, you can't take advantage of a group annuity unless your employer (or other group approved by your state insurance regulator) offers one.

The ClearCourse Program

One of these group variable annuities is the ClearCourse program developed by Genworth Financial, a Virginia-based insurance company. Like any other retirement plan, a bit of every paycheck goes into an investment fund. But that's where the similarity ends.

With ClearCourse, every contribution buys you — on paper, at least — a small chunk of guaranteed income that you'll receive throughout retirement. For instance, a $100 contribution today may lock in $5 each month for life after age 65. The younger you are and the higher the interest rate when you make a contribution, the more income your contribution will buy. Over time, the small chunks snowball into a substantial monthly income. Early withdrawals aren't penalized, but they do reduce your retirement income. If you change jobs, your right to future income goes with you. In short, you're building your own pension one paycheck at a time.

Note: Your money doesn't grow as fast in this group variable annuity as it would in a mutual fund because you pay a 1 percent annual fee to the insurance company. Every percentage point in fees knocks a percentage point off your annual rate of return. On the other hand, you may feel that the fee is worth paying. This annuity contract guarantees you a minimum future income — even if the stock market collapses between now and the time you retire.

No group annuity stops you from taking your money as a lump sum rather than receiving it as a monthly income at retirement. But if you do choose the lump sum, you have nothing to show for those extra insurance fees you paid over the years. If you don't want guaranteed income, don't buy a group annuity in the first place. Put your money in mutual funds.

TIAA-CREF: The retirement plan for teachers

If you work for a university, you probably participate in a 403(b) plan — a cousin of the 401(k) — managed by TIAA-CREF, the Teacher's Insurance and Equity Association-College Retirement Equities Fund. A nonprofit life insurance company, TIAA was founded in 1918 by industrialist-philanthropist Andrew Carnegie, who saw that workers in educational or research institutions lacked an adequate savings or pension plan. CREF, added in 1952, was the first company in the United States to offer a variable annuity (that is, an annuity whose value fluctuated with the financial markets).

Only workers (some two million or more) at educational and research institutions (about 900) may participate, although outsiders can buy a low-cost

TIAA-CREF deferred variable annuity. So, TIAA-CREF participants are the fortunate members of a semi-exclusive club with the following benefits:

- ✔ TIAA-CREF charges a low fee, about 0.35 percent per year (35 cents per $100), to manage and keep track of its members' money, which means fatter monthly checks in retirement.

- ✔ At retirement, TIAA-CREF participants can take their savings in one big payment, or in a series of periodic withdrawals, or as a guaranteed income.

TIAA-CREF works especially well for women because TIAA-CREF's life annuity, like all employer-based annuities, pays the same amount to men as to women. In contrast, private insurance companies pay women lower rates to compensate for living longer on average than men and, as a result, collecting more payments. For example, a 65-year-old woman who converts $100,000 to a life annuity from TIAA-CREF may receive nearly $100 more per month — for life — than she would from a private insurance company.

Other group annuities

Other insurers have come up with group annuity plans. For example:

- ✔ Metropolitan Life Insurance (MetLife) offers the Personal Pension Builder through 401(k) plans managed by Merrill Lynch.

- ✔ Hartford Life Insurance offers the Hartford Lifetime Income Plan.

- ✔ In 2006, Prudential Insurance designed Capital Guarantee Funds. If you promise not to touch your money until a certain date (like 2010, 2015, 2020, or 2025), your savings will be worth a guaranteed minimum (or more) when you take it out.

Buying Your Annuity Direct or Online

Folks who like to take the road less traveled can buy their annuities over the telephone or online. Even though these channels use a different medium (communicating with the agent or broker by phone or e-mail rather than face to face), the messages are largely the same.

Working with a phone rep

People looking for rock-bottom costs may want to work with direct marketers like The Vanguard Group, Fidelity Investments, or T. Rowe Price. Through one of their phone representatives, you can choose from a modest selection of immediate, deferred, fixed, or variable annuities (not index annuities) that have low annual fees but no up-front commission.

Buying direct isn't for everybody. In fact, it represents only about 7 percent of all annuity purchases. These annuities tend to offer a smaller selection of options and riders than the annuities from large insurance companies.

The biggest difference is that the licensed phone representative works for a salary rather than a commission, which offers two positives:

✔ You don't get a hard sell.

✔ You avoid a fee (an extra 0.50 to 1 percent annually) because the insurance company doesn't have to earn back a commission from you.

Shopping for an annuity online

You can get almost anything you want on the Internet, and that includes annuities. The number of Web sites that discuss and offer annuities has grown rapidly over the years, although it's not clear how many people actually use them. I've visited a number of these sites and talked to the sales personnel by phone. The quality (and the level of sales pressure) they provide seems — at best — inconsistent.

The site `Annuityfyi.com` is one of the more helpful ones for the average consumer. The owners say they review all the estimated 15,000 annuity products on the market and winnow out the best 300 or so. The site's charts make it easy to compare similar products from different issuers and to order information kits about specific products. The site also provides pages of useful, unbiased information about annuities.

A toll-free number allows you to talk at length with one of Annuityfyi's licensed, registered representatives who, according to the site, have at least ten years of experience and no complaints filed against them by FINRA. Still, you have to take Annuityfyi's product recommendations with a grain or two of salt — the owners acknowledge that they accept fees from some of the companies whose annuities they tout.

Most people need the presence, assistance, and encouragement of a live salesperson when buying an annuity. Executing any transaction involving hundreds of thousands of dollars without meeting the seller face to face is downright rare! The SEC recommends that you interview several financial advisers in person before choosing one.

Buying an annuity on your own can be scary and requires a lot of homework, but working with a salaried phone representative can save you money and give you peace of mind, knowing that she isn't motivated by the commission. In addition, you may experience a sense of control that you can't get if you rely solely on an agent or broker.

Chapter 17

Avoiding Annuity Pitfalls

In This Chapter

▶ Dodging common annuity problems

▶ Recognizing errors with income annuities

▶ Previewing the pitfalls of deferred variable annuities

▶ Preventing silly mistakes

*F*lying a small airplane isn't more dangerous than other sports, someone once said — it's just less forgiving. You might say the same about annuities. Mistakes can be irrevocable and expensive. Much better not to make them in the first place.

In this chapter, I identify some of the most common errors that people make when shopping for and buying annuities. Some are errors of commission, like buying an indexed annuity with a 15-year surrender period. Others are errors of omission like not shopping around for a SPIA before you buy. Any of them can lead to deep regret. All are avoidable.

The problem boils down to this: Baby boomers are the first generation of Americans who must design and build their own pensions. With the decline of the traditional pension system, the responsibility for creating lifetime income has shifted from highly-skilled pension fund managers at big companies to individual retirees — most of whom have no preparation for the task. They will plunge into the world of annuities without reading the directions, and mistakes will be made.

After reading this chapter, you will be able to spot the worst of the hazards before they snare you. The biggest mistake of all would be to give up in frustration and avoid the world of annuities entirely. Like private planes, they usually don't crash, and they can take you where you need to go.

Watching Out for Common Annuity Missteps

The four dumbest mistakes you can make when buying an annuity are: locking up too much of your savings, overlooking the impact of fees, failing to understand the surrender period, and not thinking clearly when you name your beneficiaries.

If you make all four mistakes at once, you won't be able to pay for your daughter's wedding, your purchasing power will be swallowed up by inflation, you'll pay an arm and a leg to get out of your contract, and your ex-wife will get the money your widow was counting on. But you can easily avoid those fates by following the advice in the next section.

Converting too much of your savings to income

Suppose you put your entire nest egg into an income annuity that pays $2,500 a month and five years later your grandson needs a life-saving operation that insurance won't cover. You ask the insurance company for permission to break the contract, but they say no. Your mistake: not reading the fine print that said your decision was irrevocable.

As a general rule, you shouldn't put all of your money in an income annuity where you can't reach it. How much of your total wealth should be in any combination of annuities? There are several rules of thumb, ranging from "no more than 30 percent" to "as much as you have to." For details, see Chapter 8.

Forgetting about fees

Most people are willing to go an extra mile to save 10 cents on a gallon of gasoline. So why do so many investors allow themselves to be snookered into paying outrageously high fees when they buy financial products and services? It's a mystery.

This problem is not unique to annuities. You can pay excessive sales loads, investment management fees, and marketing costs when buying mutual funds. You can pay excessive fees to trade stocks or bonds. Over many years, the fees undermine your chances of getting ahead of the inflation game.

The remedies are fairly simple: When buying a variable annuity, read the expense page of the prospectus (fixed annuities don't have prospectuses or fees stated separately from the guaranteed return or income payout) and remember that if your investments are earning 9 percent before fees and you're paying 3 percent in fees, your net return is 6 percent. Your fees, in effect, are 33 percent of your gain.

Surrendering to a long surrender period

Surrender periods are a necessary evil. When you buy an annuity, the insurance company is making a long-term commitment; it wants you to do the same. As a result, it penalizes you for early withdrawal in order to recover the cost — including the broker's commission — of setting up the annuity. Without these restrictions on withdrawals, fixed annuities probably wouldn't be feasible for the insurance companies.

Deferred annuities generally have surrender periods that last from 3 to 15 years. In many cases, if you withdraw more than 10 percent of the value of your annuity during the surrender period, you'll pay a penalty equal to a percentage of your contract's value.

In most cases, the penalty in the first year is equal to the number of years in the surrender period. That is, if the surrender period is seven years long, the first year's penalty is 7 percent.

You don't need to mess with long surrender periods when you shop for a *variable* annuity. Lots of deferred variable annuity contracts offer short or no surrender periods. You may pay higher annual fees for a no-surrender-period variable annuity, but if you want to maintain access to your money, it may be worth it.

Mis-structuring your contract

Did you hear the one about the man who mistakenly left his entire fortune to his ex-wife, leaving his widow and children bereft? It's not very funny. But it can happen to people who structure their annuity contracts wrong.

When you buy a deferred annuity, you must designate an owner, an owner's beneficiary, an annuitant, and an annuitant's beneficiary (as though you intend to convert the contract to a lifelong income). If you make these designations carelessly and then die unexpectedly, the money in the annuity can end up in the wrong hands.

Stories of ex-wives rather than current wives and children or mothers receiving money are not uncommon. For example, an owner may name his wife as his annuitant and his son as his beneficiary, thinking that his wife will become the owner if he dies. But in many contracts, the beneficiary will control the contract. For tips on proper contract structure, see Chapter 11.

Heading Off Income Annuity Errors

When you buy a car, what do you do? You shop around and compare prices. You try to buy only the options you really want. You wait until the end of the year, when the dealers are desperate to meet their sales goals. If you're concerned about mileage and gas consumption, you don't buy the V-6.

You need to apply the same common-sense principles when you buy an income annuity. Your worst mistakes, as I explain in this section, will be: not shopping around, not understanding what your options are, buying in the wrong interest rate climate, and choosing the wrong AIR.

Buying a fixed income annuity when interest rates are low

In the last 30 years, the best time to buy a fixed income annuity — where you exchange a big chunk of money for an immediate, guaranteed lifetime income — was in the early 1980s, when the Federal Reserve raised prime interest rates above 12 percent to cool down inflation.

The worst time to buy was in the early 2000s, when the Federal Reserve lowered interest rates to 1 percent to prevent the economy from falling into recession after the stock market crash in the spring of 2000.

Buying an income annuity (not a deferred annuity) is like getting a mortgage, but in reverse. Locking your money into an annuity when rates are low is as costly as buying a house when interest rates are high. It's worse: You can refinance a mortgage when rates go down, but generally you can't refinance an income annuity when rates go up.

Granted, you can't always delay the purchase of a home until interest rates come down, and you may not be able to delay the purchase of an income annuity until rates go up. (And you may not care. When buying homes or income annuities, most people focus on monthly payments, not rates, without understanding the link between the two.) But trust me. If interest rates are historically low, consider postponing your SPIA purchase until they bob back up again. Eventually they will.

Providing specific advice about rates is very hard. When rates are low, your stocks will probably be worth a lot, so it might be a *good* time to sell stocks and buy an annuity with the money. If you wait until rates are high, your stocks may have lost value by then, and you'll have less money to buy your annuity with.

Ignoring the "period certain" and refund options

Many people refuse to consider an income annuity because they're concerned that the insurance company, and not their beneficiaries, will get their money if they die. But if that's your fear, you can easily prevent it from happening.

By using the *joint and survivor, period certain,* or *refund* options available on virtually every income annuity contract, you can make sure your money doesn't just revert to the carrier if you die when your annuity contract is in force. The following are brief explanations of each:

- ✔ **Joint and survivor option:** This option ensures that annuity payments keep coming as long as either of two spouses is living.

- ✔ **Period certain option:** With this option, you can keep payments coming for no less than a specific number of years. If you die, your beneficiaries will receive the remaining payments.

- ✔ **Refund option:** This option, paid either in cash or monthly installments, ensures that your heirs receive the difference between your original payment for the annuity and what you received before you died.

Of course, these options have a trade-off. You receive lower monthly payments than you would have if all payments stopped at your death. By their nature, annuities offer the highest monthly benefits when all payments stop at your death.

An alternative solution to the *bequest motive* problem (the reluctance to buy an annuity because you want your money to go your heirs) is to buy a smaller annuity and set aside the difference for your heirs. Instead of converting 40 percent of your savings to guaranteed income, for instance, convert 30 percent and put the balance in trust for your kids.

Talking about these topics can be gruesome; many people are repelled by income annuities because, as one expert put it, "Annuities have the smell of death." On the contrary, an income annuity is a wager that you're going to live a long life *and* have enough income to finance it.

Getting only one or two SPIA quotes

When I went shopping for a new car, I visited several dealers and got a variety of prices. I surfed the Internet for bargains. Finally, I went back to the first (and nearest) dealer and told him the lowest bid I'd found. He matched it.

Like new cars, single premium immediate fixed annuities (SPIAs; see Chapter 8) don't all have the same price. In exchange for $100,000, one company may offer you $650 a month while another offers $618 and another offers $688. If $70 a month for the rest of your life matters to you (it amounts to about $8,200 over ten years), then be sure you shop around before you decide on a SPIA.

As a consumer, you have no way of knowing how a carrier determines its rates or quotes on a given day. Many factors affect the offer . . . and those factors change by the hour.

The company that offers the highest SPIA rate today may offer the lowest rate tomorrow. If you've set your heart on buying an annuity from a certain carrier and don't investigate further, you'll never know whether you've picked a good day or a bad one (or frankly, a good SPIA or a bad one).

Executives at Hueler Investment Services, a consumer-oriented company in Eden Prairie, Minnesota, decided a few years ago to offer an alternative to this roulette of annuity shopping. They set up a Web site, incomesolutions. com, where people near retirement age can submit requests for SPIA quotes to several insurance companies at once. The near-retirees receive the quotes through the Web site and pick the most attractive choice.

Unfortunately, you can only benefit from this method if you work for a large employer (IBM is one) that makes the service available to participants in their 401(k) plans. (However, the site does offer plenty of free valuable information if you just want to beef up your knowledge of annuities.) If you're not one of these participants, you can still look up competing SPIA quotes on a Web site like comparativeannuityreports.com.

Back in the late 1990s, annuity scholars found SPIA payout rates to be utterly unpredictable. At any given time, a 65-year-old man wanting to pay a premium of $100,000 for lifetime income could receive quotes ranging from as much as $872 to as little as $725 a month. That's a difference of about $1,800 per year. During retirement, that could buy quite a few rounds of golf.

So how do you make sure you don't buy a SPIA with the lowest rate in town? You can

✔ Visit lots of insurance company Web sites and get lots of quotes from their online SPIA calculators.

✔ Go to a Web site that offers comparative rates, like `www.immediate annuity.com`.

✔ Consult a financial adviser who subscribes to a professional SPIA database that tracks the latest prices, like `www.cannex.com`.

✔ Shop at a SPIA supermarket like Fidelity Investments (`www.fidelity.com`), where you can compare SPIAs from five different carriers.

✔ Use Hueler Associates' supermarket, called Income Solutions, at `www.incomesolutions.com` (but only if your employer participates in it).

Choosing the wrong AIR

The assumed interest rate (AIR) confuses many people. As a result, some people are unpleasantly surprised at the low amount of their monthly variable annuity payment because they don't fully understand how the AIR works.

When you buy an immediate variable annuity or convert a deferred annuity to an income stream, the insurance carrier has to calculate your first payment. But how? Insurers can't predict the future course of the stock market, and they don't know how fast or slowly your investments will grow over the next 15, 20, or 25 years.

So they have to *assume* a growth rate. Actually, they let you choose one of two possible AIRs (for instance, a 3.5 or 5.0 percent). The AIR you pick (along with your age and the amount of money you put in the annuity) determines the size of your first immediate variable annuity payment:

✔ If you like to avoid disappointment by lowering your expectations, you should probably choose the 3.5-percent AIR.

Your first payment will be lower than the one with the 5 percent AIR, but your payments will rise whenever your investment gains are higher than 3.5 percent. They won't shrink unless your investments — the money in those subaccounts you chose when you bought the contract — earn less than 3.5 percent.

✔ If you're an optimist and believe stocks will go ever higher, you may choose the 5-percent AIR.

Your first payment will be higher than the contract with 3.5 percent, but your payments will only increase if your investments grow faster than 5 percent.

In the end, it will all even out. If you live long enough, you'll receive the same amount of money either way. (Picture the staggered starts of a 400-meter run. The runners on the outer lanes start out farther down the track than the runners on the inside lanes. But they all end up running exactly 400 meters.) In the meantime, a 4-percent growth rate gives you something to cheer about if you chose a 3.5-percent AIR but causes you pain if you picked the 5-percent AIR. It's up to you.

The point is to avoid surprise or disappointment with the size of your payments by understanding the effect the AIR will have on your payments before you settle on its percentage for your policy.

Deflecting Deferred Variable Annuity Problems

Few, if any, annuity products are more complicated than variable annuities with guaranteed lifetime withdrawal benefits. Buried deep inside the prospectuses, printed in a legal font too small to be read by anyone over 40, are dense paragraphs of information that you won't understand even after you don your trifocals.

Tripping over step-up fees

Always be alert for hidden fees. By law, the prospectus must disclose them, but they aren't always easy to find. For instance, in some deferred variable annuities, the insurance carrier offers to *step up* (raise) your *benefit base* (the figure that your annual guaranteed lifetime income benefit is based on) when the actual value of your investments rises. Sounds good. But in some cases, this offer causes your rider fee to go up.

Suppose you invest $100,000 in a variable annuity that guarantees 5-percent withdrawals for life. Your withdrawals start at $5,000 and can never fall below $5,000. But then your account grows to $120,000. Two events may occur:

- ✔ If you bought a step-up rider for, say, 0.65 percent ($650) per year, you now have the right to increase your base to $120,000 and thereby increase your annual payment to $6,000.

- ✔ If you exercise the rider, the company may exercise its right to raise your rider fee — perhaps to 1.2 percent ($1,440) per year. Your net gain? Negligible.

Moral of the story? Check the fine print!

Confusing the account value with the benefit base

Variable annuities with lifetime income benefits can be very useful. They protect you against the risk of outliving your savings *and* allow you access to your savings during a financial emergency. But they can also be complex and confusing.

What's confusing about them? They define *money* in several different ways. When reading a variable annuity prospectus, you'll find four or five definitions for what you thought was a discrete stack of money sitting somewhere with your name on it. It's important to keep the meanings straight. Otherwise, you won't know how much money you're actually entitled to. Know how to recognize:

- ✔ **Account value**: The current market value of the subaccounts (similar to mutual funds) where your money is invested. Think of it as the value of your annuity contract. This is real money.

- ✔ **Bonus value:** The value of your original investment plus any bonus that the insurance company may have tacked on to your account value to reward you for buying its annuity. The bonus may disappear if you break the terms of the contract.

- ✔ **Guaranteed benefit base**: The figure that your future income payments will be based on. Your contract might specify that you'll receive 5 percent of your guaranteed benefit base every year from age 65 on, and that your benefit base will grow at a certain rate each year until then, even if your account value doesn't grow.

    Here's an example. You buy your contract with a purchase payment of $100,000 at age 55. This particular contract guarantees that your benefit base will be at least $200,000 when you reach age 65, and that you can receive 5 percent of it ($10,000) each year for life. Meanwhile, your account value moves up and down with the markets. At age 65, it might be $180,000. It might be $235,000.

    At age 65, you have a choice between your account value (whatever it may be) and $10,000 for life. Do not make the mistake of thinking that you can choose between your account value and $200,000. *There is no $200,000.* The benefit base is just the number on which your guaranteed 5-percent payout is calculated under the terms of your contract.

✔ **Guaranteed death benefit:** The amount your beneficiaries will receive if you die while the contract is in force.

Depending on whether you have a standard, enhanced, or super-enhanced death benefit, your heirs will receive different sums:

- **Standard benefit:** They receive your account balance.

- **Enhanced benefit:** They receive your original premium (the amount you originally put into the annuity) or your account balance, whichever is more. Under some contracts, this might be the standard benefit.

- **Super-enhanced benefit:** They receive the account balance's highest value on any anniversary of the purchase date.

✔ **Step-up value**: Your account value on the day you are eligible to raise or "step up" your guaranteed benefit base to your account value (assuming that the account value is higher than the benefit base on the that day).

Suppose that at age 65, your account value was $191,000 but your guaranteed benefit base was $200,000. You chose to begin receiving $10,000 a year for life — 5 percent of the benefit base. But what if your account value later exceeds $200,000? On the anniversary of your contract, you may be allowed to "step up" your benefit base to your account value. *On that day*, your account value is called your "step-up" value. If, in the same example, your account value was $214,000 on your contract anniversary, you could increase your benefit base to $214,000. From then on (until the next step opportunity), you'd receive 5 percent of $214,000 per year, or $10,700.

✔ **Surrender value:** The amount you receive if you break the contract during the surrender period. It will equal your original contribution minus any surrender charges you were required to pay. If you received an up-front bonus, you will forfeit the bonus.

The "account value" is your money. You can withdraw as much of it as you want at any time. All the other terms mentioned in this section describe amounts to which you may be entitled in certain situations. Read the fine print. You may be dazzled by the promise that your guaranteed withdrawal benefit base will at least double in ten years. But you are not entitled to the benefit base itself — only to a small percentage of its value each year.

Preventing Silly Mistakes

Why is Homer Simpson so popular? Is it possible that we recognize something of ourselves in him? Homer would commit any and all the following violations of everyday common sense. You don't have to.

Buying an index annuity that you don't understand

As I mention in Chapter 9, most people don't understand how index annuities work — and, unfortunately, neither do many agents. If you don't fully comprehend index annuities, you should probably stay away from them.

Indexed annuities are creatures that evolved for a specific environment — the ultra-low interest rate environment and dodgy stock market climate in the four to five years after the dot-com crash of 2000. They offered a small, risk-free return with a chance to benefit from an increase in stock prices at a time when stocks and bonds seemed to offer only risk and no return. Since then, stocks prices and bond yields (interest rates) have recovered and sales of index annuities, not coincidentally, have fallen.

Falling for an annuity postcard come-on

A company in Ohio sends out tens of thousands of postcards each year to older people throughout the United States to trick them into calling an 800 number. The company's goal is to get an agent into their homes and convince these folks to swap their existing annuity for a new index annuity or to buy other insurance products. A few trusting souls always get snared.

 If you receive such a postcard, don't call the 800 number. Instead, call your state insurance commissioner's toll-free fraud hotline. It's illegal to send a postcard through the mail for the purpose of finding out what investments a person holds. This type of abuse, which helps give annuities a bad name, belongs to the category of senior scams. Such schemes target older people, taking advantage of their isolation, age, or infirmities to separate them from their savings.

Underestimating your own (or your spouse's) longevity

Boomers try to stay healthy in so many ways: wearing jogging shoes, hydrating with green tea, and buttering themselves with sunblock. You'd think they'd realize how much longer they will live as a result of it. But no.

Surveys in the United States and England show that

✔ People tend to underestimate their own life expectancies by about five years.

✔ Baby boomers think of themselves as 14.5 years younger than their true chronological age.

But no one knows the effect these collective delusions will have on their individual longevity. What's the reality?

According to the Society of Actuaries, among American couples who reach age 65 together:

✔ The chance that at least one spouse will reach age 85: 78.4 percent

✔ The chance that one will reach age 90: 70 percent

✔ The chance that one will reach age 95: 30.9 percent

In other words, if you're married, you and your spouse are only a coin flip away from living to age 90. Unless you have a traditional pension, you'll need to ration your savings or put aside a chunk of money in the event you enjoy extreme longevity. This is called *self-insuring*.

Or, you can buy longevity insurance (see Chapter 10). With this type of annuity, you pay an insurance company about 10 percent of your savings in return for its guarantee that you and your spouse will receive an income starting at age 85 or 90. Because many people don't live to claim these benefits (just like many people don't receive benefits from fire or flood insurance on their homes), longevity insurance tends to be inexpensive compared to the potential benefit.

Ignoring the impact of inflation

When the wind is at your back, you forget how hard it's blowing. Inflation is like that. As long as you work and your salary rises with inflation, you don't notice its effect. But when you retire, and your income levels off, inflation is in your face. That's when it stings. To make sure that your retirement income keeps up with inflation, you need to prepare.

Take advantage of one of these strategies:

✔ If you buy a fixed income annuity, consider one with an inflation rider that provides a rising level of income. Some riders allow your payments to track the Consumer Price Index. Others allow you to prearrange a 1-, 2-, or 3-percent annual increase in your payments.

✔ Invest in stocks. Because stock market prices tend to rise with inflation, investing in them is a time-tested way to keep up with the rising cost of food, shelter, and transportation.

If you buy an income annuity, consider a variable contract or a contract that lets you receive *combination payments* where part of your income is fixed and the rest fluctuates with the value of your investments in mutual funds.

Avoiding annuities entirely

In the past, annuities (mainly deferred annuities) have been sold to the wrong people for the wrong reasons. Mistakes have been made. This fact, coupled with so much potential for errors, leads too many people away from annuities. But that decision may be the biggest mistake of all. Today's annuities — income-producing annuities — have the potential to help millions of people finance their retirement.

Part V
The Part of Tens

The 5th Wave   By Rich Tennant

"That reminds me — I have to figure out how to save for retirement _and_ send these two to college."

In this part . . .

The world's most accomplished people use lists to increase their productivity. So why mess with success? Each of these chapters offers a list of ten questions, factors, Web sites, or terms that can instantly double your annuity IQ. Chapter 20, which focuses on health and longevity, reflects this book's implicit wish for every reader: May you live long and prosper.

Chapter 18

Ten Essential Annuity Expressions

"**G**uaranteed living benefit." "Annuitization." "Survivorship credit."

Linguistically, the world of annuities can seem like a foreign country. If you've just arrived, you'll find new words with new meanings, and familiar words — like "surrender" — with unfamiliar meanings.

In this chapter, I translate some of the most important annuity expressions and briefly define them. In most cases, I introduce two related terms and try to explain the distinctions between them.

Feel free to refer to this chapter, and to the glossary in this book, whenever you need to refresh your understanding of the technical terms that I use throughout this book.

Annuities and Annuitization

In the most literal sense, an *annuity* is a bond-like investment that you pay for all at once or over time and which pays you (or you and your spouse) a guaranteed annual income for life, starting right away or at some future date. Social Security, for instance, is an annuity.

All annuity contracts offer their owners the right to convert the money in their annuity to a guaranteed lifetime income. If the owner buys an *immediate* annuity, the conversion takes place within a year of the purchase date. If the owner buys a *deferred* annuity, he has the right to convert at some future date.

The act of converting a deferred annuity to an income stream is called *annuitization*. If you've never heard that term, it's because very few — less than 5 percent — of the people who own annuities ever annuitize them. Instead, they simply treat the annuity as if it were a savings account or mutual fund account and withdraw money when they need it.

Why don't they annuitize? Because conversion or annuitization is more or less irreversible. After you convert the lump sum (usually $50,000 or more) to monthly income, your access to your cash is highly restricted. It may be limited to the check you receive every month for life. As a general rule, people prefer not to turn liquid assets (cash, stocks, mutual funds) into illiquid assets (stuff that's hard to sell, like a house or annuity).

That's why Guaranteed Lifetime Withdrawal Benefits (GWLBs) have become so popular. GWLBs are the latest options on variable deferred annuity contracts. They offer some of the safety of annuitization while still allowing the owner to withdraw some or all of his money in an emergency. ***Note:*** GLWBs do not provide *survivorship credits* (also known as *mortality credits),* which I define later in this chapter.

Contract Owners and Annuitants

The *contract owner* pays for the annuity and directs the investments. The *annuitant* is the person whose life expectancy is used to calculate the annuity payments if the contract is annuitized — that is, converted to a guaranteed income stream. In most but not all contracts, the owner and annuitant are the same person. (It's simpler that way.)

For example, a 50-year-old man may buy a contract and name his 75-year-old mother as the annuitant. If the contract's value is converted to income right away, the insurance company will plan on making payments for about 15 years (the 75-year-old annuitant's life expectancy) rather than 29 years (the 50-year-old owner's life expectancy).

Before you buy an annuity, find out whether the contract is *owner-driven* or *annuitant-driven.* The answer determines who receives the *death benefit* (described below) in the event of an unforeseen death. For more on this topic, see Chapter 11.

Contract or Policy versus Investment

Strictly speaking, annuities are *insurance contracts,* not *investments.* The owners are "contract owners" rather than "investors." What's the difference? In an investment, you take *risks* with your money in hopes of high returns. In an insurance contract, you avoid risk by purchasing one or more *guarantees*.

When you buy an annuity, for instance, you enter into a binding agreement with a life insurance company. The agreement obligates you to obey certain rules and obligates the insurance carrier to provide certain benefits (such as a guaranteed minimum return or a death benefit).

What makes it so confusing is that annuities are investments and contracts rolled into one. In short, your annuity is an investment with a guarantee attached to it. For instance, you might think of your $30,000 car as an investment, and your $2,000 extended warranty as an insurance contract. Most annuities are like the car and the warranty rolled into one $32,000 product.

If you persist in thinking of annuities as investments, you'll compare them to other investments, and they will look expensive and complicated by comparison. The costs and the complexity make sense only when you recognize that an annuity is a contract, and involves guarantees, restrictions, obligations, and costs that investments do not have.

In an investment, the owner of the security undertakes risk in search of rewards. Also, in an annuity, the contract owner buys securities (directly or indirectly) but also pays the insurer to assume certain risks (such as the risk that the stock market might crash during his retirement or that he might live too long and run out of money.)

Death Benefits versus Living Benefits

Until recently, most people bought deferred variable annuities (which are clusters of mutual funds, essentially; see Chapter 7) for the tax benefits, which allowed them to defer (postpone) taxes on their investment gains until after they retired. Such contracts typically offered only one insurance feature: the *death benefit.*

Death benefit is simply a technical term for the payment that the beneficiary of the owner of an annuity (or the beneficiary of the annuitant, in an annuitant-driven contract) receives if the owner (or annuitant) dies before the annuity is converted to a lifelong income stream. The death benefit, traditionally, is the value of the annuity when the owner (or annuitant) dies.

Over the past ten years or so, insurance carriers have made the death benefit more valuable. For an added fee, you can make sure that the death benefit will be equal to no less than the owner's initial investment, or the contract's highest value on any anniversary of the day the contract was purchased (minus any withdrawals made or fees deducted).

Few, if any, people ever purchased a deferred variable annuity just for the death benefit. But it was a nice feature to have if the owner happened to die during a stock market slump. For instance, suppose you bought your variable annuity in 1999 when stocks were overvalued and died in 2001 after stock prices dropped off a cliff. If you had purchased an enhanced death benefit, your beneficiary would have received the contract's pre-crash value and wouldn't have been hurt by the market's collapse.

Today, insurance companies are more likely to promote the living benefits of their deferred annuities than their death benefits. These benefits provide guarantees that, for example, the value of your contract will grow at a certain minimum rate over a ten-year period, or that you can receive guaranteed life-time income. For a full discussion of living benefit options, see Chapter 8.

Understanding the Exclusion Ratio

When you buy an income annuity that pays you a fixed monthly income in retirement, the contract issuer (an insurance company) provides you with an *exclusion ratio*. It indicates the percentage of your annuity income that will be exempt from income tax.

The higher the exclusion ratio, the lower your income tax. The exclusion ratio depends on how much after-tax and pretax money you used when buying your annuity:

- ✔ If you bought your annuity with after-tax money — money from an ordinary taxable mutual fund account, for instance — your exclusion ratio will be high and your income tax bill will be low.

- ✔ If you bought your annuity with pre-tax money — money from a tradi-tional IRA or qualified retirement plan such as a 401(k) — your exclusion ratio will be zero. You'll owe ordinary income tax on all of your annuity income.

- ✔ If you bought your annuity with tax-deferred money — money from a deferred annuity — your exclusion ratio will fall somewhere in the middle of the scale. The exact figure depends on how much your deferred annuity has grown since you bought it. You'll owe income tax on the tax-deferred growth, but not on your original investment.

An income annuity can help you spread your tax burden evenly across the length of your retirement. Let me explain. Consider two retirees, A and B, who own deferred variable annuities that they purchased 20 years ago for $100,000. Both contracts are now worth $250,000, of which $150,000 ($250,000 minus $100,000) will be subject to income tax as it is withdrawn.

With his $250,000, Retiree A buys an income annuity that will pay him about $1,800 a month for life. His exclusion ratio (as calculated by the insurance company that issued his contract) is about 24 percent. Every year, 24 percent of his annuity income is exempt from income tax.

Retiree B decided to leave his $250,000 in the deferred variable annuity and make withdrawals whenever he needs cash. He will owe income tax on 100 percent of his withdrawals until there's $100,000 left in his contract. After that, his withdrawals are tax exempt.

Fortunately, you do not have to calculate your exclusion ratio when you buy an income annuity, or even when you ask for a quote. The issuer does that for you.

If you buy an income annuity with a variable monthly payout (one that fluctuates with the markets), the insurance company won't provide an exclusion ratio.

Instead, it will simply ask you how much after-tax money you're using to buy the annuity. Then it will divide that amount by the number of payments you're expected to receive. (That's usually the average number of months a person your age is expected to live.)

For instance, the typical 65-year-old male purchaser of an income annuity might be expected to live almost 20 more years, according to insurance company mortality tables. If he puts $200,000 ($100,000 in after-tax money and $100,000 in pre-tax money) into a variable income annuity with a lifetime payout:

- His first monthly payment will be about $1,188 a month.
- From each payment, about $417 ($100,000 divided by 239 months) will be exempt from income tax.*

*Source: www.vanguard.com, September 2007.

If you are both the owner and annuitant of a life annuity contract — that is, if you're getting income for life — everything you receive after you reach your life expectancy will be fully taxed. If you're a 65-year-old man and you bought a life annuity for yourself, all annuity income after you reach age 85 or so will be taxed as ordinary income.

Fixed versus Variable

The words *fixed* and *variable* are fertile sources of confusion in Annuityville because they each have dual meanings. They depend on whether you're discussing deferred annuities or income annuities.

If you're talking about deferred annuities, which are mainly investments, you can receive either a fixed or variable rate of return. You receive a fixed return if the insurance company invests your money in bonds. You receive a variable return if you invest your money in subaccounts, which are similar to mutual funds. Eventually, you take your money out.

If you're talking about income (also known as immediate) annuities, which are personal pensions, you receive either a fixed or variable monthly income in return for your nonrefundable premium. You receive a fixed income if the insurance company invests your money in bonds. You receive a variable income if you invest your money in subaccounts. You don't (unless you die, or in certain emergencies) take all of your money out.

When brokers, bankers, insurance agents, and journalists talk about annuities, they may refer to "fixed annuities" or "variable annuities" without making it clear that they mean deferred or income annuities. If you don't keep the differences straight, you can end up buying the wrong product. Or you may become confused, lose patience, and not buy an annuity at all.

Reaping the Survivorship Credits

Lifetime income annuities, like any kind of insurance, are based on the principle of risk pooling. Here's how it works. All annuity purchasers of a certain age throw their money into a big pot, and every year the ones who are still alive receive payments from the pot.

The pot consists of the initial premiums or investments — including the investments of those who die along the way — and the appreciation of those investments. To put it another way, the owners who live share the assets of those who have died. It's like car insurance: The premiums of those who don't get into accidents are paid to those who do.

The technical name for the shares that go from the deceased annuity owners to the living ones are *mortality credits.* I prefer to use the more positive-sounding term — *survivorship credits* — that Jeffrey K. Dellinger uses in his book, *The Handbook of Variable Income Annuities* (Wiley). (**Note:** Mortality credits are not related to death benefits in any way.)

Of course, you never see survivorship credits. They aren't reported on any monthly or annual statement. No checks get mailed to survivors from the estates of the deceased. The monthly payments to survivors don't change. On the contrary. From its mortality tables, the insurance company knows in advance how many annuity owners will live or die every year. It factors those statistics into its calculation of the quote it offers you when you shop for a contract.

Many people worry that if they die before receiving at least as much money as they put into the annuity, the insurance company will get the rest of their money. That's why so few people buy life annuities. But, as I mentioned above, the money simply stays in the pool from which the surviving contract owners draw their income.

That's the nature of mortality pooling. It's the only way that an insurance company can afford to guarantee that every contract owner will receive income for his or her entire life.

The survivorship credit gets bigger as you get older and your fellow contract owners are passing away at a faster rate. That's why your Social Security payments will be about 60 percent larger if you start taking them at age 70 rather than at age 62. It's also why some people think it makes sense to delay the purchase of a life annuity until age 70 or 75, or even to buy an advanced life deferred annuity (ALDA), which pays no benefits until or unless you reach age 80 or 85. (For details on ALDAs, see Chapter 10.)

Qualified versus Nonqualified

When you put your money in a *qualified* plan or account, your contributions are tax deductible (up to certain limits). You don't pay income tax on your contributions or the earnings on those contributions until you start taking withdrawals. All other accounts, and the money in them, are *nonqualified*.

Employer-sponsored retirement plans such as 401(k)s, 403(b)s, Keoghs, Tax-Sheltered Annuities (TSAs), and defined benefit pensions are all qualified plans. Traditional IRAs offer similar tax benefits, but they're technically not called *qualified* because a different statute governs them.

Qualified plans were created by Uncle Sam to encourage people to save for retirement and to spend the savings during retirement. To make sure that people use the plans as Congress intended, qualified plans contain rules that:

- ✔ Discourage early withdrawals by levying a 10-percent penalty tax on most withdrawals before age 59½

- ✔ Encourage people to spend them down during retirement by requiring investors to start withdrawing by age 70½ (in amounts no less than total assets divided by years of remaining life expectancy).

See Chapter 14 for more discussion on these requirements.

General Accounts and Separate Accounts

Insurance companies put your annuity and other insurance premiums into two kinds of accounts. When you buy a fixed deferred annuity, your investment goes into the carrier's *general account*, where it mingles with other people's money. When you buy a variable annuity, your investment first goes into the carrier's *separate account*.

The difference is subtle but significant. If a carrier declares bankruptcy, its creditors can claim the money in the general account but not the money in the separate account. (Fortunately, bankruptcies among major insurance companies are extremely rare.)

Inside the separate account are *subaccounts*, which are like mutual funds. After you buy a variable annuity, you can choose which subaccounts to put your money in, just as you choose which mutual funds to put your 401(k) money in. You manage your subaccounts exactly as you would manage mutual funds:

- ✔ You make tax-free exchanges between subaccounts when you want to invest more aggressively or conservatively.

- ✔ You rebalance your portfolio if it drifts from your asset allocation formula.

- ✔ You set up a regular drip of contributions from a mutual fund or bank account.

Subaccounts are also taxed differently from mutual funds:

- ✔ At least once a year, mutual-fund managers distribute the fund's taxable dividends, interest, and capital gains. Those gains get taxed even if you use them to buy more mutual fund shares.

- ✔ Subaccount earnings aren't distributed or taxed immediately. Instead, they're retained in the account, adding to the value of each annuity unit.

Even when a subaccount and a mutual fund hold identical sets of stocks or bonds, the value of a subaccount share (its accumulation unit value, or AUV) will differ from the value of the mutual fund share (its net asset value, or NAV).

Surrender Period and Surrender Charge

Only insurance companies can issue (or "manufacture," in industry jargon) annuities, but they distribute them through networks of wholesale marketing organizations, brokerages, or banks, which in turn give them to individual agents, brokers, or bankers to sell to people like you. In many cases, the insurance company pays the wholesaler and the salesman a commission.

When there's a commission involved, there will be a surrender charge period, often lasting the same number of years as the size of the commission that was paid. (That is: 9-percent commission = 9-year surrender charge period.) If you withdraw too much money in a single year (more than 10 percent of your initial investment, for instance) during this period, you'll have to pay a surrender charge.

The threat of the surrender charge is intended to discourage you from canceling your annuity before the insurance carrier can recover the sales commission from you by charging you annual fees. As each year passes and you pay fees to the carrier, the surrender charge usually declines. By the last year of a nine-year surrender charge period, for instance, the surrender charge may be only 1 percent. The surrender charge is also called a *contingent deferred sales charge,* or CDSC.

Some deferred annuity contracts don't have surrender charge periods or surrender charges at all. If you pay the sales commission yourself in advance, there is no surrender charge period. If you buy your contract from a direct seller like Vanguard or Fidelity, there is no commission and no surrender charge period. See Chapter 16 for details on direct providers.

Chapter 19

Ten Questions to Ask Before You Sign a Contract

* *

In This Chapter

▶ Determining your risk tolerance

▶ Assessing the fees

▶ Identifying the exit strategy

* *

*S*uitability is one of the annuity world's favorite buzzwords. State and federal regulators are constantly pressuring annuity marketers not to pressure their clients into buying annuities that aren't "suitable" for them. So, if you buy an annuity, you'll probably have to read and sign a *suitability statement*.

But instead of relying on the regulators to protect you from annuity salesmen, you should plan to have some questions of your own. Here are a few to ask the seller — and yourself — before buying an annuity. Keep this in mind: Your first objective is to understand the products; the second is to make sure that the annuity you buy is the one you need.

"How Will This Annuity Reduce My Risks?"

When you buy an annuity, you shift risk from yourself to an insurance company. So you need to determine which financial risks bother you so much that you're willing to pay an insurer to take them off your hands.

For instance, maybe you worry about having an income after age 90. Or you worry that a bear market will start just before or after you retire. Or maybe you want to prevent yourself from over- or under-spending your savings during retirement.

By identifying your risks, you can determine the kind of annuity to buy, when to buy it, and how much money to contribute to it. But first you need to view annuities as insurance — something you pay fees for. Otherwise, they'll probably strike you as an odd and unnecessarily expensive kind of investment.

"What Is My Risk Tolerance?"

Your personal tolerance for risk should help guide your choice of an annuity because you can't guess the future, but you do know your risk tolerance. Along with unique genetic codes, each person has a highly subjective risk profile. Some people can't sleep well if all their money is in stocks. Some can't sleep well with half their money in stocks and half in bonds. And for others, bonds and bond funds aren't safe enough; they need guaranteed lifetime income. Knowing your risk tolerance helps you figure out the right annuity for you.

In 2006, researchers sponsored by the Michigan Retirement Research Center rated investors on a scale of 1 to 10, with the 10s having the lowest tolerance for risk. The results showed the following:

- People with a risk tolerance between 1 and 3.5 didn't seem to need annuities. They were comfortable investing in stocks and bonds, and they could tolerate the possibility of a recession.

- People who were higher on the risk-aversion scale (3.6 to 10) could benefit from keeping part of their money in stocks and bonds and part in an income annuity.

   Of that group, those who were less risk-averse (with scores of 4.0 to 6.0) weren't tempted to buy annuities unless interest rates were high or they were in their 80s. In other words, they were willing to wait for less expensive annuities.

   Virtually no one was so risk-intolerant that they would benefit from locking all their money in an income annuity as soon as they retired.

"How Much of My Assets Should I Put into an Annuity?"

The answer to this question depends on whether you're considering a deferred annuity (a savings tool) to take advantage of tax deferral or an income annuity (a retirement income tool) to prevent you from running out of money in your old age.

✔ If you buy a deferred annuity, you shouldn't put more than about 30 percent of your assets into the contract. By deferred annuity, I mean a fixed deferred annuity (similar to a bond) or a variable deferred annuity (similar to mutual funds, but with insurance-related bells and whistles).

✔ If you're younger than age 55 or so, you shouldn't put any money into a deferred annuity unless you're in a high tax bracket and have not yet put the maximum into a tax-deferred employer-sponsored retirement plan or an IRA.

✔ If you don't have much money, and the only realistic way for you to generate enough monthly income in retirement is by converting 80 or 90 percent of your savings to an income annuity, you may have to do so.

✔ If regular withdrawals from savings can provide you with an adequate retirement income, but you're afraid you might live to age 95 or 100 and run out of money, you should put about 40 percent of your savings into an income annuity when you retire or 20 percent into an advanced life deferred annuity (ALDA) that starts paying an income if or when you reach age 80 or age 85.

Beware of anyone who pressures you to put all of your retirement savings in an annuity. He might try to sell you a multipurpose, high-fee product that offers some of everything you need — lifetime income, long-term care coverage, and an inheritance for your heirs — but not enough of anything.

In any case, putting all of your money into an annuity is rarely a good idea. Be wary of any broker or adviser who suggests that you do.

"What Is the Strength and Integrity of the Issuer?"

Buy an annuity contract only from an insurance company whose financial strength — that is, its likely ability to pay claims, fulfill guarantees, and meet all of its obligations — has received a high rating from the agencies that rate insurance companies (for example, Standard & Poor's, Fitch & Co., and A.M. Best).

Most annuity sales come from the largest and most-stable insurance companies; these companies generally have *excellent*, *strong*, or *superior* ratings. However, the rating shouldn't be your only consideration — you don't necessarily have to choose the company with the very highest rating.

To determine the integrity of a specific company, simply search the Internet to check for civil, criminal, or administrative actions against it. Your state insurance commissioner, state attorney general, or the National Association of Securities Dealers, may have records of such actions. *Note:* Unfortunately, many prestigious carriers have paid fines for misconduct in at least one of their many lines of business. If you prefer relatively unblemished integrity, consider a direct marketer like Vanguard or Fidelity or a mutually-owned carrier. These firms aren't publicly held, don't have stock traded on the New York Stock Exchange, and aren't under pressure to please Wall Street at the expense of their customers. (A mutually-owned insurance company is owned by its policyholders.)

"What Are the Fees?"

When you're buying an annuity, you may be concentrating so much on the living benefits or the potential earnings of the investments that you don't notice the fees. Or maybe you don't see a clear correlation between the benefits and the fees you pay. Keep in mind:

✔ The fees associated with fixed deferred annuities are included in the interest rates the issuer offers you. The fees associated with income annuities are included in the monthly payment that the carrier offers you. The fees aren't expressed separately.

✔ With variable deferred annuities, you can't always see the link between the fees you pay the insurance company and the sales commission that the insurance company pays the agent or broker. See Chapter 7 for more information.

If the annuity pays an up-front bonus or commission to the seller, find out how the insurance company plans to recoup those costs from you:

✔ The issuer of an equity-indexed annuity (a fixed deferred annuity whose returns are linked to the stock market) generally earns back its costs by limiting your potential gains.

✔ The issuer of a variable annuity may charge a higher mortality-and-expense-risk fee.

One of the most obvious but most-frequently overlooked facts in the financial service industry is that fees (sometimes called *expense ratios*) are based on *assets*, not *profits*. So, if your variable annuity charges a total annual fee of 3 percent and your portfolio earns 9 percent, your net return is 6 percent. The fees consume a whopping 33 percent of your gain.

Recently, L-share variable annuities have become popular because they pay the seller a smaller up-front commission and the surrender period is only about three years rather than the usual seven. But these annuities may charge a 1-percent annual *trailing fee* (an annual commission deducted from your account and paid to the salesman after the sale), which can be more expensive for the client in the long run.

Many fees are not visible at first. For example:

- ✔ Variable annuities that offer living benefits with step-up options (which allow you to capture market gains and increase your guaranteed annual income) may raise the fee on the living benefit if you exercise that option (see Chapter 7).

- ✔ The crediting formulas of equity-indexed annuities and the renewal rates of fixed annuities are subject to change without your approval.

- ✔ The few annuities that require annuitization (that is, force you to convert your account into a monthly income) don't reveal the fees that help determine the monthly payment. If the carrier offers you a $685-a-month income in exchange for your $100,000 in savings, for instance, you won't know the role that fees played in calculating that figure.

"What's My Upside Potential?"

All annuities are part insurance, part investment, so find out how much growth you can expect from your contract. The answer depends on the type of annuity you intend to buy:

- ✔ **Fixed annuity with a guaranteed multiyear rate:** The seller will tell you your annual rate of return before you buy, and the rate will never change.

- ✔ **Variable annuity:** Your returns will depend on the performance of the stock or bond market, the investment methodologies of the investment managers, and the size of your fees.

- ✔ **Equity-indexed annuity:** Good luck! Given the many crediting methods of these products and their relatively short track record, you'll find it almost impossible to predict your investment return. At most, you can expect to earn about half what you would have earned by investing the same amount in stocks. (For help on these annuities, see Chapter 9.)

"How Do I Get My Money Out?"

If you're looking for a highly liquid investment, then you're not in the market for an annuity. Annuities, designed specifically for retirement savings and retirement income, are one of the most illiquid investments you can imagine. Before buying one, make sure you have other savings that you can tap for emergencies, opportunities, and gifts.

Note: Annuities have different degrees of liquidity. For example, most variable annuities allow withdrawals up to 10 percent per year without surrender fees. But two-tiered, equity-indexed annuities and variable annuities with guaranteed minimum income benefits (GMIBs) require you to annuitize — you can never get your money out in a lump sum unless you die (see Chapter 8 for more on these specifics). On the other hand, an increasing number of annuities are available with no surrender period and no penalty for early withdrawals.

Many annuities are *more* liquid than you think. For instance, some people think that when you annuitize a deferred annuity or buy an income annuity (and exchange a large sum for a guaranteed monthly income), you have no access to your cash other than the monthly check. Not necessarily. An increasing number of contract options allow you to make sure that your heirs will receive at least part of your money if you die early, or allow you to take emergency withdrawals in excess of your monthly payments. If you use those options, you may receive a bit less in monthly income. But the flexibility may be worth the price.

Illiquidity has an upside. An insurance company can't hold up its side of the bargain (guaranteeing you a fixed return, for instance) if you don't hold up your side (not taking withdrawals for a predictable number of years). That's why a fixed rate annuity that guarantees its rate for seven years has a seven-year surrender period. That's also why you should avoid a fixed rate annuity whose surrender period is longer than the guaranteed period.

"Where Can I Get More Information about This Annuity?"

Even after listening to a broker's explanation of an annuity product, you may not immediately understand how the product works. Brokers themselves don't necessarily understand the latest annuity products. Try asking for a copy of the contract prospectus, where you'll find all the details (see Chapter 17). By law, you must receive (and read, ideally) a prospectus before buying a variable annuity. Fixed annuities do not have prospectuses because they are contracts, and do not involve the purchase of securities.

Prospectuses — especially those for variable annuities with guaranteed living benefits — are notoriously confusing. They can lead you on endlessly circular and futile searches for the explanations and definitions that you need. But the prospectus is your best source of information about a variable annuity. If you don't have time to read the prospectus cover to cover, then read the fee section, the rider section, and anything in boldface type.

"Am I Better Off Exchanging My Annuity for Another One?"

In 2006, about $130 billion worth of variable annuities were sold. But most of those sales were transfers of annuity assets from one contract to another through a 1035 exchange (see Chapter 13 for more info on this transaction). In other words, the variable annuity industry has turned into a merry-go-round; lots of contract owners are changing ponies in the middle of the ride, but few new customers are getting on.

Most exchanges are instigated by commission-hungry annuity salesmen, not by contract owners. But at least two situations can justify an exchange. If you're paying 2.5 percent in annual fees on your variable annuity, you may save thousands of dollars a year by switching to a dirt-cheap Vanguard or Fidelity contract. And if your old annuity doesn't offer the fancy new living benefits of the new variable annuities, you might consider an upgrade. Remember that you may owe a surrender fee to the old carrier if you switch annuities. The seller of the new annuity may offer you a "bonus" that appears to offset the surrender fee, but don't go there.

"What Are the Tax Implications?"

Never buy an annuity without considering all the tax implications. From a tax perspective, annuities are a double-edged sword. The money you invest in an annuity grows tax-deferred, and isn't subject to taxes at all until you withdraw it in retirement. Tax deferral can enhance your savings rate. On the other hand, the investment gains that you withdraw from an annuity are taxed at a higher rate (as income rather than as capital gains) than gains that you would withdraw from, say, a mutual fund account. The purchase of an annuity always has tax implications, and what you don't know can hurt you later. See Chapter 14 for more on this topic.

My advice: consult a tax expert or trusted investment adviser before you buy an annuity.

If you use an annuity to provide yourself with guaranteed lifetime income, you'll probably purchase either a deferred variable annuity with guaranteed lifetime withdrawal benefits (GMWB) or an income annuity (SPIA). Withdrawals from these two types of contracts are taxed very differently.

Think of your initial investment to an annuity as skim milk and your earnings (the interest, dividends, and capital gains that accumulate over time) as cream. When you own a GMWB annuity, you must first withdraw all the cream and pay income taxes on it. After you've drawn off all the cream, you can withdraw the skim tax-free. When you own an income annuity, every monthly payment contains a precise blend of both skim and cream. At the end of each year, you will owe income tax only on the cream you've received. In short, a GMWB requires you to pay more tax early in retirement, while an income annuity spreads the tax liability over the entire course of your retirement.

Chapter 20

Ten Factors that Determine Longevity

. . . .

In This Chapter

▶ Identifying your risk factors

▶ Calculating your longevity risk

▶ Adjusting for adverse selection

. . . .

Annuities arose as a response to an inconvenient uncertainty, one that has always fascinated and terrified humankind: We don't know how long we'll live. In retirement, this uncertainty becomes *longevity risk*. That's a fancy name for the risk that you'll spend your savings too fast and run out of money before you die, or under-spend during retirement and deprive yourself of certain pleasures — like spoiling your grandchildren.

Life annuities (income annuities) insure you against longevity risk. They allow you to spend at a rate that assumes you'll live to the average age; if you live longer, they keep on paying you. So the bigger your longevity risk, the more sense it makes to insure against it.

Only you can estimate how much longevity risk you have. The insurance company doesn't send a nurse to your house to estimate your life expectancy, as it does when you buy life insurance. But don't think you can put one over on good ol' Monolithic Life — insurers already know that annuity buyers tend to outlive their neighbors! (To find out about annuities that are tailored for people with life-shortening illnesses, see Chapter 15.)

This chapter helps you gauge your own longevity risk. I include ten of the major determinants of long life and identify a couple of Web sites that offer longevity calculators. Keep in mind that your life expectancy at age 65, 70, or 75 — the age you may choose to annuitize — is a much more important indicator of your longevity risk than your life expectancy at birth.

By the end of this chapter, you may end up thinking, "Even if I'm a thin woman of Asian descent who has a PhD, is married or widowed, loves Mediterranean food, but never smoked and don't belong to a motorcycle club, I could still get run over by a bus and lose all the benefits of an annuity." It's true. And there are plenty of stories about fitness fanatics and organic food aficionados who've died unexpectedly young. That's why they call it longevity *risk*. You can't be sure how long you'll live. Fortunately, you can tailor an income annuity so that, even if you do die prematurely, you won't lose all the benefits. See Chapter 8 for details.

Earning (Somewhat) Big Bucks

"The rich are different from you and me," Scott Fitzgerald wrote in *The Great Gatsby*. For one thing, they tend to live longer. John D. Rockefeller, the oil baron, lived to age 97. Brooke Astor, the heiress and philanthropist, lived to 105. Actor George Burns, who starred in vaudeville, radio, and TV, died at 101. No one knows why wealthier people seem to live longer — they may simply have obeyed Ben Franklin's famous advice and been "early to bed and early to rise."

But people with more wealth may also have greater access to benefits associated with longevity: good healthcare, safe neighborhoods, and stress-relieving vacations. Likewise, life expectancies are invariably longer in wealthier countries, partly because of access to safer drinking water, better healthcare, and lower rates of infant mortality.

In the United States, the National Institutes of Health documented the wealth-longevity relationship in the early 1990s and showed that higher-income men live about four years longer than lower-income men. At the time of the study, 65-year-old, low-income men could expect to live to age 78, but high-income men could expect to live to age 82. However, women in the highest income bracket lived only one year longer than women in the lowest bracket.

Having the Right Demographics

Certain types of Americans live longer than others. In 2006, the Harvard School of Public Health published statistics showing a stunning 21-year longevity gap between the longest-lived and the shortest-lived Americans. Some of the specifics include the following:

- American women of Asian descent live the longest, with a life expectancy at birth of 87.4 years.

- Many live in Hawaii, the state in the Union in which people live the longest.

✔ Men of African American descent living in urban areas or in the rural South have a life expectancy of only about 67 years.

✔ The life expectancy of most Americans — the 214 million residents of "white middle America," as researchers refer to them — is about 78 years.

If you belong to a demographic group with a shorter average life expectancy, you can always increase your longevity by doing what long-lived people everywhere do: avoid tobacco and alcohol, get plenty of exercise, and eat a diet rich in fruits, vegetables, and whole grains.

The study identified eight different longevity groups in the United States. From longest- to shortest-lived, they are: Asian Americans, rural whites in the Northern Plains and Dakotas, white middle America, low-income whites in Appalachia, Western Native Americans (the smallest group), and African Americans living in middle America, the rural South, or cities. The following ten states report the longest life spans (beginning with the longest):

✔ Hawaii

✔ Minnesota

✔ Utah

✔ Colorado

✔ Massachusetts

✔ New Hampshire

✔ Iowa

✔ North Dakota

✔ Rhode Island

✔ California

The ten states reporting the shortest life spans are (beginning with the shortest):

✔ Mississippi

✔ Louisiana

✔ Alabama

✔ South Carolina

✔ West Virginia

✔ Tennessee

✔ Oklahoma

✔ Arkansas

  ✔ Kentucky

  ✔ Georgia

Watching Your Weight

Few 80-somethings and 90-somethings are overweight. In fact, severely obese people live up to 20 years fewer than people who aren't overweight. So maintaining an ideal weight for your height is an important longevity factor.

But people of ideal weight are in the minority in America. On the average, two-thirds to three-quarters of Americans are overweight (heavier than ideal weight for age, height, and body type), and one-third of those are obese (30 percent over ideal weight). Studies by the National Institutes of Health show that, if current trends continue for several more decades, death rates from obesity may reduce the average American's life expectancy by five years.

Explanations for the inverse relationship between weight and longevity are countless. Directly or indirectly, obesity tends to wear out your hips and knees sooner and contributes to the development of diabetes, cancers of the colon and other organs, high blood pressure, hardening of the arteries, and so on.

Given the thousands of books on the topics of obesity and diet, I won't try to address them here. Well, okay, maybe just one comment . . .

Epidemiologists and public health researchers have long been fascinated by the longer, more disease-free lives of people in Mediterranean countries like Italy and Spain. And the American Medical Association affirms that you can't go wrong with whole grains, green vegetables, fruits, nuts, olive oil, and moderate consumption of alcohol, all elements of a Mediterranean diet.

A study in the New England Journal of Medicine in 2003 showed that, in Greece, such a diet (along with other factors, such as not smoking and exercising regularly) was associated with an 83 percent lower risk of heart disease, a 91-percent lower risk of diabetes in women, and a 71-percent lower risk of colon cancer in men, compared to people who did not follow a healthy diet.

Getting Hitched

Married people live longer than single people. According to The Rand Corporation's Center for the Study of Aging, 65-year-olds who are divorced or have never married are more than twice as likely to die at that age than 65-year-olds who are married.

In the 1990s, Center for the Study of Aging reviewed the medical histories of 11,000 Americans to figure out why married people live longer. Although they identified many intriguing *effects* of marriage on health, they found no specific *causes*. Nevertheless, two factors came out of the study:

✔ Married men's risk of dying appears to drop as their wives' education level rises — possibly because educated women run healthier households or because these women select healthier, more stable mates.

✔ Although widowers are more likely to die at any specific age than married men, widows, it turns out, are merrier — they're no likelier to die than married women.

It appears that when wives die, their husbands lose the protective effect of marriage. But when husbands die, their wives retain it.

Going Easy on the Vices

Insurance professionals who sell annuities often have a dark sense of humor. One of them suggested that, as an alternative to an annuity, you can reduce your chance of outliving your savings by engaging in reckless, life-shortening behaviors. His name for this strategy: *vice management*.

For instance, you're less likely to need an annuity if you drink more than three servings of alcohol a day, ride a motorcycle, sit on your seatbelt in a car, parachute out of airplanes, climb steep mountains, or use drugs for nonmedicinal purposes.

Being Female

Visit a retirement community and you quickly notice that women far outnumber men. (Why do men die earlier? "Because they want to," goes the old, sexist, joke.) After age 85, good men are hard to find; good men who can still drive a car at night at 85 are even harder to find. Only one out of every seven people (or 15 percent) aged 100 or older is a man.

In 2004, the average life expectancy for a 65-year-old American man was about 81 years. For women, it was two to three years longer. Each year from age 65 to age 85 or so, roughly three men die for every two women who die:

✔ At age 65, 21.5 men die for every 13.3 women.

✔ At age 70, 32 men die for every 20 women.

✔ At age 75, 47 men die for every 30 women.

✔ At age 80, 76 men die for every 49 women.

Extending the years from cradle to grave

In the past, reductions in infant mortality accounted for most of the increases in a country's average lifespan. In the future, new treatments for chronic diseases will keep people alive longer. Insurance company executives worry that some unforeseen Nobel-Prize-winning cure will enable large numbers of annuity owners to live much longer than expected — and claim far more in annuity benefits than the companies can pay.

No one knows why more men than women die at each level. According to one theory, women have lower levels of iron prior to menopause, and high iron levels are linked to harmful levels of *free radicals* (chemical compounds in the body that vandalize chromosomes and turn normal cells into cancer cells) and *low-density lipoproteins* (particles associated with heart disease).

The enhanced longevity of women means that married men can think of life annuities with joint-and-survivor options as gifts to their wives. It also means that annuities are more expensive for women than for men; different mortality tables and different payout rates are applied. *Note:* This is not true for annuities purchased through a 401(k) or 403(b) retirement plan; by law, these plans must use unisex mortality tables that factor women the same as men.

Exercising Regularly

Regular exercisers appear to be good candidates for annuities. Exercise is associated with lower rates of cardiovascular disease, the most common cause of premature death in the United States. Researchers at RAND Corporation studied 44,542 men for 12 years (1986 to 1998) and found that men who ran for an hour or more per week had a 42-percent lower risk for a heart attack or dying from heart disease than men who didn't run. In simple terms, they cut their risk nearly in half!

In the study, other types of exercise helped, but to a lesser degree:

- Lifting weights for 30 minutes or more per week reduced the risk of a heart attack by 23 percent.
- Rowing for 30 minutes or more every week or walking briskly for 30 minutes every day reduced the risk by 18 percent.

The benefits of exercise held true even when researchers took into account other factors such as age, smoking habits, and other heart disease risks.

Know when to hold (an annuity), know when to fold

Insurers have found that people who buy income annuities at age 65 tend to live about 20 percent longer (to age 83 rather than age 80) than 65-year-olds who don't buy income annuities. Carriers have also discovered that the mortality rate for 75-year-old annuity owners is only about 70 percent of the general population's. In other words, for every 100 people who die at age 75 without annuities, only about 70 people who are covered by annuities die. Why the differences in life expectancy? Because unhealthy people don't buy annuities. The tendency for only healthier people to buy annuities is called adverse selection. Insurers know that annuity owners live longer than average, and they mark up the price of annuities accordingly.

My advice? Try to estimate your longevity risk *before* you buy an annuity. People with average life expectancies are at a disadvantage from the get-go and are, therefore, less likely to get their money's worth out of an annuity. But that's not necessarily bad. If you're sure you won't outlive your neighbors, don't bother with an annuity.

Exercise tends to lower blood pressure, and people with normal blood pressure live longer. The landmark Framingham Heart Study (a long-term study, begun in 1948, of the cardiovascular health of 5,209 adult citizens of Framingham, Massachusetts, by Boston-area health professionals) found that people with normal blood pressure:

- ✔ Lived an average of five years longer than people with high blood pressure
- ✔ Delayed the onset of heart disease by 7.2 years
- ✔ Spent two years fewer with heart disease

Note: High blood pressure was defined as systolic pressure higher than 140mm and diastolic pressure higher than 90mm.

Wearing Good Genes

Researchers have found strong evidence that longevity runs in families. Siblings of people who live to age 100 have about half the risk of dying at any age as the average person. Whether the linkage is due to similar environments or similar genetic makeup, no one knows for sure.

At Boston University and elsewhere, researchers continue to search for *longevity* genes — ones that predispose a long life, protect against disease, delay the onset of disease, or increase a person's ability to live with disease. According to one study, the average set of genes prepares a person to live into his late 80s. Unfortunately, harmful lifestyle factors account for the average American's life expectancy of about 10 years less.

Play the longevity game

A number of Web sites offer *wizards* that invite you to calculate your life expectancy by inputting your personal data. In addition to your current age, you may need to provide your cholesterol count, lifestyle habits, and diseases that run in your family. Try one. You may be surprised with your results. Here are three links worth clicking:

✔ *Welcome to The Longevity Game* at www. nmfn.com/tn/learnctr--life events--longevity

✔ *Life Expectancy Calculator* at www.life expectancy.com/asp/Calculator/

✔ *Health Age Questionnaire* at www.exrx. net/Calculators/HealthAge.html

In the following chart, the percentages indicate the relative weight or impact given to each set of factors in determining life expectancy.

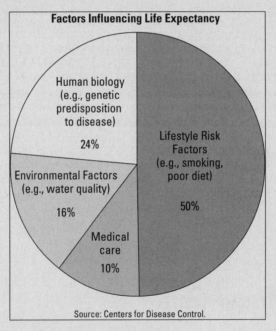

Factors Influencing Life Expectancy

Human biology (e.g., genetic predisposition to disease) 24%

Lifestyle Risk Factors (e.g., smoking, poor diet) 50%

Environmental Factors (e.g., water quality) 16%

Medical care 10%

Source: Centers for Disease Control.

Avoiding Tobacco

If you smoke cigarettes, don't bother buying an annuity. The anti-tobacco organization, Action on Smoking and Health, estimates that a 30-year-old smoker can expect to live only about 35 more years, on average. That's 18 years less than a 30-year-old nonsmoker and barely long enough to retire at all. The jury is still out on the impact of parental smoking on the health of their nonsmoking children. Smoking a pipe and chewing tobacco have been associated with oral cancers.

Several studies have attempted to calculate the life expectancy lost per cigarette. As a result, the recognized estimates include the following:

- ✔ Each cigarette costs 11 minutes of life.
- ✔ Every pack takes an average of 28 minutes off a lifetime.
- ✔ Each carton of cigarettes represents a day and a half of lost life.
- ✔ A pack-a-day smoker shortens his life by an average of two months for every year he smokes.

Staying in School

People with more years of education generally earn higher incomes and tend to live longer than people with less education. According to the National Institutes of Health, 65-year-old men with the least education — reaching the fourth grade at most — live another 14.8 years on average. Men of the same age with some graduate-school training can expect to live more than three years longer than the uneducated men.

In determining longevity, education is a bigger factor than race. A study in North Carolina several years ago showed that, at age 65, regardless of race or sex, people with 12 or more years of education had an active life expectancy between 2.4 and 3.9 years longer than people with less education.

Chapter 21

Ten Web Sources for More Annuity Information

In This Chapter

▶ Finding the top Web sites for annuity education

▶ Identifying Web sites that provide detailed product information

▶ Avoiding Web sites that phish for sales leads

*I*f you Google the keyword *annuities*, you'll net about 14 million Web addresses. In this chapter, I try to save you a bit of legwork by sharing the addresses of a few annuity-related sites that I've found informative, insightful, or just plain interesting.

This list of ten recommended sites should provide you with a few departure points for your own annuity surfing safari. I don't claim this selection to be comprehensive or authoritative, and I don't necessarily endorse the opinions, products, or services they feature.

In compiling this list, I intentionally omitted the sites of well-known corporations like Fidelity, Vanguard, MetLife or The Hartford. You'll understand the promotional material on those sites better after you've read the unbiased, educational material on the sites I mention here.

Annuity Web sites typically fall into one of these categories:

✔ **Manufacturers:** Sites that are sponsored by insurance and financial services companies and intended for use by the public or by annuity salesmen

✔ **Retail:** Sites where individuals can find out about and purchase annuities online

✔ **Industry associations and regulatory agencies:** Sites that offer information and consumer tips to the public

- ✔ **Annuity databases:** Sites that sell detailed annuity contract information to industry professionals

- ✔ **Wholesalers:** Sites where the annuity manufacturers promote their wares to independent advisers, brokers, and agents

As you surf, beware of these common traps and pitfalls. Avoid sites that

- ✔ Ask you to provide your name, address, and phone number on the first page

- ✔ Use domain names that are copycats of the names of good sites and that merely cut and paste information from other sites

- ✔ Use gaudy attention grabbers like blazing patriotic colors, flashing arrows, dancing doodlebugs, and exaggerated claims such as, "14.38 percent guaranteed first year" or "absolutely no market risk"

In my experience, such sites are usually sponsored by someone hawking a product you don't need, such as a bonus annuity or a book that reveals the "truth about annuities" or "the seven secrets of successful investing." If you provide your name and address, you'll soon get a call from an agent or broker. When in doubt, click the About Us button at the top of the home page. It may reveal the site sponsor's identity and motives.

Advantage Compendium

This site, www.indexannuity.org, is hosted by the respected Jack Marrion and his St. Louis-based research firm, Advantage Compendium. It is the acknowledged mother of all equity-indexed annuity (also known as EIAs or indexed annuities) sites. (A former stockbroker, Marrion wrote *Index Annuities - Power & Protection* (Advantage Compendium, 2003.)

His site is full of specific product information collected directly from the insurance companies that issue EIAs. You can look up a company's EIAs and their surrender periods, minimum investments, crediting and adjustment methods, indexes, and other details. The site offers free info on what you need to know most about a product.

Note: The site doesn't promote or sell EIAs, but it also makes no claims of objectivity. For example, in response to one reader's inquiry, Marrion wrote: "Now, I hate to disappoint you, but I am biased. Advantage Compendium doesn't sell any financial products, nor will we endorse or recommend anybody over anybody else, but we are biased. You see I like the index annuity concept. I've done a lot of research on index annuities and I believe they offer a very realistic shot at earning higher yields than you'd get on other instruments that provide the same protection of principal."

Annuity Advantage

Annuity Advantage, www.annuityadvantage.com, is one of the few places you can find the renewal rate histories for fixed annuities. You can simply use its free information or you can buy an annuity over the phone.

Annuity Advantage has splashy, multicolor ads for annuities-of-the-month on its home page. It will also solicit your name and address. But you can easily bypass those seductions by clicking on one of the menu buttons at the top of the page: Fixed Annuities, CD-Type Annuities, and Equity-Indexed Annuities.

When you click on one of these three buttons, you're greeted by long, scrollable lists of specific products and their most important details such as rates and surrender periods.

Click on a specific product name, and you'll find much more nitty-gritty information: the company's rate history, rules regarding penalty-free withdrawals, the states in which it is issued, and other details.

Annuity Advantage was launched in 1999 by Ken Nuss, a Medford, Oregon, insurance man and financial planner. A disclosure on the site claims, "Every annuity offered by the company is filtered, screened, and analyzed for client suitability."

Annuity FYI

Advisers at Burgess Wever, the Portland, Oregon-based company that operates Annuity FYI, www.annuityfyi.com, believe that only 2 percent of the 15,000 annuity products on the market are worth buying. As a result, their site recommends only the fixed, variable, and immediate annuities that meet their high standards. At their site, you can

- Find product recommendations
- Understand annuities better
- Use the toll-free number to speak to someone knowledgeable on annuities
- Buy an annuity over the phone or request a referral for an independent adviser in your area

During my anonymous phone conversations with the site's representatives, I found them to be forthcoming, impartial, and generous with their time. They answered my questions without nudging me toward a transaction. I was even more impressed by the types of annuities they chose *not* to recommend than the types of annuities they recommended.

Note: The site's sponsors are compensated by insurance companies, but Burgess Wever claims its recommendations are customer driven and objective. In any case, you can get a lot of good, free information at this site.

ELM Income Group

The silhouette of a stately elm tree greets visitors on the home page of www.elmannuity.com, where you quickly discover that ELM stands for *Expect to live more.* Two insurance industry veterans, Cliff O'Flinn and Frank Schirripa, developed the site primarily as a place for retirement-plan participants to understand EIAs and single premium immediate annuities (SPIAs) as ways to convert their savings to retirement income. Apparently to avoid confusion with too many options, the site leads readers to only two products: an EIA from Nationwide Financial and a SPIA from Principal Financial.

That limited offering is a weakness of the site, but not a fatal one. The site's real value is the way it unfurls the annuity-purchase story in a logical, non-pushy way, supporting its explanations with strong graphics and providing links to worthwhile research studies about retirement income. At the end of the education process, it directs you to a customer service representative at Nationwide or Principal. After visiting the site, you may be interested in those products, but I recommend you compare them to other products before you buy.

Errold F. Moody

The sponsor of this site, www.efmoody.com/insurance/annuity.html, is Errold F. Moody, an adviser, lecturer, and author of *No Nonsense Finance* (McGraw Hill) in San Leandro, California. He is no fan of annuities; like most financial advisers, he regards them as poor investments and practically discounts their insurance value. But his extensive site — some 4,000 pages — contains thorough, critical analyses of annuity payouts that you're not likely to find anywhere else.

Immediate Annuities

Immediate Annuities, www.immediateannuities.com, sponsored by WebAnnuities, an Englishtown, New Jersey, company owned by Hersh Stern, a former insurance executive, serves much the same purpose and audience as Annuity Advantage (see this section earlier in the chapter). Stern sponsors a family of sites:

✔ **Total Return Annuities** at `www.totalreturnannuities.com`

This site offers quick answers to questions about all types of annuities. You can find information about specific products. The site also provides a calculator for determining how much lifetime income you can generate from a given amount of savings.

✔ **Annuity Shopper** at `www.annuityshopper.com`

View current and back issues of Stern's free, semiannual magazine. It has vast amounts of information, all of it sympathetic to annuities but not noticeably partial to any individual insurance company or product.

✔ **Annuity Museum** at `www.immediateannuities.com/annuity museum/`

This may be the most extensive, if not only, repository of annuity memorabilia on the Internet. For example, at this site you find out that annuities were the only compensation given to Native American tribes for much of their land.

If you want to see fixed annuity rates and SPIA rates for dozens of companies, you can consult current or past issues of the *Comparative Annuity Reports* at `www.immediateannuities.com/comparativeannuityreports/`. Or click on Annuity Shopper Library (`www.immediateannuities.com/content_pages/library.htm`) to find a compendium of articles about annuities, many of them Medicare- and tax-related.

Path to Investing, `www.pathtoinvesting.org`, wants to help you understand annuities *and* the entire world of investing to boot! It was created by the Securities Industry Association (SIA), which became the Securities Industry and Financial Markets Association (SIMFA) in a merger with the Bond Association. (SIMFA distributes *The Stock Market Game,* a board game that teaches students about investments and financial markets.)

There's no selling at this site. It doesn't even recommend products or attempt to harvest your name and address. Instead, the site contains a reasonably comprehensive dictionary of financial terms, calculators, worksheets, and even games. I was particularly impressed with the detailed tutorials about investing by such financial industry experts as Roger Ibbotson, founder of Ibbotson Associates, the financial research and consulting firm that is now part of Morningstar, Inc.

Internal- and Federal-Governing Sites

I include three sites here, one from the industry itself (FINRA) and two federal agencies (the Securities Exchange Commission and the United States Treasury). Both FINRA and the Securities Exchange Commission sites have general investment education, investor warnings, instructions on filing complaints, and information about annuities.

- ✔ **Financial Industry Regulatory Authority (FINRA),** www.finra.org: This site belongs to the securities industry's internal self-policing agency. Prior to June 2007, FINRA was known as the National Association of Securities Dealers, or NASD.

  Choose the Investor Information tab from the main menu across the top of the home page, and then click on Investment Choices at the top of the page for no-nonsense articles about variable and equity-indexed annuities.

- ✔ **Securities and Exchange Commission (SEC),** www.sec.gov: This federal agency regulates the United States' securities markets, including variable annuities.

  On the home page, click For Seniors in the Investor Information section. Then click Products to Know About for links to Variable Annuities and Equity-Indexed Annuities. The links contain sober, unsentimental descriptions of both products and intersperses them with special alerts, hypothetical examples, and links to other sections of the SEC and FINRA site (see the previous bullet).

- ✔ **United States Treasury Department,** www.ustreas.gov: Find out the prevailing interest rates for risk-free government bonds of every available maturity. Then use these rates to measure the value of annuity rates you're offered.

You may wonder whether there's annuity software that streamlines the process of choosing annuities (similar to Turbo Tax or Quicken that streamlines the tax filing process). Not to my knowledge. Most of the current software for comparing, analyzing, and researching annuities has been developed for and marketed to advisers and brokers, not individuals. However, many Web sites have *wizards,* built-in calculators that help you determine how big a premium is necessary to generate a certain amount of monthly income or vice versa. Some wizards even let you choose income annuity options so you can see your monthly income under those options.

If your computer is older or has limited power or if you have a slow dial-up Internet connection, you'll probably find flipping through Web sites or opening large prospectuses to be slow and frustrating. Consider upgrading your computer before you start your search or try one of the terminals at your local public library or university.

Mutual Fund Sites

A firm called Dalbar regularly reviews the Web sites of insurance and financial companies for quality and publishes "top 10" lists on its Web site, `dalbar.com`. Here are some of Dalbar's recent rankings (4th quarter, 2006), starting with the highest:

- T. Rowe Price (`www.troweprice.com`)
- Wells Fargo (`www.wellsfargo.com`)
- Fidelity (`www.fidelity.com`)
- Franklin Templeton (`www.franklintempleton.com`)
- Vanguard (`www.vanguard.com`)
- American Century (`www.americancentury.com`)
- USAA (`www.usaa.com`)
- Mainstay (`www.nylim.com/mainstayfunds`)
- Oppenheimer (`www.oppenheimerfunds.com`)
- E*Trade (`www.etrade.com`)

The top ten insurance company sites, 4th quarter 2006, are

- New York Life (`www.newyorklife.com`)
- Lincoln Life (`www.lfg.com`)
- Northwestern Mutual (`www.nmfn.com`)
- AXA Advisors (`www.axaonline.com`)
- MassMutual (`www.massmutual.com`)
- Fidelity (`www.fidelity.com`)
- Pacific Life (`www.pacificlife.com`)
- TIAA-CREF (`www.tiaa-cref.org`)
- Guardian Investor (`www.guardianinvestor.com`)
- Western Southern (`www.westernsouthern.com`)

Source: `www.dalbar.com`

Trade Association Sites

The following sites are all sponsored by trade associations that directly or indirectly support the insurance and annuity industries:

- ✔ **American Council of Life Insurers, `acli.org`:** To understand annuitization better, download *Managing Money for Life: How Annuitization Works* at `www.acli.org/ACLI/Industry+Products/Annuities/`. On the same page, at left, under Tools, click Publications List. In the index, under "I", you can find a useful downloadable article called, *The Individual Annuity: a Resource in Your Retirement.*

- ✔ **Insurance Information Institute, `www.iii.org`:** In addition to articles on annuity fundamentals, the III's section on Annuities (`www.iii.org/individuals/annuities`) includes two short videos about annuities: *Are You Ready for Retirement?* and *Fixed versus Variable Annuities.*

- ✔ **The National Association for Fixed Annuities (NAFA), `www.nafa.us`:** You can download detailed articles about how equity-indexed annuities work, but most of these articles are for insurance agents.

- ✔ **The Association for Insured Retirement Solutions (NAVA; formerly the National Association of Variable Annuities), `www.navanet.org`:** This site contains a number of educational pamphlets about variable annuities (you may need to pay for some of them), and it publishes an annual *Annuity Fact Book* that provides as much general information about variable annuities as you'll ever need.

- ✔ **The National Retirement Planning Coalition (NRPC), `www.retireon yourterms.org`:** Ben Stein, the actor, economist, and *New York Times* columnist, is the spokesman for this group, which is affiliated with NAVA. In one of three videos available on this site, he explains the role of variable annuities in retirement income planning.

Variable Annuities Knowledge Center (VAKC)

If you're looking for a quiet, tastefully appointed reading room where you can understand the role of variable annuities in a stable retirement income, this is the spot. VAKC, `www.variableannuityfacts.org`, is an educational site with an implicit bias toward variable annuities and no explicit commercial intent. It discusses the risks, benefits, fees, and optional features of variable annuities and offers a primer on finding an adviser.

Most helpful are the hypothetical case studies, which illustrate various strategies without an obvious bias toward any specific course of action. The site is ostensibly sponsored by Smarter Consumer, a not-for-profit group whose advisory board includes Ellie Lowdser, (former director of education at the National Tax-Sheltered Accounts Association) and Cindy Hounsell (an attorney and director of the National Financial Partners' Women's Institute for a Secure Retirement (WISER). The financial sponsor of the site, however, is AXA Equitable, one of the most prominent issuers of variable annuity contracts. Despite this for-profit sponsorship, VAKC is a useful resource.

Appendix A

Key Research Sources

● ●

*I*f you're going to be married for 10, 20, or 30 years, then you'd better choose your partner carefully. That's as true for insurance as it is for affairs of the heart. When you're relying on an annuity for the rest of your life, you want to buy it from a solid company.

Although you have hundreds of life insurance companies to choose from in the United States, you'll probably buy your annuity from one of the two dozen or so mega-carriers that sell most of the annuities every year. It's a concentrated industry and, thanks to corporate mergers, it's getting more so.

This appendix introduces you to a few of the giants of the annuity industry and the sales categories they dominate. Although I can't begin to give detailed contact information about every company in this chapter, I do provide info for the top three companies in each category — a good starting place for your research. I also include information about their products and financial ratings.

Note: This book was written during 2007, and 2006 was the last full year for which data was available from insurance companies. Annual sales figures will therefore be for 2006. Although those figures may be a year old when the book appears, the rankings based on the sales data are likely to remain the same.

Factors to Keep in Mind While Researching

When you're researching an insurance carrier (or mutual fund company in partnership with the carrier), remember these important points:

✔ **In insurance, credit ratings mean everything.** Because the relationships you form with insurance companies can last a couple of decades, you have to be sure of a company's ability to meet its obligations to you now and in the future.

Your best — and only — reliable indications of a company's financial strength are its ratings from the major rating agencies: Moody's, Standard & Poor's, A.M. Best, and Fitch (see Table A-1). Their standards are easy to understand: Look for companies that have all As in their ratings, no Bs, and absolutely no Cs. A+ is better than A-, but as long as you see all As, the company is *strong, very strong, exceptionally strong, superior,* or *exceptional,* depending on the exact lingo of each rating agency.

B-rated companies may tantalize you with better terms (how else can they compete?), but you'll be treading in riskier waters. With so many strong issuers to choose among, don't settle for a company with less than all As. If you have a yen for risk, you shouldn't be shopping for an annuity; you should be out buying stocks.

Table A-1	Three Ratings Agencies and Their Grading Scales	
Moody's	*Standard & Poor's*	*A.M. Best*
Aaa (Exceptional)	AAA (Extremely strong)	A++, A+ (Superior)
Aa1, Aa2, Aa3 (Excellent)	AA+, AA (Very strong)	A, A- (Excellent)
A1, A2, A3 (Good)	AA-, A+, A (Strong)	B++, B+ (Very good)
Baa1, Baa2, Baa3 (Adequate)	A-, BBB+, BBB (Good)	B, B- (Fair)
Ba1, Ba2, Ba3 (Questionable)	BBB-, BB+, BB (Marginal)	C++, C+ (Marginal)

✔ **Hunt for bargains.** Variable annuities have a wide range of insurance costs and investment costs. For example, you may pay less than 1 percent per year in total fees for a deferred annuity but more than 3 percent per year for a variable annuity with living benefit options. On a $100,000 annuity, that 2-percent difference can cost or save you more than $20,000 over ten years.

✔ **Service counts.** Before you choose an annuity issuer, find out whether it has a good reputation for customer services. Go to the Web site; is it easy to use? Call a phone representative; how fast can you reach an operator and how friendly or knowledgeable is the phone rep? Check out the company's *Dalbar* ratings; how good are they? (See the later section of this appendix, "Dalbar Ratings," for more info on this consumer tool.)

Several Web sites can also help you with research. If you'd like more information about variable annuities, you will find sites like AnnuityIQ.com (www.annuityiq.com; see Figure A-1) and the Variable Annuities Knowledge Center (www.variableannuityfacts.org; see Figure A-2) very informative. For fixed annuities, I recommend visiting AnnuityFYI (www.annuityfyi.com; see Figure A-3) for the latest information.

Figure A-1: AnnuityIQ.com offers information on variable annuities and tips on finding an agent.

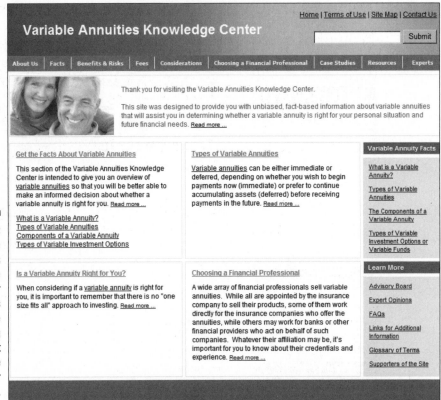

Figure A-2:
The Variable
Annuities
Knowledge
Center
contains
great advice
on picking
out the right
variable
annuity for
you.

Biggest doesn't always mean the best. In theory, a tiny carrier that sells annuities only in Kentucky may be as good as one with offices in New York, Tokyo, and Amsterdam. Whichever you choose, insist on these three qualities: strong financial ratings, low costs, and a record of reliable service.

Variable Annuity Leaders

The number of companies selling deferred variable annuities has been shrinking. That's no mystery. Only the largest companies can afford to keep up with the variable-annuity arms race where insurers are promising ever-more-generous living benefits and lots of mutual fund investment choices.

The trend is for fewer carriers to offer more products. Between 2001 and 2005, the number of unique variable annuities more than doubled (from 523 to 1,008). But during that same period, the number of firms issuing variable annuity contracts dropped from 60 to 45.

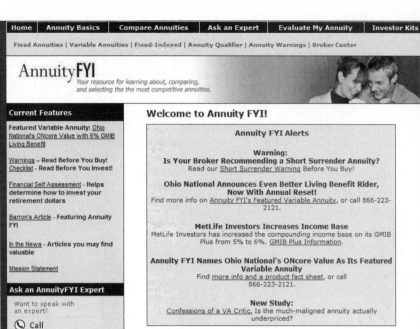

The top ten issuers accounted for 70 percent of all variable-annuities sales in 2006 (See Table A-2; *LIMRA International, 2007*). The top 20 accounted for 92 percent. ***Note:*** The top seller, TIAA-CREF, is a group annuity that's limited to the retirement plans of universities and research institutions.

Table A-2	Variable Annuity Sales Leaders, 2006	
Insurance Carrier	*Best-Selling Variable Annuity*	*2006 Sales (In $ Billions)*
TIAA-CREF	Retirement Annuity	13.87
AXA Equitable	Accumulator Elite 2004	13.48
MetLife	Preference Plus	13.47
Hartford Life	Leaders	12.20
ING	Golden Select Premium Plus	11.54
Lincoln Financial Life	American Legacy III View	10.46
Prudential/ American Skandia/ Allstate	APEX II	9.54
Pacific Life	Innovations Select	9.50
RiverSource Life	Golden Select Premium Plus	9.43
John Hancock	Venture III	9.11

Almost all variable annuities sold in the U.S. in 2006 were issued by 20 carriers, including the 10 companies in the table along with the 10 equally reputable companies listed below:

- ✔ AIG
- ✔ Jackson National Life
- ✔ Allianz Life
- ✔ AEGON USA
- ✔ New York Life
- ✔ Genworth Financial
- ✔ Sun Life of Canada
- ✔ Thrivent Financial for Lutherans
- ✔ Fidelity Investments

The top three sellers of variable annuities in 2006 were AXA-Equitable, Metropolitan Life (MetLife), and Hartford Life. Following are their contact and background information and key features.

AXA Equitable Life Insurance Company

AXA Financial, Inc.

1290 Avenue of the Americas

New York, NY 10104

Phone 212-554-1234

Web site www.axa-equitable.com

Financial ratings: Moody's Aa3; S&P, AA-; A.M. Best A+; Fitch, AA

Background: Known for over a century as The Equitable Life Assurance Society of the United States, this company became AXA Equitable after it merged with the AXA Group, a global company that manages investments worth $1.73 trillion. AXA Financial (the parent of AXA Equitable) also owns Alliance Capital Management, L.P., Sanford C. Bernstein & Co., LLC, MONY Life Insurance Company, U.S. Financial Life Insurance Company, and Advest, Inc.

Key features of its variable annuities: AXA Equitable sells the *Accumulator* series of variable annuities for people saving for retirement and the *Retirement Income for Life* variable annuity for people age 55 or older who want income right away. For instance, if you pay $100,000 for your Retirement Income contract at age 65, you're guaranteed at least $5,000 a year for as long as you live. If you start at age 75, you get at least $6,000 a year for life. Your payments can rise if your investments appreciate, but they can't fall unless you withdraw more than your allotted yearly amount.

Metropolitan Life Insurance Company

200 Park Avenue

New York, NY 10166

Phone 800-MET-LIFE (638-5433)

Web site www.metlife.com

Financial ratings: Moody's, Aa2; S&P, AA; A.M. Best, A+

Background: Metropolitan Life Insurance Company was founded in New York State in 1868. Its corporate parent, MetLife, is consistently among the largest sellers of many kinds of group and individual insurance plans and policies in the United States. It has operations in 15 countries on 5 continents, with 38,000 employees in the United States and 65,500 worldwide.

Key variable annuity features: MetLife's *Preference Plus* variable annuity offers living benefits that protect your investments from losing value while allowing you to benefit from rising stock values. Fees range from 0.25 to 1.5 percent. The Guaranteed Minimum Income Benefit rider, which costs from 0.80 to 1.5 percent, assures you that your original investment will grow by at least 6 percent per year.

Hartford Life Insurance Company

Hartford Plaza, 690 Asylum Avenue

Hartford, CT 06115

Phone 1-860-547-5000

Web site www.hartfordlife.com

Financial ratings: Moody's, Aa3; S&P, AA-; A.M. Best, A+

Background: Hartford Life is one of the patriarchs of the insurance industry, with a history traceable to 1810. The company managed $322 billion in assets as of the end of 2005. It sells annuities through banks, brokerages, and agents; it manages corporate retirement programs; and it's the largest provider of variable annuities in Japan.

Key features of its variable annuities: The Hartford *Leaders* series of variable annuities includes the *Leaders Access* contract, which lets you withdraw 100 percent of your assets at any time without paying a surrender fee for early withdrawal. It has a $10,000 minimum investment (at least $5,000 in each fund you invest in), an annual insurance fee of 1.50 percent, and annual investment management fees of 0.48 percent to 2.76 percent. Hartford variable annuities offer mutual funds from American Funds, Franklin Templeton, MFS, and (in some products) AIM.

Fixed Annuity Leaders

Fixed annuities (including index annuities) resemble certificates of deposits or bond investments, promising a specific annual return over a specific period of time. They are considered insurance products, not securities, and because of that they can be sold by insurance agents and are regulated by state insurance commissions. Table A-3 (*LIMRA International, 2007*) shows the ten top fixed annuity sales leaders with their 2006 sales numbers. *Note:* The sales totals include fixed indexed annuities.

Table A-3	Fixed Annuity Sales Leaders, 2006
Insurance Carrier	*2006 Sales (In Billions)*
AIG	8.83
Allianz Life	6.91
Allstate Financial	6.22
New York Life	5.07
Aviva	3.47
ING	2.85
MetLife	2.83
Old Mutual Financial Network	2.48
Midland National	2.35
Jackson National Life	2.28

In 2006, the 20 largest sellers accounted for 78 percent of the $75.6 billion worth of fixed and indexed annuities sold in the United States in 2006. The next ten largest fixed annuity issuers, all as reputable as the top ten, were, beginning with the largest:

- ✔ Lincoln Financial
- ✔ American Equity Investment Life
- ✔ Hartford Life
- ✔ Genworth Financial
- ✔ Principal Financial
- ✔ Western Southern Group
- ✔ John Hancock
- ✔ AEGON USA
- ✔ Sun Life of Canada
- ✔ Bankers Life & Casualty

The top three sellers of fixed annuities in 2006 were AIG VALIC, Allianz Life Insurance Company of North America, and Allstate Financial. Following are their contact and background information and key features.

AIG VALIC

American International Group, Inc. (AIG)

70 Pine Street

New York, NY 10270

Phone 800-448-2542

Financial ratings: Moody's, Aa1; S&P, AA+; A.M. Best, A+; Fitch, AA+

Background: VALIC (Variable Annuity Life Insurance Company) helped pioneer group variable annuities for employees of education, healthcare, government, the public sector, and other organizations back in the 1950s and 1960s. VALIC was acquired in 2001 by American International Group, Inc. (AIG), a financial conglomerate with activities in 130 countries.

Key fixed annuity features: AIG VALIC's *Portfolio Director* variable annuity offers a feature called IncomeLOCK. For a fee of 0.65 percent per year *and* provided you take no withdrawals for 10 years (20 optionally), your account will be valued at its highest value on any anniversary of the purchase date. After age 65, you can begin receiving a guaranteed 5 percent of that value each year for life.

Allianz Life Insurance Company of North America

P.O. Box 1344

Minneapolis, MN 55416-1297

Phone 800-950-5872

Web site www.allianzlife.com

Financial ratings: Moody's, A2; S&P, AA-; A.M. Best, A

Background: Allianz Life of North America started out as North American Casualty in 1896. In 1979 it was acquired by Germany-based Allianz SE, which was ranked as the 16th largest company in the world by *Forbes* magazine in 2006. For several years, Allianz has produced *MasterDex,* the top-selling index annuity, and sold it through its national network of independent insurance agents.

Key fixed annuity features: Like other equity-index annuities (also called *fixed index* or *index* annuities), Allianz Life's *MasterDex* series offers lower guaranteed returns than standard fixed annuities but provides an opportunity for much higher returns if the stock market goes up. These products have been criticized for their lack of *liquidity* (ability to get your money out), high commissions (up to 9 percent), and complex methods for calculating returns.

Allstate Financial

Lincoln Benefit Life Company

2940 South 84th St.

Lincoln, NE 68506-4142

Phone 800-525-9287

Web site www.allstate.com

Financial ratings: (Allstate Life Insurance) Moody's, Aa2; S&P, AA+; A.M. Best, AA

Background: Allstate annuities are produced and sold by Lincoln Benefit Life Company. The parent company, Allstate Insurance Company, was founded 75 years ago. It describes itself as "the largest publicly held personal lines insurance company in America" and the second largest property and casualty insurance company.

Key fixed annuity features: Allstate offers a *Treasury-Linked* fixed annuity that protects contract holders from the possibility that they will be stuck in a low-interest-bearing annuity when interest rates are rising. Generally, if the interest rate paid by United States Treasury 5-year notes goes up by a certain amount after you buy your contract, Allstate will raise your rate by the same amount.

Direct Sellers

If you're looking for bargains, three mutual fund companies, Vanguard, Fidelity Investments, and T. Rowe Price, sell variable annuities that cost less than many mutual funds. They save money by eliminating brokers or agents and selling direct to the public (by phone, mail, fax, or Internet). Fidelity has its own insurance company, but Vanguard and T. Rowe Price get their annuities from insurance company partners.

You can save tens of thousands of dollars over the long run by shopping at one of these companies. As a result, you don't get the personalized advice that you might get from a broker, and you don't always get the latest product innovations.

Buying annuities direct isn't for everybody (which explains why only about 10 percent of annuities are sold through this channel). You do have to be well informed and somewhat confident to buy direct, but these products rarely have hidden traps. What you see is usually what you get.

Following are the contact and background information and key features of these three mutual fund companies.

The Vanguard Group

Vanguard Annuity and Insurance Services

P.O. Box 1110

Valley Forge, PA 19482-1110

Phone 800-522-5555

Web site www.vanguard.com

Background: Vanguard, which manages about $1 trillion in mutual fund assets, also has a department that sells fixed annuities, variable annuities, and single premium immediate annuities that it obtains from a variety of insurance companies.

Since the mid-1970s, Vanguard has specialized in mutual funds and other products with extremely low costs. The company also manages many corporate 401(k) retirement plans. Unlike most financial services companies, Vanguard is neither publicly nor privately owned; it is run by the board of directors of a consortium of mutual-fund management companies.

Key annuities at Vanguard include the following:

✔ **Vanguard Variable Annuity**

Financial ratings: (People's Benefit Life and Transamerica Financial) Moody's, Aa3; S&P, AA; A.M. Best, A+; Fitch, AA+

Key variable annuity features: If you buy a Vanguard variable annuity, expect low costs and not a lot of options. You can only put your money in 15 selected Vanguard investment portfolios, which, like Vanguard funds, are managed for thrift, consistency, and reliability, not for extraordinary returns.

The mortality and expense risk charge for the Vanguard variable annuity is only 0.20 percent (0.25 or 0.32 percent if you want a death benefit that guarantees a more generous payout to your heirs); investment management fees average well under 1 percent a year.

You can convert the value of the annuity to a retirement income, but Vanguard doesn't offer any of the popular guaranteed living benefits that other variable annuities have. But it also has no front-end loads (sales commissions) or surrender fees for early withdrawal.

✔ **Vanguard Lifetime Income Program**

Financial ratings: (AIG and American International) Moody's, Aa1; S&P, AA+; A.M. Best, A++; Fitch, AA+

Key immediate annuity features: Vanguard's single premium immediate annuity (SPIA) lets you turn a chunk of money into a lifetime of monthly payments. You can receive a fixed monthly income for life, or an income that fluctuates based on the performance of the Vanguard funds you choose, or a combination of the two.

The annuity comes with an optional inflation adjustment to increase your income over time. In return for a smaller income, you are guaranteed that your heirs will receive the unpaid balance if you die before receiving payments that are equal to your initial investment.

✔ **Vanguard Single 5**

Financial ratings: (Jefferson Pilot Life) S&P, AA; A. M. Best, A+; Fitch, AA

Key fixed annuity features: This fixed annuity offers competitive — neither the highest nor the lowest — interest rates. The only term available is five years, and the surrender charge starts at 6 percent the first year and declines to zero after five years. You may withdraw up to 10 percent of your money each year without a penalty. The initial purchase premium is $10,000.

Fidelity Investments

1 Boston Place

Boston, MA 02108

Phone 617-563-7000 or 800-FIDELITY

Web site www.fidelity.com

Financial ratings: (Fidelity Investments Life Insurance) S&P, AA; A.M. Best, A+

Background: Fidelity is the largest investment management company in the United States, managing over $1.5 trillion in individual savings and group retirement plans, serving some 23 million shareholders, and offering about 300 mutual funds. Privately owned and managed by Edward "Ned" Johnson III and his daughter, Abigail, Fidelity is universally known and respected. In contrast to investor-owned companies, Fidelity releases little information about itself.

Key annuities at Fidelity include the following:

✔ **The Fidelity Personal Retirement Annuity**

This deferred variable annuity has an annual insurance fee of only 0.25 percent. It offers no guaranteed minimum death benefit; upon your death, your heirs receive the current value of your investment.

If you don't want to choose investments on your own, you can put yours in a Fidelity *FundsManager* portfolio (a mix of many different Fidelity funds) or an *Investor Freedom* fund, which automatically reduces the risk level of your portfolio as you get older and approach retirement.

✔ **Fidelity Guaranteed Growth and Income**

This product, introduced in October 2007, is Fidelity's first variable annuity with a guaranteed lifetime withdrawal benefit (GWLB). At about 2 percent per year, its costs are lower than most GWLB contracts.

✔ **Fidelity Lifetime Income and Fidelity Income Advantage**

Fidelity offers two immediate variable annuities that provide guaranteed lifetime incomes that fluctuate with the value of your investments in mutual funds:

• The *Fidelity Lifetime Income* annuity aims for simplicity and low cost. It gives you three investment options, allowing you to allocate your money to a fund that's 36-, 50-, or 62-percent invested in domestic stocks. The basic insurance fee is only 0.60 percent per year.

• The *Fidelity Income Advantage* costs a bit more (an annual insurance charge of 1 percent) but offers a wider selection of investments for the retiree who wants to manage his portfolio actively and creatively. The plan has 42 investment choices including mutual funds from Suisse, Lazard Freres, Morgan Stanley, Old Mutual, and Wells Fargo.

✔ **A choice of five different income annuities**

Fidelity also offers immediate fixed income annuities. In fact, it offers five — its own brand and the products of four other insurance companies.

Recognizing that people like choice, Fidelity executives decided to invite John Hancock, The Principal, The Hartford, and ING to sell their fixed annuities alongside the product from Fidelity Investments Life. *Note:* You can't get an immediate variable annuity from those companies through Fidelity.

This *open architecture* approach, pioneered by Hueler Investment Services in 2005 (see Chapter 16), is Fidelity's way of recognizing that people like lots of choices and the ease of one-stop shopping. At the Fidelity Web site, you can get an instant estimate of your future income. For example, for $100,000, a 65-year-old man can receive a guaranteed income of $655 a month for life or for ten years, whichever is longer.

T. Rowe Price

P.O. Box 17300

Baltimore, MD 21297-1300

Phone 800-638-5660

Web site www.troweprice.com

Financial ratings: (Security Benefit Life Insurance) A.M. Best, A

Background: Headquartered in Baltimore, Maryland, T. Rowe Price was founded by its namesake in 1937. According to its Web site, "The T. Rowe Price investment approach strives to achieve superior performance but is always mindful of the risks incurred relative to the potential rewards."

Key variable annuity features: T. Rowe Price offers a basic immediate variable annuity with insurance fees of 0.55 percent per year. But it also offers *Option 9,* which includes living benefits that combine guaranteed minimum lifetime income with access to your money during the first 5 years of the contract and a death benefit for your heirs if you die during the first 15 years of the contract.

Distribution Channel Champs

Certain marketers of fixed annuities dominate particular *distribution channels* (sales settings). At a bank, for instance, AIG annuities are the most common. On the other hand, an independent insurance agent will probably offer you an Allianz product. Table A-4 shows each channel, the issuer of the top fixed annuity, the product name, and its fixed annuity type.

Table A-4	Top Annuity Issuers in Six Distribution Channels		
Distribution Channel	Company Issuing the Top Fixed Annuity	Product	Fixed Annuity Type
Banks and savings & loans	AIG Annuity	Flex (5- or 7-year term)	Book value
Career insurance agents	New York Life	Preferred Fixed	Book value
Independent insurance agents	Allianz Life	MasterDex	Index annuity
Small, independent brokerage firms	John Hancock	GPA Plus	Book value
Regional brokerage firms	Protective Life	ProSave Platinum	Market value-adjusted
National brokerage firms (wirehouses)	The Hartford	CRC	Market value-adjusted

An index annuity offers a guaranteed return plus the potential for greater returns linked to a stock market index. For details, see Chapter 9. A market value adjusted fixed annuity requires contract owners to bear interest rate risk if they end their contract when interest rates rise. For more, see Chapter 6.

Dalbar Ratings

When you want to buy a lawnmower or a camcorder, you can look up the performance ratings of various manufacturers in *Consumer Reports* magazine. With annuities, you have a similar advantage: the Dalbar scores of insurance companies.

Dalbar, Inc., a Boston-based consulting firm, ranks financial service companies on the quality of their customer service. You can check out some of their ratings at www.dalbarinc.com. Following are recent Dalbar rankings of insurance companies' Web sites and their overall service quality.

Top annuity Web sites for consumers

In Dalbar's evaluations, not all Web sites are created equal. Some companies' sites are easier to read, easier to navigate, and better at anticipating where your eyeballs will go next. Table A-5 (*Dalbar, Inc., 2007*) shows the ten annuity sites that Dalbar ranks highest. (The top six have an *excellent* rating and the next four have a *very good* rating.)

Table A-5	Dalbar's Top Ten Annuity Web Sites	
Annuity Issuer	*Dalbar Score Out of 100*	*Company Web Site*
New York Life	88.63	www.newyorklife.com
Lincoln Life	84.66	www.lfg.com
AXA Advisors	83.03	www.axa-equitable.com
Northwestern Mutual	82.31	www.nmfn.com
MassMutual	81.09	www.massmutual.com
Pacific Life	80.50	www.pacificlife.com
Western Southern	79.35	www.westernsouthern.com
TIAA-CREF	79.32	www.tiaa-cref.org
Guardian Investor	79.23	www.guardianinvestor.com
Fidelity	76.79	www.fidelity.com

Top companies for annuity customer service, 2006

Just as some airlines do a better job of making sure your luggage doesn't end up in Seattle when you're flying to Miami, some financial services companies are better at customer service than others. Their phone representatives answer the phone faster, they make fewer mistakes on your contract applications (a common problem in the annuity world), and their literature is easier to understand. ***Note:*** Some of the companies in Table A-6 are mutual fund companies, but the service rating refers to their variable annuity service.

Table A-6	Dalbar's Top Ten Service Providers
Financial Services Company	*Dalbar Score (Out of 100)*
Mainstay Annuities (New York Life)	98.97
New York Life	98.39
Hartford Life	97.55
AEGON/Transamerica	97.04
Putnam Investments	96.30
RiverSource (Ameriprise Financial)	95.79
The Equitable EQUI-VEST	95.41
Guardian Life & Annuity Co.	95.30
Prudential Financial	94.12
Pacific Life	94.07

Income Annuity Leaders

Only a few billion dollars of income annuities (also known as single premium immediate annuities, or SPIAs) are sold in the United States each year — a trifle compared to the $160 billion or so spent on variable annuities.

Even though SPIAs offer a remarkably sensible way to stretch a finite amount of money across an indefinite period of time (a lifetime!), most people resist the idea of exchanging a large portion of their savings for a modest monthly income, even if that income is guaranteed for life. (For more on SPIAs, see Chapter 8.)

But many experts believe (as do I) that increasing numbers of Americans will see the benefits of converting their 401(k) or 403(b) retirement accounts into lifelong incomes, especially when they enter retirement without a traditional pension. The only question is whether insurance companies will be able to offer more attractive income annuity — for instance, one that pays $2,000 instead of $1,600 for a $250,000 premium.

When you shop for an income annuity, you should look for the highest monthly payout from the most financially strong carrier you can find. Strength is especially important, because you'll be relying on that company to provide you with a monthly income for the next 20 to 30 years. All the companies listed below are financially strong. Your challenge will be to find the highest rates.

According to Beacon Research, the income annuity sales leaders in 2006 included:

- ✔ New York Life
- ✔ Genworth Financial
- ✔ AIG American General
- ✔ Protective Life
- ✔ MetLife
- ✔ Old Mutual Financial Network
- ✔ Aviva Life
- ✔ American National Insurance
- ✔ Thrivent Financial for Lutherans
- ✔ Nationwide Financial

Following are the top three, along with their contact and background information, financial ratings, and key policy features.

New York Life Insurance Company

51 Madison Ave.

Suite 3200

New York, NY 10010

Phone 212-576-7000 or 800-710-7945

Web site www.newyorklife.com

Financial ratings: Moody's, Aaa; S&P, AA+; AM Best, A++; Fitch AAA

Background: Founded in 1845, New York Life is one of the few remaining large mutual insurance companies. The company, which manages some $169 billion in assets, still has an army of career agents at a time when many companies have dispensed with the cost of a large sales force.

Key immediate annuity features: New York Life's product includes the *Income Enhancement Option,* which offers an increase in monthly annuity payments if interest rates have risen by at least 2 percent on the fifth anniversary of your purchase date. (The rates are measured by the ten-year Constant Maturity Treasury Index, a United States government yardstick.) The option costs 3.5 percent of the initial investment or premium.

This feature is an enticement for the many people who resist buying an immediate annuity when rates are low, just as they resist buying a mortgage when interest rates are high. The Income Enhancement Option provides an opportunity to refinance the annuity when rates go up, just as a mortgage can be refinanced when rates go down.

Genworth Financial

Genworth Financial, Inc.

6620 W. Broad St.

Richmond, VA 23230

Phone 888-Genworth (436-9678)

Web site www.genworth.com

Financial ratings: (Genworth Life and Annuity Insurance Company) Moody's, Aa3; S&P, AA-; A.M. Best, A+; Fitch, AA-

Background: Genworth traces its roots to 1871 and the Life Insurance Company of Virginia, but before it became a public company in 2004, it was an insurance subsidiary of General Electric Company. It is now one of America's largest insurance companies, with $110 billion in assets and 15 million customers in 25 countries.

Key immediate annuity features: Genworth offers the _SecureLiving Income Provider_ single premium immediate annuity with a minimum purchase amount of $5,000.

If you buy your contract with nonqualified money (not from a tax-deferred retirement plan), you can have the payment increased by as much as 6 percent each year to offset the effects of inflation. (Inflation protection doesn't provide more benefits; you merely receive more of your benefits in the latter years of the contract.)

AIG American General Life

American International Group, Inc.

70 Pine St.

New York, NY 10270

Phone 212-770-3144

Web site www.aigag.com

Financial ratings: Moody's, Aa1; S&P, AA+ ; A.M. Best, A++; Fitch, AA+

Background: American General Life Insurance Company, like its parent company, AIG, has grown through mergers and acquisitions. In 2002 and 2003, All American Life Insurance Company, The American Franklin Life Insurance Company, The Franklin Life Insurance Company, and The Old Line Life Insurance Company were merged into American General.

Key immediate annuity features: American General's *Platinum Income Annuity* offers medical underwriting. Under this option, someone whose life expectancy is reduced by a serious illness such as diabetes, emphysema, or congestive heart failure can receive higher annuity payments than a person of average health.

Appendix B

Protection from Insurer Default

* * *

*B*ankruptcy is a rare event among large insurance companies. When it does occur, it's nice to know that there's a safety net for a bankrupt company's policyholders.

Every state in the Union, along with Puerto Rico and the District of Columbia, has a *guaranty association* that gives you some, all, or most of your money back if the life insurance company that issued your contract goes bankrupt. These associations all belong to the National Organization of Life & Health Guaranty Associations (NOLHGA; www.nolhga.org).

You don't hear much about this service because governments are afraid it will be perceived as a bailout fund for financially weak insurers. Such secrecy is unfortunate. More people might buy immediate annuities if they knew this protection existed.

Because every state regulates the sale of insurance within its borders, each state establishes its own limits on the coverage it extends to annuity owners who are the victims of insurer bankruptcy.

The limits range from $100,000 to as much as $500,000. Some states provide one level of coverage in the *accumulation* stage (still growing) and a higher level in the *income* stage (available only as monthly or quarterly payments).

Here's a list of the benefit limits in all 50 states, plus the District of Columbia and Puerto Rico, as of September 2007:

> Alabama $300,000

The state guaranty association provides $300,000 coverage if the annuity is in payout status. Otherwise, the cash value limit is $100,000.

> Alaska $100,000
> Arizona $100,000
> Arkansas $300,000

California $100,000

Benefits for annuity policies in California are 80 percent of the guaranteed amount, up to $100,000.

Colorado $100,000

Connecticut $500,000

Delaware $100,000

District of Columbia $300,000

Florida $300,000

Georgia $300,000

Hawaii $100,000

Idaho $300,000

Illinois $100,000

Indiana $100,000

Iowa $300,000

Kansas $100,000

Kentucky $100,000

Louisiana $100,000

Maine $100,000

Maryland $100,000

Massachusetts $100,000

Michigan $100,000

Minnesota $120,000

In Minnesota, benefits are indexed to inflation. If the annuity is in payout status, the limit is $360,000.

Mississippi $100,000

Missouri $100,000

Montana $100,000

Nebraska $100,000

Nevada $100,000

New Hampshire	$100,000
New Jersey	$500,000
New Mexico	$300,000
New York	$500,000
North Carolina	$300,000
North Dakota	$100,000
Ohio	$100,000
Oklahoma	$300,000
Oregon	$100,000
Pennsylvania	$300,000
Puerto Rico	$100,000
Rhode Island	$100,000
South Carolina	$300,000
South Dakota	$300,000
Tennessee	$100,000
Texas	$100,000
Utah	$200,000
Vermont	$100,000
Virginia	$100,000
Washington	$500,000
West Virginia	$100,000
Wisconsin	$300,000
Wyoming	$100,000

This list, although believed to be correct as of September 1, 2007, is based on the most current statutory materials available online to NOLHGA and is not intended as legal advice. No liability is assumed in connection with its use. Users should seek advice from a qualified attorney and should not rely on this compilation when considering any questions relating to Guaranty Association coverage. For more information, contact NOLHGA, 13873 Park Center Rd., Suite 329, Herndon, VA 20171.

Appendix C

General Rule for Pensions and Annuities

· ·

*I*RS Publication 939 explains how you can determine the taxable portion of your pension or annuity. I can't present you with the entire publication in this book, because it takes up a total of 81 pages. However, the pages immediately following this one — about 15 total — are a good starting point if you want an understanding of annuity and pension taxes.

The complete document is available at the IRS Web site: www.irs.gov/pub/irs-pdf/p939.pdf. Publication 939 is in Adobe Acrobat PDF (Portable Document Format) form, so you need to install Adobe Acrobat Reader on your computer to use it. You can download the most recent version of Adobe Reader from the following Web site, free of charge: www.adobe.com/products/acrobat/readstep2.html

PAGER/SGML

Userid: _____
Fileid: P939.cvt (14-Apr-2003)
Filename: D:\USERS\RLBake00\documents\Epicfiles\03P939 sgml.sgm

Leading adjust: 0%

☐ Draft ☐ Ok to Print
(Init. & date) _____

Page 1 of 81 of Publication 939

14:39 - 14-APR-2003

The type and rule above prints on all proofs including departmental reproduction proofs. MUST be removed before printing.

Department of the Treasury
Internal Revenue Service

Publication 939
(Rev. April 2003)
Cat. No. 10686K

General Rule for Pensions and Annuities

Get forms and other information faster and easier by:

Computer • www.irs.gov or **FTP** • ftp.irs.gov

FAX • 703-368-9694 (from your FAX machine)

Contents

Introduction

This publication gives you the information you need to determine the tax treatment of your pension and annuity income under the General Rule. Generally, each of your monthly annuity payments is made up of two parts: the tax-free part that is a return of your net cost, and the taxable balance.

What is the General Rule. The General Rule is one of the two methods used to figure the tax-free part of each annuity payment based on the ratio of your investment in the contract to the total expected return. The other method is the Simplified Method, which is discussed in Publication 575, *Pension and Annuity Income*.

Who must use the General Rule. Use this publication if you receive pension or annuity payments from:

1) A **nonqualified plan** (for example, a private annuity, a purchased commercial annuity, or a nonqualified employee plan),

2) A qualified plan **if:**

   a) Your annuity starting date is *before* November 19, 1996 (and after July 1, 1986), and you do not qualify to use, or choose not to use, the Simplified Method, or

   b) You are 75 or over and the annuity payments are guaranteed for at least 5 years (regardless of your annuity starting date).

The following are qualified plans.

- A qualified employee plan.
- A qualified employee annuity.
- A tax-sheltered annuity (TSA) plan or contract.

If you cannot use the General Rule. If your annuity starting date is after November 18, 1996, you must use the Simplified Method for annuity payments from a qualified plan. This method is covered in Publication 575.

If, at the time the annuity payments began, you were at least 75 and were entitled to annuity payments from a qualified plan with fewer than 5 years of guaranteed payments, you must use the Simplified Method.

Topics not covered in this publication. Certain topics related to pensions and annuities are not covered in this publication. They include:

- **Simplified Method.** This method is covered in Publication 575. That publication also covers nonperiodic payments (amounts not received as an annuity) from a qualified pension or annuity plan, rollovers, special averaging and capital gain treatment of lump-sum distributions, and special additional taxes on early distributions, excess distributions, and excess accumulations (not making required minimum distributions).

- **Individual retirement arrangements (IRAs).** Information on the tax treatment of amounts you receive from an IRA is included in Publication 590, *Individual Retirement Arrangements (IRAs)*.

- **Life insurance payments.** If you receive life insurance payments because of the death of the insured person, get Publication 525, *Taxable and Nontaxable Income*, for information on the tax treatment of the proceeds.

Help from IRS. If, after reading this publication, you need help to figure the taxable part of your pension or annuity, the IRS can do it for you for a fee. For information on this service, see *Requesting a Ruling on Taxation of Annuity*, later.

Comments and suggestions. We welcome your comments about this publication and your suggestions for future editions.

You can e-mail us while visiting our web site at **www.irs.gov.**

You can write to us at the following address:

Internal Revenue Service
Individual Forms and Publications Branch
W:CAR:MP:T:I
1111 Constitution Ave. NW
Washington, DC 20224

We respond to many letters by telephone. Therefore, it would be helpful if you would include your daytime phone number, including the area code, in your correspondence.

Useful Items
You may want to see:

Publication

❏ **524** Credit for the Elderly or the Disabled

❏ **525** Taxable and Nontaxable Income

❏ **571** Tax-Sheltered Annuity Plans (403(b) Plans)

❏ **575** Pension and Annuity Income

❏ **590** Individual Retirement Arrangements (IRAs)

❏ **721** Tax Guide to U.S. Civil Service Retirement Benefits

❏ **910** Guide To Free Tax Services

Form (and Instructions)

❏ **1099-R** Distributions From Pensions, Annuities, Retirement or Profit-Sharing Plans, IRAs, Insurance Contracts, etc.

See *How To Get Tax Help*, near the end of this publication for information about getting these publications and forms.

General Information

Some of the terms used in this publication are defined in the following paragraphs.

- A **pension** is generally a series of payments made to you after you retire from work. Pension payments are made regularly and are for past services with an employer.

- An **annuity** is a series of payments under a contract. You can buy the contract alone or you can buy it with the help of your employer. Annuity payments are made regularly for more than one full year.

Types of pensions and annuities. Particular types of pensions and annuities include:

1) **Fixed period annuities.** You receive definite amounts at regular intervals for a definite length of time.

2) **Annuities for a single life.** You receive definite amounts at regular intervals for life. The payments end at death.

3) **Joint and survivor annuities.** The first annuitant receives a definite amount at regular intervals for life. After he or she dies, a second annuitant receives a definite amount at regular intervals for life. The amount paid to the second annuitant may or may not differ from the amount paid to the first annuitant.

4) **Variable annuities.** You receive payments that may vary in amount for a definite length of time or for life. The amounts you receive may depend upon such variables as profits earned by the pension or annuity funds or cost-of-living indexes.

5) **Disability pensions.** You are under minimum retirement age and receive payments because you retired on disability. If, at the time of your retirement, you were permanently and totally disabled, you may be

eligible for the credit for the elderly or the disabled discussed in Publication 524.

If your annuity starting date is after November 18, 1996, **the General Rule cannot be used** for the following qualified plans.

- A **qualified employee plan** is an employer's stock bonus, pension, or profit-sharing plan that is for the exclusive benefit of employees or their beneficiaries. This plan must meet Internal Revenue Code requirements. It qualifies for special tax benefits, including tax deferral for employer contributions and rollover distributions.

- A **qualified employee annuity** is a retirement annuity purchased by an employer for an employee under a plan that meets Internal Revenue Code requirements.

- A **tax-sheltered annuity** is a special annuity plan or contract purchased for an employee of a public school or tax-exempt organization.

The General Rule is used to figure the tax treatment of various types of pensions and annuities, including nonqualified employee plans. A **nonqualified employee plan** is an employer's plan that does not meet Internal Revenue Code requirements. It does not qualify for most of the tax benefits of a qualified plan.

Annuity worksheets. The worksheets found near the end of the text of this publication may be useful to you in figuring the taxable part of your annuity.

Request for a ruling. If you are unable to determine the income tax treatment of your pension or annuity, you may ask the Internal Revenue Service to figure the taxable part of your annuity payments. This is treated as a request for a ruling. See *Requesting a Ruling on Taxation of Annuity* near the end of this publication.

Withholding tax and estimated tax. Your pension or annuity is subject to federal income tax withholding unless you choose not to have tax withheld. If you choose not to have tax withheld from your pension or annuity, or if you do not have enough income tax withheld, you may have to make estimated tax payments.

Taxation of Periodic Payments

This section explains how the periodic payments you receive under a pension or annuity plan are taxed under the General Rule. Periodic payments are amounts paid at regular intervals (such as weekly, monthly, or yearly) for a period of time greater than one year (such as for 15 years or for life). These payments are also known as *amounts received as an annuity.*

 *If you receive an amount from your plan that is a **nonperiodic payment** (amount not received as an annuity), see Taxation of Nonperiodic Payments in Publication 575.*

In general, you can recover your net cost of the pension or annuity tax free over the period you are to receive the payments. The amount of each payment that is more than the part that represents your net cost is taxable. Under the General Rule, the part of each annuity payment that represents your net cost is in the same proportion that your investment in the contract is to your expected return. These terms are explained in the following discussions.

Investment in the Contract

In figuring how much of your pension or annuity is taxable under the General Rule, you must figure your investment in the contract.

First, find your *net cost* of the contract as of the annuity starting date (defined later). To find this amount, you must first figure the total premiums, contributions, or other amounts paid. This includes the amounts your employer contributed if you were required to include these amounts in income. It also includes amounts you actually contributed (except amounts for health and accident benefits and deductible voluntary employee contributions).

From this **total cost** you subtract:

1) Any refunded premiums, rebates, dividends, or unrepaid loans (any of which were not included in your income) that you received by the later of the annuity starting date or the date on which you received your first payment.

2) Any additional premiums paid for double indemnity or disability benefits.

3) Any other tax-free amounts you received under the contract or plan before the later of the dates in (1).

The annuity starting date is the later of the first day of the first period for which you receive payment under the contract or the date on which the obligation under the contract becomes fixed.

Example. On January 1 you completed all your payments required under an annuity contract providing for monthly payments starting on August 1, for the period beginning July 1. The annuity starting date is July 1. This is the date you use in figuring your investment in the contract and your expected return (discussed later).

Adjustments

If any of the following items apply, adjust (add or subtract) your total cost to find your net cost.

Foreign employment. If you worked abroad, your cost includes amounts contributed by your employer that were not includible in your gross income. The contributions that apply were made either:

1) Before 1963 by your employer for that work, or

2) After 1962 by your employer for that work if you performed the services under a plan that existed on March 12, 1962.

The type and rule above prints on all proofs including departmental reproduction proofs. MUST be removed before printing.

Death benefit exclusion. If you are the *beneficiary* of a deceased employee (or former employee), who died *before* August 21, 1996, you may qualify for a death benefit exclusion of up to $5,000. The beneficiary of a deceased employee who died after August 20, 1996, will not qualify for the death benefit exclusion.

How to adjust your total cost. If you are eligible, treat the amount of any allowable death benefit exclusion as additional cost paid by the employee. Add it to the cost or unrecovered cost of the annuity at the annuity starting date. See *Example 3* under *Computation Under General Rule* for an illustration of the adjustment to the cost of the contract.

Free IRS help. If you are eligible for this exclusion and need help computing the amount of the death benefit exclusion, see *Requesting a Ruling on Taxation of Annuity*, near the end of this publication.

Net cost. Your total cost plus certain adjustments and minus other amounts already recovered before the annuity starting date is your net cost. This is the unrecovered investment in the contract as of the annuity starting date. If your annuity starting date is after 1986, this is the maximum amount that you may recover tax free under the contract.

Refund feature. Adjustment for the value of the refund feature is only applicable when you report your pension or annuity under the General Rule. Your annuity contract has a refund feature if:

1) The expected return (discussed later) of an annuity depends entirely or partly on the life of one or more individuals,

2) The contract provides that payments will be made to a beneficiary or the estate of an annuitant on or after the death of the annuitant if a stated amount or a stated number of payments has not been paid to the annuitant or annuitants before death, and

3) The payments are a refund of the amount you paid for the annuity contract.

If your annuity has a refund feature, you must reduce your net cost of the contract by the value of the refund feature (figured using Table III or VII at the end of this publication, also see *How To Use Actuarial Tables*, later) to find the investment in the contract.

Zero value of refund feature. For a joint and survivor annuity, the value of the refund feature is *zero* if:

1) Both annuitants are age 74 or younger,

2) The payments are guaranteed for less than 2½ years, *and*

3) The survivor's annuity is at least 50% of the first annuitant's annuity.

For a single-life annuity without survivor benefit, the value of the refund feature is *zero* if:

1) The payments are guaranteed for less than 2½ years, *and*

2) The annuitant is:

   a) Age 57 or younger (if using the new (unisex) annuity tables).

   b) Age 42 or younger (if male and using the old annuity tables), or

   c) Age 47 or younger (if female and using the old annuity tables).

If you do not meet these requirements, you will have to figure the value of the refund feature, as explained in the following discussion.

Examples. The first example shows how to figure the value of the refund feature when there is only one beneficiary. Example 2 shows how to figure the value of the refund feature when the contract provides, in addition to a whole life annuity, one or more temporary life annuities for the lives of children. In both examples, the taxpayer elects to use Tables V through VIII. If you need the value of the refund feature for a joint and survivor annuity, write to the Internal Revenue Service as explained under *Requesting a Ruling on Taxation of Annuity*, near the end of this publication.

Example 1. At age 65, Barbara bought for $21,053 an annuity with a refund feature. She will get $100 a month for life. Barbara's contract provides that if she does not live long enough to recover the full $21,053, similar payments will be made to her surviving beneficiary until a total of $21,053 has been paid under the contract. In this case, the contract cost and the total guaranteed return are the same ($21,053). Barbara's investment in the contract is figured as follows:

Net cost	$21,053
Amount to be received annually $1,200	
Number of years for which payment is guaranteed	
($21,053 divided by $1,200) 17.54	
Rounded to nearest whole number of years 18	
Percentage from Actuarial Table VII for age 65 with	
18 years of guaranteed payments 15%	
Value of the refund feature (rounded to the nearest dollar)—	
15% of $21,053	3,158
Investment in the contract, adjusted for value of refund	
feature	**$17,895**

If the total guaranteed return were less than the $21,053 net cost of the contract, Barbara would apply the appropriate percentage from the tables to the lesser amount. For example, if the contract guaranteed the $100 monthly payments for 17 years to Barbara's estate or beneficiary if she were to die before receiving all the payments for that period, the total guaranteed return would be $20,400 ($100 × 12 × 17 years). In this case, the value of the refund feature would be $2,856 (14% of $20,400) and Barbara's investment in the contract would be $18,197 ($21,053 minus $2,856) instead of $17,895.

The type and rule above prints on all proofs including departmental reproduction proofs. MUST be removed before printing.

Example 2. John died while still employed. His widow, Eleanor, age 48, receives $171 a month for the rest of her life. John's son, Elmer, age 9, receives $50 a month until he reaches age 18. John's contributions to the retirement fund totaled $7,559.45, with interest on those contributions of $1,602.53. The guarantee or total refund feature of the contract is $9,161.98 ($7,559.45 plus $1,602.53).

The adjustment in the investment in the contract is figured as follows:

A) Expected return:*
  1) Widow's expected return:
    Annual annuity ($171 × 12) $2,052
    Multiplied by factor from Table V
    (nearest age 48) 34.9 $71,614.80
  2) Child's expected return:
    Annual annuity ($50 × 12) $600
    Multiplied by factor from
    Table VIII (nearest age 9
    for term of 9 years) 9.0 5,400.00
  3) Total expected return $77,014.80

B) Adjustment for refund feature:
  1) Contributions (net cost) $7,559.45
  2) Guaranteed amount (contributions of $7,559.45 plus
    interest of $1,602.53) $9,161.98
  3) Minus: Expected return under child's (temporary life)
    annuity (A(2)) 5,400.00
  4) Net guaranteed amount $3,761.98
  5) Multiple from Table VII (nearest age 48 for 2 years
    duration (recovery of $3,761.98 at $171 a month to
    nearest whole year)) 0%
  6) Adjustment required for value of refund feature
    rounded to the nearest whole dollar
    (0% × $3,761.98, the smaller of B(3) or B(6)) 0

*Expected return is the total amount you and other eligible annuitants can expect to receive under the contract. See the discussion of expected return, later in this publication.

Free IRS help. If you need to request assistance to figure the value of the refund feature, see *Requesting a Ruling on Taxation of Annuity,* near the end of this publication.

Expected Return

Your expected return is the total amount you and other eligible annuitants can expect to receive under the contract. The following discussions explain how to figure the expected return with each type of annuity.

 A person's age, for purposes of figuring the expected return, is the age at the birthday nearest to the annuity starting date.

Fixed period annuity. If you will get annuity payments for a fixed number of years, without regard to your life expectancy, you must figure your expected return based on that fixed number of years. It is the total amount you will get beginning at the annuity starting date. You will receive specific periodic payments for a definite period of time, such as a fixed number of months (but not less than 13). To figure your expected return, multiply the fixed number of months for which payments are to be made by the amount of the payment specified for each period.

Single life annuity. If you are to get annuity payments for the rest of your life, find your expected return as follows.

You must multiply the amount of the annual payment by a multiple based on your life expectancy as of the annuity starting date. These multiples are set out in actuarial Tables I and V near the end of this publication (see *How To Use Actuarial Tables,* later).

You may need to adjust these multiples if the payments are made quarterly, semiannually, or annually. See *Adjustments to Tables I, II, V, VI, and VIA* following Table I.

Example. Henry bought an annuity contract that will give him an annuity of $500 a month for his life. If at the annuity starting date Henry's nearest birthday is 66, the expected return is figured as follows:

Annual payment ($500 × 12 months) $6,000
Multiple shown in Table V, age 66 . . . . × 19.2
Expected return $115,200

If the payments were to be made to Henry quarterly and the first payment was made one full month after the annuity starting date, Henry would adjust the 19.2 multiple by +.1. His expected return would then be $115,800 ($6,000 × 19.3).

Annuity for shorter of life or specified period. With this type of annuity, you are to get annuity payments either for the rest of your life **or** until the end of a specified period, whichever period is shorter. To figure your expected return, multiply the amount of your annual payment by a multiple in Table IV or VIII for temporary life annuities. Find the proper multiple based on your sex (if using Table IV), your age at the annuity starting date, and the nearest whole number of years in the specified period.

Example. Harriet purchased an annuity this year that will pay her $200 each month for five years or until she dies, whichever period is shorter. She was age 65 at her birthday nearest the annuity starting date. She figures the expected return as follows:

Annual payment ($200 × 12 months) $2,400
Multiple shown in Table VIII, age 65, 5-year term . . . . × 4.9
Expected return $11,760

 She uses Table VIII (not Table IV) because all her contributions were made after June 30, 1986. See Special Elections, later.

Joint and survivor annuities. If you have an annuity that pays you a periodic income for life and after your death provides an *identical* lifetime periodic income to your spouse (or some other person), you figure the expected return based on your combined life expectancies. To figure the expected return, multiply the annual payment by a multiple in Table II or VI based on your joint life expectancies. If your payments are made quarterly, semiannually, or annually, you may need to adjust these multiples. See *Adjustments to Tables I, II, V, VI, and VIA* following Table I near the end of this publication.

Example. John bought a joint and survivor annuity providing payments of $500 a month for his life, and, after his death, $500 a month for the remainder of his wife's life. At John's annuity starting date, his age at his nearest birthday

The type and rule above prints on all proofs including departmental reproduction proofs. MUST be removed before printing.

is 70 and his wife's at her nearest birthday is 67. The expected return is figured as follows:

Annual payment ($500 × 12 months)	$6,000
Multiple shown in Table VI, ages 67 and 70	× 22.0
Expected return	$132,000

Different payments to survivor. If your contract provides that payments to a survivor annuitant will be *different* from the amount you receive, you must use a computation which accounts for both the joint lives of the annuitants and the life of the survivor.

Example 1. Gerald bought a contract providing for payments to him of $500 a month for life and, after his death, payments to his wife, Mary, of $350 a month for life. If, at the annuity starting date, Gerald's nearest birthday is 70 and Mary's is 67, the expected return under the contract is figured as follows:

Combined multiple for Gerald and Mary, ages 70 and 67 (from Table VI)		22.0
Multiple for Gerald, age 70 (from Table V)		16.0
Difference: Multiple applicable to Mary		6.0
Gerald's annual payment ($500 × 12)	$6,000	
Gerald's multiple	16.0	
Gerald's expected return		$96,000
Mary's annual payment ($350 × 12)	$4,200	
Mary's multiple	6.0	
Mary's expected return		25,200
Total expected return under the contract		$121,200

Example 2. Your husband died while still employed. Under the terms of his employer's retirement plan, you are entitled to get an immediate annuity of $400 a month for the rest of your life or until you remarry. Your daughters, Marie and Jean, are each entitled to immediate temporary life annuities of $150 a month until they reach age 18.

You were 50 years old at the annuity starting date. Marie was 16 and Jean was 14. Using the multiples shown in Tables V and VIII at the end of this publication, the total expected return on the annuity starting date is $169,680, figured as follows:

Widow, age 50 (multiple from Table V—33.1 × $4,800 annual payment)	$158,880
Marie, age 16 for 2 years duration (multiple from Table VIII—2.0 × $1,800 annual payment)	3,600
Jean, age 14 for 4 years duration (multiple from Table VIII—4.0 × $1,800 annual payment)	7,200
Total expected return	$169,680

No computation of expected return is made based on your husband's age at the date of death because he died before the annuity starting date.

Computation Under the General Rule

Under the General Rule, you figure the taxable part of your annuity by using the following steps:

Step 1. Figure the amount of your investment in the contract, including any adjustments for the refund feature and the death benefit exclusion, if applicable. See *Death benefit exclusion,* earlier.

Step 2. Figure your expected return.

Step 3. Divide Step 1 by Step 2 and round to three decimal places. This will give you the *exclusion percentage.*

Step 4. Multiply the *exclusion percentage* by the first regular periodic payment. The result is the tax-free part of each pension or annuity payment.

The tax-free part remains the same even if the total payment increases or you outlive the life expectancy factor used. If your annuity starting date is after 1986, the total amount of annuity income that is tax free over the years cannot exceed your net cost.

Each annuitant applies the same exclusion percentage to his or her initial payment called for in the contract.

Step 5. Multiply the tax-free part of each payment (step 4) by the number of payments received during the year. This will give you the tax-free part of the total payment for the year.

 In the first year of your annuity, your first payment or part of your first payment may be for a fraction of the payment period. This fractional amount is multiplied by your exclusion percentage to get the tax-free part.

Step 6. Subtract the tax-free part from the total payment you received. The rest is the taxable part of your pension or annuity.

Example 1. You purchased an annuity with an investment in the contract of $10,800. Under its terms, the annuity will pay you $100 a month for life. The multiple for your age (age 65) is 20.0 as shown in Table V. Your expected return is $24,000 (20 × 12 × $100). Your cost of $10,800, divided by your expected return of $24,000, equals 45.0%. This is the percentage you will not have to include in income.

Each year, until your net cost is recovered, $540 (45% of $1,200) will be tax free and you will include $660 ($1,200 − $540) in your income. If you had received only six payments of $100 ($600) during the year, your exclusion would have been $270 (45% of $100 × 6 payments).

Example 2. Gerald bought a joint and survivor annuity. Gerald's investment in the contract is $62,712 and the expected return is $121,200. The exclusion percentage is 51.7% ($62,712 ÷ $121,200). Gerald will receive $500 a month ($6,000 a year). Each year, until his net cost is recovered, $3,102 (51.7% of his total payments received of $6,000) will be tax free and $2,898 ($6,000 − $3,102) will be included in his income. If Gerald dies, his wife will receive $350 a month ($4,200 a year). If Gerald had not recovered all of his net cost before his death, his wife will use the same exclusion percentage (51.7%). Each year, until the entire net cost is recovered, his wife will receive $2,171.40 (51.7% of her payments received of $4,200) tax free. She will include $2,028.60 ($4,200 − $2,171.40) in her income tax return.

Example 3. Using the same facts as Example 2 under *Different payments to survivor,* you are to receive an an-

The type and rule above prints on all proofs including departmental reproduction proofs. MUST be removed before printing.

nual annuity of $4,800 until you die or remarry. Your two daughters each receive annual annuities of $1,800 until they reach age 18. Your husband contributed $25,576 to the plan. You are eligible for the $5,000 death benefit exclusion because your husband died before August 21, 1996.

Adjusted Investment in the Contract

Contributions	$25,576
Plus: Death benefit exclusion	5,000
Adjusted investment in the contract	$30,576

The total expected return, as previously figured (in Example 2 under *Different payments to survivor),* is $169,680. The exclusion percentage of 18.0% ($30,576 ÷ $169,680) applies to the annuity payments you and each of your daughters receive. Each full year $864 (18.0% × $4,800) will be tax free to you, and you must include $3,936 in your income tax return. Each year, until age 18, $324 (18.0% × $1,800) of each of your daughters' payments will be tax free and each must include the balance, $1,476, as income on her own income tax return.

Part-year payments. If you receive payments for only part of a year, apply the exclusion percentage to the first regular periodic payment, and multiply the result by the number of payments received during the year. If you received a fractional payment, follow Step 5, discussed earlier. This gives you the tax-free part of your total payment.

Example. On September 28, Mary bought an annuity contract for $22,050 that will give her $125 a month for life, beginning October 30. The applicable multiple from Table V is 23.3 (age 61). Her expected return is $34,950 ($125 × 12 × 23.3). Mary's investment in the contract of $22,050, divided by her expected return of $34,950, equals 63.1%. Each payment received will consist of 63.1% return of cost and 36.9% taxable income, until her net cost of the contract is fully recovered. During the first year, Mary received three payments of $125, or $375, of which $236.63 (63.1% × $375) is a return of cost. The remaining $138.37 is included in income.

Increase in annuity payments. The tax-free amount remains the same as the amount figured at the annuity starting date, even if the payment increases. All increases in the installment payments are fully taxable.

Example. Joe's wife died while she was still employed and, as her beneficiary, he began receiving an annuity of $147 per month. In figuring the taxable part, Joe elects to use Tables V through VIII. The cost of the contract was $7,938, consisting of the sum of his wife's net contributions, adjusted for any refund feature. His expected return as of the annuity starting date is $35,280 (age 65, multiple of 20.0 × $1,764 annual payment). The exclusion percentage is $7,938 ÷ $35,280, or 22.5%. During the year he received 11 monthly payments of $147, or $1,617. Of this amount, 22.5% × $147 × 11 ($363.83) is tax free as a return of cost and the balance of $1,253.17 is taxable.

Later, because of a cost-of-living increase, his annuity payment was increased to $166 per month, or $1,992 a year (12 × $166). The tax-free part is still only 22.5% of the annuity payments as of the annuity starting date (22.5% × $147 × 12 = $396.90 for a full year). The increase of $228 ($1,992 – $1,764 (12 × $147)) is fully taxable.

Variable annuities. For variable annuity payments, figure the amount of each payment that is tax free by dividing your investment in the contract (adjusted for any refund feature) by the total number of periodic payments you expect to get under the contract.

If the annuity is for a definite period, you determine the total number of payments by multiplying the number of payments to be made each year by the number of years you will receive payments. If the annuity is for life, you determine the total number of payments by using a multiple from the appropriate actuarial table.

Example. Frank purchased a variable annuity at age 65. The total cost of the contract was $12,000. The annuity starting date is January 1 of the year of purchase. His annuity will be paid, starting July 1, in variable annual installments for his life. The tax-free amount of each payment, until he has recovered his cost of his contract, is:

Investment in the contract	$12,000
Number of expected annual payments (multiple for age 65 from Table V)	20
Tax-free amount of each payment ($12,000 ÷ 20)	$600

If Frank's first payment is $920, he includes only $320 ($920 – $600) in his gross income.

If the *tax-free amount for a year is more than the payments you receive* in that year, you may choose, when you receive the next payment, to refigure the tax-free part. Divide the amount of the periodic tax-free part that is more than the payment you received by the remaining number of payments you expect. The result is added to the previously figured periodic tax-free part. The sum is the amount of each future payment that will be tax free.

Example. Using the facts of the previous example about Frank, assume that after Frank's $920 payment, he received $500 in the following year, and $1,200 in the year after that. Frank does not pay tax on the $500 (second year) payment because $600 of each annual pension payment is tax free. Since the $500 payment is less than the $600 annual tax-free amount, he may choose to refigure his tax-free part when he receives his $1,200 (third year) payment, as follows:

Amount tax free in second year	$600.00
Amount received in second year	500.00
Difference	$100.00
Number of remaining payments after the first 2 payments (age 67, from Table V)	18.4
Amount to be added to previously determined annual tax-free part ($100 ÷ 18.4)	$5.43
Revised annual tax-free part for third and later years ($600 + $5.43)	$605.43
Amount taxable in third year ($1,200 – $605.43)	$594.57

If you choose to refigure your tax-free amount, you must file a statement with your income tax return stating that you are refiguring the tax-free amount in accordance with the rules of section 1.72–4(d)(3) of the Income Tax Regulations. The statement must also show the following information:

The type and rule above prints on all proofs including departmental reproduction proofs. MUST be removed before printing.

1) The annuity starting date and your age on that date.

2) The first day of the first period for which you received an annuity payment in the current year.

3) Your investment in the contract as originally figured.

4) The total of all amounts received tax free under the annuity from the annuity starting date through the first day of the first period for which you received an annuity payment in the current tax year.

Exclusion Limits

Your annuity starting date determines the total amount of annuity income that you can exclude from income over the years.

Exclusion limited to net cost. If your annuity starting date is after 1986, the total amount of annuity income that you can exclude over the years as a return of your cost cannot exceed your net cost (figured without any reduction for a refund feature). This is the **unrecovered investment in the contract** as of the annuity starting date.

If your annuity starting date is after July 1, 1986, any unrecovered net cost at your (or last annuitant's) death is allowed as a miscellaneous itemized deduction on the final return of the decedent. This deduction is not subject to the 2%-of-adjusted-gross-income limit.

Example 1. Your annuity starting date is after 1986. Your total cost is $12,500, and your net cost is $10,000, taking into account certain adjustments. There is no refund feature. Your monthly annuity payment is $833.33. Your exclusion ratio is 12% and you exclude $100 a month. Your exclusion ends after 100 months, when you have excluded your net cost of $10,000. Thereafter, your annuity payments are fully taxable.

Example 2. The facts are the same as in Example 1, except that there is a refund feature, and you die after 5 years with no surviving annuitant. The adjustment for the refund feature is $1,000, so the investment in the contract is $9,000. The exclusion ratio is 10.8%, and your monthly exclusion is $90. After 5 years (60 months), you have recovered tax free only $5,400 ($90 x 60). An itemized deduction for the unrecovered net cost of $4,600 ($10,000 net cost minus $5,400) may be taken on your final income tax return. Your unrecovered investment is determined without regard to the refund feature adjustment, discussed earlier, under *Adjustments.*

Exclusion not limited to net cost. If your annuity starting date was before 1987, you could continue to take your monthly exclusion for as long as you receive your annuity. If you choose a joint and survivor annuity, your survivor continues to take the survivor's exclusion figured as of the annuity starting date. The total exclusion may be more than your investment in the contract.

How To Use Actuarial Tables

In figuring, under the General Rule, the taxable part of your annuity payments that you are to get for the rest of your life (rather than for a fixed number of years), you must use one or more of the actuarial tables in this publication.

Unisex Annuity Tables

Effective July 1, 1986, the Internal Revenue Service adopted new annuity Tables V through VIII, in which your sex is not considered when determining the applicable factor. These tables correspond to the old Tables I through IV. In general, Tables V through VIII must be used if you made contributions to the retirement plan after June 30, 1986. If you made no contributions to the plan after June 30, 1986, generally you must use only Tables I through IV. However, if you received an annuity payment after June 30, 1986, you may elect to use Tables V through VIII (see *Annuity received after June 30, 1986,* later).

Special Elections

Although you generally must use Tables V through VIII if you made contributions to the retirement plan after June 30, 1986, and Tables I through IV if you made no contributions after June 30, 1986, you can make the following special elections to select which tables to use.

Contributions made both before July 1986 and after June 1986. If you made contributions to the retirement plan both before July 1986 and after June 1986, you may elect to use Tables I through IV for the pre-July 1986 cost of the contract, and Tables V through VIII for the post-June 1986 cost. (See the examples below.)

Making the election. Attach this statement to your income tax return for the first year in which you receive an annuity:

"I elect to apply the provisions of paragraph (d) of section 1.72–6 of the Income Tax Regulations."

The statement must also include your name, address, social security number, and the amount of the pre-July 1986 investment in the contract.

If your investment in the contract includes post-June 1986 contributions to the plan, and you do not make the election to use Tables I through IV and Tables V through VIII, then you can only use Tables V through VIII in figuring the taxable part of your annuity. You must also use Tables V through VIII if you are unable or do not wish to determine the portions of your contributions which were made before July 1, 1986, and after June 30, 1986.

Advantages of election. In general, a lesser amount of each annual annuity payment is taxable if you separately figure your exclusion ratio for pre-July 1986 and post-June 1986 contributions.

TIP *If you intend to make this election, save your records that substantiate your pre-July 1986 and post-June 1986 contributions. If the death benefit exclusion applies (see discussion, earlier), you do not have* *to apportion it between the pre-July 1986 and the post-June 1986 investment in the contract.*

The following examples illustrate the separate computations required if you elect to use Tables I through IV for your pre-July 1986 investment in the contract and Tables V through VIII for your post-June 1986 investment in the contract.

Example 1. Bill, who is single, contributed $42,000 to the retirement plan and will receive an annual annuity of $24,000 for life. Payment of the $42,000 contribution is guaranteed under a refund feature. Bill is 55 years old as of the annuity starting date. For figuring the taxable part of Bill's annuity, he chose to make separate computations for his pre-July 1986 investment in the contract of $41,300, and for his post-June 1986 investment in the contract of $700.

	Pre-July 1986	Post-June 1986
A. Adjustment for refund feature		
1) Net cost	$41,300	$700
2) Annual annuity—$24,000		
($41,300/$42,000 × $24,000)	$23,600	
($700/$42,000 × $24,000)		$400
3) Guarantee under contract	$41,300	$700
4) No. of years payments guaranteed (rounded), A(3) ÷ A(2)	2	2
5) Applicable percentage from Tables III and VII	1%	0%
6) Adjustment for value of refund feature, A(5) × smaller of A(1) or A(3)	$413	$0
B. Investment in the contract		
1) Net cost	$41,300	$700
2) Minus: Amount in A(6)	413	0
3) Investment in the contract	$40,887	$700
C. Expected return		
1) Annual annuity receivable	$24,000	$24,000
2) Multiples from Tables I and V	21.7	28.6
3) Expected return, C(1) × C(2)	$520,800	$686,400
D. Tax-free part of annuity		
1) Exclusion ratio as decimal, B(3) ÷ C(3)	.079	.001
2) Tax-free part, C(1) × D(1)	$1,896	$24

The tax-free part of Bill's total annuity is $1,920 ($1,896 plus $24). The taxable part of his annuity is $22,080 ($24,000 minus $1,920). If the annuity starting date is after 1986, the exclusion over the years cannot exceed the net cost (figured without any reduction for a refund feature).

Example 2. Al is age 62 at his nearest birthday to the annuity starting date. Al's wife is age 60 at her nearest birthday to the annuity starting date. The joint and survivor annuity pays $1,000 per month to Al for life, and $500 per month to Al's surviving wife after his death. The pre-July 1986 investment in the contract is $53,100 and the post-June 1986 investment in the contract is $7,000. Al makes the election described in Example 1.

For purposes of this example, assume the refund feature adjustment is zero. If an adjustment is required, IRS will figure the amount. See *Requesting a Ruling on Taxation of Annuity* near the end of this publication.

	Pre-July 1986	Post-June 1986
A. Adjustment for refund feature		
1) Net cost	$53,100	$7,000
2) Annual annuity—$12,000		
($53,100/$60,100 × $12,000)	$10,602	
($7,000/$60,100 × $12,000)		$1,398
3) Guaranteed under the contract	$53,100	$7,000
4) Number of years guaranteed, rounded, A(3) ÷ A(2)	5	5
5) Applicable percentages	0%	0%
6) Refund feature adjustment, A(5) × smaller of A(1) or A(3)	0	0
B. Investment in the contract		
1) Net cost	$53,100	$7,000
2) Refund feature adjustment	0	0
3) Investment in the contract adjusted for refund feature	$53,100	$7,000
C. Expected return		
1) Multiple for both annuitants from Tables II and VI	25.4	28.8
2) Multiple for first annuitant from Tables I and V	16.9	22.5
3) Multiple applicable to surviving annuitant, subtract C(2) from C(1)	8.5	6.3
4) Annual annuity to surviving annuitant	$6,000	$6,000
5) Portion of expected return for surviving annuitant, C(4) × C(3)	$51,000	$37,800
6) Annual annuity to first annuitant . . .	$12,000	$12,000
7) Plus: Portion of expected return for first annuitant, C(6) × C(2)	$202,800	$270,000
8) Expected return for both annuitants, C(5) + C(7)	$253,800	$307,800
D. Tax-free part of annuity		
1) Exclusion ratio as a decimal, B(3) ÷ C(8)	.209	.023
2) Retiree's tax-free part of annuity, C(6) × D(1)	$2,508	$276
3) Survivor's tax-free part of annuity, C(4) × D(1)	$1,254	$138

The tax-free part of Al's total annuity is $2,784 ($2,508 + $276). The taxable part of his annuity is $9,216 ($12,000 − $2,784). The exclusion over the years cannot exceed the net cost of the contract (figured without any reduction for a refund feature) if the annuity starting date is after 1986.

After Al's death, his widow will apply the same exclusion percentages (20.9% and 2.3%) to her annual annuity of $6,000 to figure the tax-free part of her annuity.

Annuity received after June 30, 1986. If you receive an annuity payment after June 30, 1986, (regardless of your annuity starting date), you may elect to treat the entire cost of the contract as post-June 1986 cost (even if you made no post-June 1986 contributions to the plan) and use Tables V through VIII. Once made, you cannot revoke the election, which will apply to all payments during the year and in any later year.

Make the election by attaching the following statement to your income tax return.

"I elect, under section 1.72–9 of the Income Tax Regulations, to treat my entire cost of the contract as a post-June 1986 cost of the plan."

The statement must also include your name, address, and social security number.

You should also indicate you are making this election if you are unable or do not wish to determine the parts of your contributions which were made before July 1, 1986, and after June 30, 1986.

Disqualifying form of payment or settlement. If your annuity starting date is after June 30, 1986, and the contract provides for a disqualifying form of payment or settlement, such as an option to receive a lump sum in full discharge of the obligation under the contract, the entire investment in the contract is treated as post-June 1986 investment in the contract. See regulations section 1.72–6(d)(3) for additional examples of disqualifying forms of payment or settlement. You can find the Income Tax Regulations in many libraries and at Internal Revenue Service Offices.

The type and rule above prints on all proofs including departmental reproduction proofs. MUST be removed before printing.

Worksheet I
For Determining Taxable Annuity Under Regulations Section 1.72-6(d)(6)
Election For Single Annuitant With No Survivor Annuity

	Pre-July 1986	**Post-June 1986**
A. Refund Feature Adjustment		
1) Net cost (total cost less returned premiums, dividends, etc.) .	_____	_____
2) Annual annuity allocation:		
$\dfrac{\text{Portion of net cost in A(1)}}{\text{Net cost}} \times$ annual annuity	_____	_____
3) Guaranteed under the contract	_____	_____
4) Number of years guaranteed rounded to whole years:		
A(3) divided by A(2)	_____	_____
5) Applicable percentages from Tables III and VII.	_____	_____
6) Refund feature adjustment:		
A(5) times lesser of A(1) or A(3).	_____	_____
B. Investment in the Contract		
1) Net cost:		
A(1)	_____	_____
2) Refund feature adjustment:		
A(6)	_____	_____
3) Investment in the contract adjusted for refund feature:		
B(1) minus B(2).	_____	_____
C. Expected Return		
1) Annual annuity:		
12 times monthly annuity	_____	_____
2) Expected return multiples from Tables I and V.	_____	_____
3) Expected return:		
C(1) times C(2).	_____	_____
D. Tax-Free Part of Annuity		
1) Exclusion ratio, as a decimal rounded to 3 places:		
B(3) divided by C(3)	_____	_____
2) Tax-free part of annuity:		
C(1) times D(1).	_____	_____

The type and rule above prints on all proofs including departmental reproduction proofs. MUST be removed before printing.

Worksheet II
For Determining Taxable Annuity Under Regulations Section 1.72-6(d)(6)
Election For Joint and Survivor Annuity

	Pre-July 1986	**Post-June 1986**
A. Refund Feature Adjustment		
1) Net cost (total cost less returned premiums, dividends, etc.) .	_____	_____
2) Annual annuity allocation:		
$\dfrac{\text{Portion of net cost in A(1)}}{\text{Net cost}} \times$ retiree's annual annuity . .	_____	_____
3) Guaranteed under the contract	_____	_____
4) Number of years guaranteed, rounded to whole years:		
A(3) divided by A(2)	_____	_____
5) Applicable percentages*	_____	_____
*If your annuity meets the three conditions listed in *Zero value of refund feature* in *Investment in the Contract,* earlier, both percentages are 0. If not, the IRS will calculate the refund feature percentage.		
6) Refund feature adjustment:		
A(5) times lesser of A(1) or A(3).	_____	_____
B. Investment in the Contract		
1) Net cost:		
A(1)	_____	_____
2) Refund feature adjustment:		
A(6)	_____	_____
3) Investment in the contract adjusted for refund feature:		
B(1) minus B(2).	_____	_____
C. Expected Return		
1) Multiples for both annuitants, Tables II and VI.	_____	_____
2) Multiple for retiree. Tables I and V	_____	_____
3) Multiple for survivor:		
C(1) minus C(2)	_____	_____
4) Annual annuity to survivor:		
12 times potential monthly rate for survivor	_____	_____
5) Expected return for survivor:		
C(3) times C(4).	_____	_____
6) Annual annuity to retiree:		
12 times monthly rate for retiree	_____	_____
7) Expected return for retiree:		
C(2) times C(6).	_____	_____
8) Total expected return:		
C(5) plus C(7)	_____	_____
D. Tax-Free Part of Annuity		
1) Exclusion ratio, as a decimal rounded to 3 places:		
B(3) divided by C(8)	_____	_____
2) Retiree's tax-free part of annuity:		
C(6) times D(1).	_____	_____
3) Survivor's tax-free part of annuity, if surviving after death of retiree:		
C(4) times D(1).	_____	_____

The type and rule above prints on all proofs including departmental reproduction proofs. MUST be removed before printing.

ACTUARIAL TABLES

Table I (One Life) applies to all ages. Tables II–IV apply to males ages 35 to 90 and females ages 40 to 95.

Table I.—Ordinary Life Annuities—One Life—Expected Return Multiples

Ages		Multiples	Ages		Multiples	Ages		Multiples
Male	Female		Male	Female		Male	Female	
6	11	65.0	41	46	33.0	76	81	9.1
7	12	64.1	42	47	32.1	77	82	8.7
8	13	63.2	43	48	31.2	78	83	8.3
9	14	62.3	44	49	30.4	79	84	7.8
10	15	61.4	45	50	29.6	80	85	7.5
11	16	60.4	46	51	28.7	81	86	7.1
12	17	59.5	47	52	27.9	82	87	6.7
13	18	58.6	48	53	27.1	83	88	6.3
14	19	57.7	49	54	26.3	84	89	6.0
15	20	56.7	50	55	25.5	85	90	5.7
16	21	55.8	51	56	24.7	86	91	5.4
17	22	54.9	52	57	24.0	87	92	5.1
18	23	53.9	53	58	23.2	88	93	4.8
19	24	53.0	54	59	22.4	89	94	4.5
20	25	52.1	55	60	21.7	90	95	4.2
21	26	51.1	56	61	21.0	91	96	4.0
22	27	50.2	57	62	20.3	92	97	3.7
23	28	49.3	58	63	19.6	93	98	3.5
24	29	48.3	59	64	18.9	94	99	3.3
25	30	47.4	60	65	18.2	95	100	3.1
26	31	46.5	61	66	17.5	96	101	2.9
27	32	45.6	62	67	16.9	97	102	2.7
28	33	44.6	63	68	16.2	98	103	2.5
29	34	43.7	64	69	15.6	99	104	2.3
30	35	42.8	65	70	15.0	100	105	2.1
31	36	41.9	66	71	14.4	101	106	1.9
32	37	41.0	67	72	13.8	102	107	1.7
33	38	40.0	68	73	13.2	103	108	1.5
34	39	39.1	69	74	12.6	104	109	1.3
35	40	38.2	70	75	12.1	105	110	1.2
						106	111	1.0
36	41	37.3	71	76	11.6	107	112	.8
37	42	36.5	72	77	11.0	108	113	.7
38	43	35.6	73	78	10.5	109	114	.6
39	44	34.7	74	79	10.1	110	115	.5
40	45	33.8	75	80	9.6	111	116	0

Adjustments to Tables I, II, V, VI and VIA. Payments Made Quarterly, Semiannually, or Annually

	Number of whole months from annuity starting date to first payment date											
	0–1	2	3	4	5	6	7	8	9	10	11	12
Payments to be made:												
Annually	+.5	+.4	+.3	+.2	+.1	0	0	-.1	-.2	-.3	-.4	-.5
Semiannually	+.2	+.1	0	0	-.1	-.2						
Quarterly	+.1	0	-.1									

The type and rule above prints on all proofs including departmental reproduction proofs. MUST be removed before printing.

Table II.—Ordinary Joint Life and Last Survivor Annuities—Two Lives—Expected Return Multiples

Ages														
	Male	35	36	37	38	39	40	41	42	43	44	45	46	47
Male	Female	40	41	42	43	44	45	46	47	48	49	50	51	52
35	40	46.2	45.7	45.3	44.8	44.4	44.0	43.6	43.3	43.0	42.6	42.3	42.0	41.8
36	41	45.7	45.2	44.8	44.3	43.9	43.5	43.1	42.7	42.3	42.0	41.7	41.4	41.1
37	42	45.3	44.8	44.3	43.8	43.4	42.9	42.5	42.1	41.8	41.4	41.1	40.7	40.4
38	43	44.8	44.3	43.8	43.3	42.9	42.4	42.0	41.6	41.2	40.8	40.5	40.1	39.8
39	44	44.4	43.9	43.4	42.9	42.4	41.9	41.5	41.0	40.6	40.2	39.9	39.5	39.2
40	45	44.0	43.5	42.9	42.4	41.9	41.4	41.0	40.5	40.1	39.7	39.3	38.9	38.6
41	46	43.6	43.1	42.5	42.0	41.5	41.0	40.5	40.0	39.6	39.2	38.8	38.4	38.0
42	47	43.3	42.7	42.1	41.6	41.0	40.5	40.0	39.6	39.1	38.7	38.2	37.8	37.5
43	48	43.0	42.3	41.8	41.2	40.6	40.1	39.6	39.1	38.6	38.2	37.7	37.3	36.9
44	49	42.6	42.0	41.4	40.8	40.2	39.7	39.2	38.7	38.2	37.7	37.2	36.8	36.4
45	50	42.3	41.7	41.1	40.5	39.9	39.3	38.8	38.2	37.7	37.2	36.8	36.3	35.9
46	51	42.0	41.4	40.7	40.1	39.5	38.9	38.4	37.8	37.3	36.8	36.3	35.9	35.4
47	52	41.8	41.1	40.4	39.8	39.2	38.6	38.0	37.5	36.9	36.4	35.9	35.4	35.0

Ages														
	Male	48	49	50	51	52	53	54	55	56	57	58	59	60
Male	Female	53	54	55	56	57	58	59	60	61	62	63	64	65
35	40	41.5	41.3	41.0	40.8	40.6	40.4	40.3	40.1	40.0	39.8	39.7	39.6	39.5
36	41	40.8	40.6	40.3	40.1	39.9	39.7	39.5	39.3	39.2	39.0	38.9	38.8	38.6
37	42	40.2	39.9	39.6	39.4	39.2	39.0	38.8	38.6	38.4	38.3	38.1	38.0	37.9
38	43	39.5	39.2	39.0	38.7	38.5	38.3	38.1	37.9	37.7	37.5	37.3	37.2	37.1
39	44	38.9	38.6	38.3	38.0	37.8	37.6	37.3	37.1	36.9	36.8	36.6	36.4	36.3
40	45	38.3	38.0	37.7	37.4	37.1	36.9	36.6	36.4	36.2	36.0	35.9	35.7	35.5
41	46	37.7	37.3	37.0	36.7	36.5	36.2	36.0	35.7	35.5	35.3	35.1	35.0	34.8
42	47	37.1	36.8	36.4	36.1	35.8	35.6	35.3	35.1	34.8	34.6	34.4	34.2	34.1
43	48	36.5	36.2	35.8	35.5	35.2	34.9	34.7	34.4	34.2	33.9	33.7	33.5	33.3
44	49	36.0	35.6	35.3	34.9	34.6	34.3	34.0	33.8	33.5	33.3	33.0	32.8	32.6
45	50	35.5	35.1	34.7	34.4	34.0	33.7	33.4	33.1	32.9	32.6	32.4	32.2	31.9
46	51	35.0	34.6	34.2	33.8	33.5	33.1	32.8	32.5	32.2	32.0	31.7	31.5	31.3
47	52	34.5	34.1	33.7	33.3	32.9	32.6	32.2	31.9	31.6	31.4	31.1	30.9	30.6
48	53	34.0	33.6	33.2	32.8	32.4	32.0	31.7	31.4	31.1	30.8	30.5	30.2	30.0
49	54	33.6	33.1	32.7	32.3	31.9	31.5	31.2	30.8	30.5	30.2	29.9	29.6	29.4
50	55	33.2	32.7	32.3	31.8	31.4	31.0	30.6	30.3	29.9	29.6	29.3	29.0	28.8
51	56	32.8	32.3	31.8	31.4	30.9	30.5	30.1	29.8	29.4	29.1	28.8	28.5	28.2
52	57	32.4	31.9	31.4	30.9	30.5	30.1	29.7	29.3	28.9	28.6	28.2	27.9	27.6
53	58	32.0	31.5	31.0	30.5	30.1	29.6	29.2	28.8	28.4	28.1	27.7	27.4	27.1
54	59	31.7	31.2	30.6	30.1	29.7	29.2	28.8	28.3	27.9	27.6	27.2	26.9	26.5
55	60	31.4	30.8	30.3	29.8	29.3	28.8	28.3	27.9	27.5	27.1	26.7	26.4	26.0
56	61	31.1	30.5	29.9	29.4	28.9	28.4	27.9	27.5	27.1	26.7	26.3	25.9	25.5
57	62	30.8	30.2	29.6	29.1	28.6	28.1	27.6	27.1	26.7	26.2	25.8	25.4	25.1
58	63	30.5	29.9	29.3	28.8	28.2	27.7	27.2	26.7	26.3	25.8	25.4	25.0	24.6
59	64	30.2	29.6	29.0	28.5	27.9	27.4	26.9	26.4	25.9	25.4	25.0	24.6	24.2
60	65	30.0	29.4	28.8	28.2	27.6	27.1	26.5	26.0	25.5	25.1	24.6	24.2	23.8

The type and rule above prints on all proofs including departmental reproduction proofs. MUST be removed before printing.

Table II.—Ordinary Joint Life and Last Survivor Annuities—Two Lives—Expected Return Multiples—Continued

Ages														
	Male	61	62	63	64	65	66	67	68	69	70	71	72	73
Male	Female	66	67	68	69	70	71	72	73	74	75	76	77	78
35	40	39.4	39.3	39.2	39.1	39.0	38.9	38.9	38.8	38.8	38.7	38.7	38.6	38.6
36	41	38.5	38.4	38.3	38.2	38.2	38.1	38.0	38.0	37.9	37.9	37.8	37.8	37.7
37	42	37.7	37.6	37.5	37.4	37.3	37.3	37.2	37.1	37.1	37.0	36.9	36.9	36.9
38	43	36.9	36.8	36.7	36.6	36.5	36.4	36.4	36.3	36.2	36.2	36.1	36.0	36.0
39	44	36.2	36.0	35.9	35.8	35.7	35.6	35.5	35.5	35.4	35.3	35.3	35.2	35.2
40	45	35.4	35.3	35.1	35.0	34.9	34.8	34.7	34.6	34.6	34.5	34.4	34.4	34.3
41	46	34.6	34.5	34.4	34.2	34.1	34.0	33.9	33.8	33.8	33.7	33.6	33.5	33.5
42	47	33.9	33.7	33.6	33.5	33.4	33.2	33.1	33.0	33.0	32.9	32.8	32.7	32.7
43	48	33.2	33.0	32.9	32.7	32.6	32.5	32.4	32.4	32.3	32.2	32.1	32.0	31.9
44	49	32.5	32.3	32.1	32.0	31.8	31.7	31.6	31.5	31.4	31.3	31.2	31.1	31.1
45	50	31.8	31.6	31.4	31.3	31.1	31.0	30.8	30.7	30.6	30.5	30.4	30.4	30.3
46	51	31.1	30.9	30.7	30.5	30.4	30.2	30.1	30.0	29.9	29.8	29.7	29.6	29.5
47	52	30.4	30.2	30.0	29.8	29.7	29.5	29.4	29.3	29.1	29.0	28.9	28.8	28.7
48	53	29.8	29.5	29.3	29.2	29.0	28.8	28.7	28.5	28.4	28.3	28.2	28.1	28.0
49	54	29.1	28.9	28.7	28.5	28.3	28.1	28.0	27.8	27.7	27.6	27.5	27.4	27.3
50	55	28.5	28.3	28.1	27.8	27.6	27.5	27.3	27.1	27.0	26.9	26.7	26.6	26.5
51	56	27.9	27.7	27.4	27.2	27.0	26.8	26.6	26.5	26.3	26.2	26.0	25.9	25.8
52	57	27.3	27.1	26.8	26.6	26.4	26.2	26.0	25.8	25.7	25.5	25.4	25.2	25.1
53	58	26.8	26.5	26.2	26.0	25.8	25.6	25.4	25.2	25.0	24.8	24.7	24.6	24.4
54	59	26.2	25.9	25.7	25.4	25.2	25.0	24.7	24.6	24.4	24.2	24.0	23.9	23.8
55	60	25.7	25.4	25.1	24.9	24.6	24.4	24.1	23.9	23.8	23.6	23.4	23.3	23.1
56	61	25.2	24.9	24.6	24.3	24.1	23.8	23.6	23.4	23.2	23.0	22.8	22.6	22.5
57	62	24.7	24.4	24.1	23.8	23.5	23.3	23.0	22.8	22.6	22.4	22.2	22.0	21.9
58	63	24.3	23.9	23.6	23.3	23.0	22.7	22.5	22.2	22.0	21.8	21.6	21.4	21.3
59	64	23.8	23.5	23.1	22.8	22.5	22.2	21.9	21.7	21.5	21.2	21.0	20.9	20.7
60	65	23.4	23.0	22.7	22.3	22.0	21.7	21.4	21.2	20.9	20.7	20.5	20.3	20.1
61	66	23.0	22.6	22.2	21.9	21.6	21.3	21.0	20.7	20.4	20.2	20.0	19.8	19.6
62	67	22.6	22.2	21.8	21.5	21.1	20.8	20.5	20.2	19.9	19.7	19.5	19.2	19.0
63	68	22.2	21.8	21.4	21.1	20.7	20.4	20.1	19.8	19.5	19.2	19.0	18.7	18.5
64	69	21.9	21.5	21.1	20.7	20.3	20.0	19.6	19.3	19.0	18.7	18.5	18.2	18.0
65	70	21.6	21.1	20.7	20.3	19.9	19.6	19.2	18.9	18.6	18.3	18.0	17.8	17.5
66	71	21.3	20.8	20.4	20.0	19.6	19.2	18.8	18.5	18.2	17.9	17.6	17.3	17.1
67	72	21.0	20.5	20.1	19.6	19.2	18.8	18.5	18.1	17.8	17.5	17.2	16.9	16.7
68	73	20.7	20.2	19.8	19.3	18.9	18.5	18.1	17.8	17.4	17.1	16.8	16.5	16.2
69	74	20.4	19.9	19.5	19.0	18.6	18.2	17.8	17.4	17.1	16.7	16.4	16.1	15.8
70	75	20.2	19.7	19.2	18.7	18.3	17.9	17.5	17.1	16.7	16.4	16.1	15.8	15.5
71	76	20.0	19.5	19.0	18.5	18.0	17.6	17.2	16.8	16.4	16.1	15.7	15.4	15.1
72	77	19.8	19.2	18.7	18.2	17.8	17.3	16.9	16.5	16.1	15.8	15.4	15.1	14.8
73	78	19.6	19.0	18.5	18.0	17.5	17.1	16.7	16.2	15.8	15.5	15.1	14.8	14.4

Glossary

Accumulated value: The sum of the premium and the earnings in an annuity contract, minus fees charged to the contract and withdrawals from the contract.

Accumulation period or savings period: The period during which the owner of a deferred annuity makes payments into the contract and accumulates assets.

Accumulation unit value (AUV): A variable annuity subaccount's unit of measure, similar to a mutual fund's net asset value (NAV). During the accumulation period, the AUV fluctuates daily with a change in the value of the subaccount (similar to a mutual fund).

Annuitant: The person (or persons) whose life expectancy is used to calculate the value of annuity payments. The contract owner and the annuitant are often, but not always, the same person.

Annuitization: The conversion of the accumulated value of the contract into a stream of monthly, quarterly, or semiannual payments, for as long as one or two persons is living, or for a specific number of years.

Annuity commencement date, annuity starting date: The date when income payments begin.

Annuity contract: The legal agreement between the annuity contract owner and the insurance company that issues the contract.

Annuity payout period: The period of time, starting on the **annuity commencement dat**e, during which the insurance company makes annuity payments.

Annuity unit value: The measurement used to determine the amount of each annuity payment to the owner of a variable income annuity. The number of units is established when the annuity is first converted to an income stream or purchased. The annuity unit value fluctuates with the value of the underlying investments.

A-Share variable annuities: Variable annuity contracts whose purchaser pays a sales charge or load at the time of purchase. A-Share contracts have no surrender charges or surrender periods, and may have lower insurance charges (M&E charges) than other types of contract share classes.

Asset allocation: The method of diversifying a portfolio by dividing the assets among investments in stocks, bonds, and cash investments. By changing the asset allocation (that is, the proportion of stocks to bonds to cash), the investor can increase or decrease the risk of the portfolio and influence its probable long-term returns.

Asset allocation funds: Mutual funds that offer the investor a pre-established asset allocation. Someone who invests in a deferred variable annuity with guaranteed living benefits may be required to put their assets in any of several asset allocation **subaccounts**.

Assumed interest rate (AIR): The hypothetical growth rate used to calculate the first payment from a variable income annuity. Subsequent payments are larger than the first payment if the underlying assets grow at a rate higher than the AIR, and smaller than the first payment if the underlying assets grow at a rate lower than the AIR.

Beneficiary: The person designated by the contact owner to receive any payments that may be due if the contract owner or the annuitant dies.

B-Share variable annuity: Variable annuity contracts that have surrender periods and charges for excess withdrawals during the surrender period. The charges typically range from 5 percent to 7 percent in the first year and decline to zero after five to seven years. B-Share contracts are the most common form of annuity contracts sold.

Cash surrender value: The amount that can be withdrawn from the contract after any surrender charge is subtracted from the **accumulated value**. Also called the cash value.

Charitable gift annuity: An annuity where an individual transfers cash, securities, or property to a charitable organization and the individual (or two people) receives a regular income from the organization for life.

Contract date, contract year: The date an annuity contract becomes effective. Each contract year begins and ends on an anniversary of the contract date.

Contingent deferred sales charge (CDSC): Also called back-end loads, these fees are charged when an annuity is liquidated during the surrender period. Back-end loads typically start at 5 percent to 7 percent of the contract value and decline by 1 percent per year until they disappear.

Contract owner: The person who pays the premium for the contract. The owner can make withdrawals, make investment decisions, surrender the contract, change the beneficiary, and convert a deferred contract to an income stream.

C-Share variable annuity: Contracts with no up-front or **contingent deferred sales charges**. Also known as no-surrender-charge annuities, they do not penalize any withdrawals.

Death benefit: The payment made to the beneficiary if the contract owner or annuitant dies during the accumulation period. The death benefit may be greater than the contract value, depending on the death benefit option chosen by the contract owner.

Deferred annuity: An annuity contract purchased to help save for retirement. The contract can be paid for with a single premium, multiple premiums, or regular contributions. The contract owner determines if or when to convert the accumulated value to a regular retirement income.

Defined benefit plan: An employer-sponsored pension plan that qualifies for special tax treatment under the Internal Revenue Code. A retiree covered by the plan receives lifetime payments based on salary, years of service, and age at retirement. The employer bears all investment risk.

Defined contribution plan: An employer-sponsored pension plan in which the employee channels part of his or her income into the plan. Contributions are tax deductible up to $15,500. The employer may match a percentage of the employee's annual contribution, but the employee bears all investment risk.

Dollar cost averaging: A program for investing a fixed amount of money in mutual funds at set intervals so that more shares are purchased when prices are low and fewer shares are purchased when prices are high. Variable annuity contract owners can practice dollar cost averaging by arranging for regular, automatic transfers from a money market subaccount to other subaccounts.

Exclusion ratio: The formula that determines what percentage of an annuity income payment is taxable and which represents the tax-free return of the original investment, or principal.

Fixed annuitization: A stream of identical, guaranteed income payments from an annuity contract in the **payout stage**.

Fixed annuity: A **deferred annuity** that guarantees that the contract owner will receive a stated rate of interest through the accumulation phase.

Fixed income annuity: An **income annuity** that makes identical payments for the life of one person, two people, or a specific period.

Flexible premium contract: A contract to which the owner can make additional payments at any time after the initial **purchase payment**.

Free-look period: The number of days after the issue of a new contract during which the owner can cancel it.

General account: All the assets of the insurance company not allocated to the separate accounts. When a fixed annuity is purchased, the premium goes into the general account.

Guarantee period: The period during which the level of interest credited to a fixed annuity is guaranteed not to change.

Guaranteed lifetime withdrawal benefit (GLWB): A variable annuity rider or option promising that the contract owner can withdraw a certain percentage (4 percent to 7 percent, depending on when payments begin) of a guaranteed benefit base every year for life, regardless of the actual account balance.

Guaranteed minimum accumulation benefit (GMAB): A promise that the contract value of a variable annuity will be equal to at least a certain minimum amount after a specified number of years.

Guaranteed minimum death benefit (GMDB): The basic **death benefit** offered in variable annuity contracts. It specifies that if the owner, or in some contracts the annuitant, dies during the **accumulation period**, the beneficiary will receive either the current contract value or the sum of the purchase payments, minus withdrawals.

Guaranteed minimum income benefit (GMIB): A guarantee that the owner may receive a guaranteed income stream whose payments are based on the highest of three amounts: the actual contract value, the original premium credited with a specific growth rate, or the highest value of the account on any previous contract anniversary.

Guaranteed minimum living benefit (GMLB): A benefit that protects the contract owner against investment risks by guaranteeing that the account value or the income payments will be no lower than a specific minimum. GMLBs include **GMIBs**, **GMABs**, and **GMWBs**.

Guaranteed minimum withdrawal benefit (GMWB): A benefit that a certain percentage (usually 5 percent to 7 percent) of a guaranteed benefit base (often the sum of the premiums) can be withdrawn annually until the base is completely paid out, regardless of market performance or the actual account value.

Immediate annuity: An annuity contract, purchased with a single premium, which begins paying an income within less than 13 months after purchase. The payments can be variable or fixed. Also call a SPIA, or single premium immediate annuity.

Income annuity: An **immediate annuity**.

Income floor guarantee: A promise that annuity payments will never be less than a specified percentage (such as 80 percent) of the first payment.

Income options, payout options: The different ways that a contract owner can receive income from an annuity. These include lump sum withdrawals, systematic withdrawals, and guaranteed lifetime income.

Indexed annuity: An annuity whose gains are indirectly linked (through options) to the performance of a broad market index, such as the S&P 500, but that also puts a limit on losses due to poor market performance.

Insurance charges: The mortality and risk expense charges plus administrative fees.

Investment management fee: The fee paid to the professional fund managers who manage the money in **variable annuity subaccounts**.

Issuer: The insurance company that issues the annuity.

Joint and survivor annuity: A **life annuity** in which there are two annuitants, usually spouses. In the **annuity payout period**, the contract makes payments as long as either of the joint annuitants is living.

Level annuity payments: Annuity payments under a variable annuity contract that change only at the end of a specified period, such as 12 months, when they reset to reflect the actual performance of the investments during the period.

Life annuity: Annuity payments that are guaranteed to continue for the life of the annuitant.

Longevity risk: The risk of outliving one's assets.

L-Share variable annuities: Variable annuity contracts that typically have shorter surrender periods, such as three or four years, but may have higher M&E charges than other contracts.

Lump sum option: The option to withdraw all the assets in the annuity in a single payment.

Market risk: The risk that an investment in stocks or bonds might lose value. Also called financial market risk.

Market value adjustment: A feature of some **fixed annuities** that adjusts the value of a withdrawal to reflect the impact of a change in interest rates since the contract was purchased. If rates have gone up, the value of the contract is adjusted downward. If rates have gone down, the value is adjusted upward.

Minimum credited interest rate: The minimum rate of interest that the owner of a fixed annuity is guaranteed to receive.

Monte Carlo simulation: A computerized analytical model that considers thousands of possible market scenarios, using hypothetical inflation rates, interest rates, and market returns. It then presents the range of probabilities that various scenarios might occur. Monte Carlo simulations are an alternative to historical performance for estimating the probability of future market performance.

Mortality & expense risk charge (M&E): A fee that pays for the insurance guarantees under the contract, such as the death benefit and the right to convert the assets into a lifetime income at rates set in the contract at the time of purchase.

Nonqualified annuity: An annuity that is not purchased as part of a retirement plan that receives special tax treatment, such as a 401(k) plan or an IRA.

Partial withdrawal: The withdrawal of an amount less than the entire cash surrender value of the contract. Many contracts permit annual withdrawals of a certain amount (such as 10 percent) without a surrender charge.

Payout phase, payout period: The period during which the money accumulated in a deferred annuity contract, or the **purchase payment** for an **immediate annuity**, is paid out as income payments.

Period certain: The number of years, usually up to 20 years, that income annuity payments are guaranteed to last. If the owner dies before the end of the period certain, the beneficiary receives payments for the rest of the period.

Portfolio rebalancing: A type of asset allocation that periodically restores the relative proportion of the investments in a variable annuity to the contract owner's desired blend. Market performance can, over time, change the balance among investments and therefore change the portfolio's risk level.

Premiums or purchase payments: The amounts of money paid into an annuity contract.

Pure life annuity or straight life annuity: An income annuity whose payments stop when the **annuitant** dies.

Qualified annuity: An annuity purchased with pre-tax dollars as part of a retirement program, such as a 401(k) plan, that receives special tax treatment.

Refund annuity: A type of annuity that guarantees that if the annuitant dies before a specific amount of premiums paid for the annuity are received as income, some or all the premiums will be refunded to the beneficiary.

Risk pooling: In income annuities, the spreading of longevity risk among a large group of individuals, some of whom will die sooner than expected and some of whom will live longer than expected.

Section 1035 exchange: The tax-free exchange of one annuity contract for another. This exchange must meet certain conditions specified under Section 1035 of the Internal Revenue Code.

Separate account: An account, consisting of mutual fund-like subaccounts, that receives the money you invest in a variable annuity. The separate account is set apart from the insurer's general account and is legally insulated from the insurer's general creditors.

Single premium annuity: An annuity contract that is purchased with a single payment. All immediate annuities and some deferred nonqualified annuities are in this category.

Stepped-up death benefit: A **death benefit** that is increased regularly to lock in the account value's investment gains.

Subaccount: The investment funds offered in variable annuity contracts. They may be identical to existing mutual funds, but are subject to different expenses and tax treatments. They are held in the insurer's **separate account**.

Surrender charge: The cost to a contract owner for withdrawals from a deferred annuity contract before the end of the surrender period.

Systematic withdrawal plan: A plan that allows owners of deferred variable annuity contracts to schedule regular withdrawals from the contract instead of converting the assets to a guaranteed income stream.

Tax-qualified retirement plan: A retirement plan such as an IRA, 401(k), or 403(b). Contributions to such plans qualify for special tax treatment under federal law.

Transfer: The movement of assets from one subaccount to another.

Transfer fee: The charge for transfers. Most issuers allow a certain amount of free transfers, and impose fees only on excessive transfers.

Unbundled contracts: Annuity contracts that permit purchasers to choose and pay for the optional features they want, such as a specific **guaranteed minimum living benefit**.

Variable annuitization: A stream of income payments that vary based on the investment performance of the underlying **subaccounts**.

Variable annuity: An annuity whose contract value or income payments vary based on the investment performance of the underlying **subaccounts**.

Variable investment options: The investment choices available to a variable annuity contract owner. These choices typically include stock, bond, and money market funds.

Withdrawal fee: An administrative fee charged on withdrawals.

Withdrawals: Any distributions from an annuity other than scheduled annuity payments.

Index

BUSINESS, CAREERS & PERSONAL FINANCE

0-7645-9847-3

0-7645-2431-3

Also available:
- Business Plans Kit For Dummies
  0-7645-9794-9
- Economics For Dummies
  0-7645-5726-2
- Grant Writing For Dummies
  0-7645-8416-2
- Home Buying For Dummies
  0-7645-5331-3
- Managing For Dummies
  0-7645-1771-6
- Marketing For Dummies
  0-7645-5600-2

- Personal Finance For Dummies
  0-7645-2590-5*
- Resumes For Dummies
  0-7645-5471-9
- Selling For Dummies
  0-7645-5363-1
- Six Sigma For Dummies
  0-7645-6798-5
- Small Business Kit For Dummies
  0-7645-5984-2
- Starting an eBay Business For Dummies
  0-7645-6924-4
- Your Dream Career For Dummies
  0-7645-9795-7

HOME & BUSINESS COMPUTER BASICS

0-470-05432-8

0-471-75421-8

Also available:
- Cleaning Windows Vista For Dummies
  0-471-78293-9
- Excel 2007 For Dummies
  0-470-03737-7
- Mac OS X Tiger For Dummies
  0-7645-7675-5
- MacBook For Dummies
  0-470-04859-X
- Macs For Dummies
  0-470-04849-2
- Office 2007 For Dummies
  0-470-00923-3

- Outlook 2007 For Dummies
  0-470-03830-6
- PCs For Dummies
  0-7645-8958-X
- Salesforce.com For Dummies
  0-470-04893-X
- Upgrading & Fixing Laptops For Dummies
  0-7645-8959-8
- Word 2007 For Dummies
  0-470-03658-3
- Quicken 2007 For Dummies
  0-470-04600-7

FOOD, HOME, GARDEN, HOBBIES, MUSIC & PETS

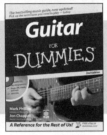

0-7645-8404-9

0-7645-9904-6

Also available:
- Candy Making For Dummies
  0-7645-9734-5
- Card Games For Dummies
  0-7645-9910-0
- Crocheting For Dummies
  0-7645-4151-X
- Dog Training For Dummies
  0-7645-8418-9
- Healthy Carb Cookbook For Dummies
  0-7645-8476-6
- Home Maintenance For Dummies
  0-7645-5215-5

- Horses For Dummies
  0-7645-9797-3
- Jewelry Making & Beading For Dummies
  0-7645-2571-9
- Orchids For Dummies
  0-7645-6759-4
- Puppies For Dummies
  0-7645-5255-4
- Rock Guitar For Dummies
  0-7645-5356-9
- Sewing For Dummies
  0-7645-6847-7
- Singing For Dummies
  0-7645-2475-5

INTERNET & DIGITAL MEDIA

0-470-04529-9

0-470-04894-8

Also available:
- Blogging For Dummies
  0-471-77084-1
- Digital Photography For Dummies
  0-7645-9802-3
- Digital Photography All-in-One Desk Reference For Dummies
  0-470-03743-1
- Digital SLR Cameras and Photography For Dummies
  0-7645-9803-1
- eBay Business All-in-One Desk Reference For Dummies
  0-7645-8438-3
- HDTV For Dummies
  0-470-09673-X

- Home Entertainment PCs For Dummies
  0-470-05523-5
- MySpace For Dummies
  0-470-09529-6
- Search Engine Optimization For Dummies
  0-471-97998-8
- Skype For Dummies
  0-470-04891-3
- The Internet For Dummies
  0-7645-8996-2
- Wiring Your Digital Home For Dummies
  0-471-91830-X

* Separate Canadian edition also available
† Separate U.K. edition also available

SPORTS, FITNESS, PARENTING, RELIGION & SPIRITUALITY

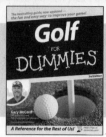

0-471-76871-5

0-7645-7841-3

Also available:

- Catholicism For Dummies
  0-7645-5391-7
- Exercise Balls For Dummies
  0-7645-5623-1
- Fitness For Dummies
  0-7645-7851-0
- Football For Dummies
  0-7645-3936-1
- Judaism For Dummies
  0-7645-5299-6
- Potty Training For Dummies
  0-7645-5417-4
- Buddhism For Dummies
  0-7645-5359-3

- Pregnancy For Dummies
  0-7645-4483-7 †
- Ten Minute Tone-Ups For Dummies
  0-7645-7207-5
- NASCAR For Dummies
  0-7645-7681-X
- Religion For Dummies
  0-7645-5264-3
- Soccer For Dummies
  0-7645-5229-5
- Women in the Bible For Dummies
  0-7645-8475-8

TRAVEL

0-7645-7749-2

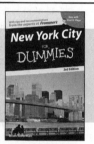

0-7645-6945-7

Also available:

- Alaska For Dummies
  0-7645-7746-8
- Cruise Vacations For Dummies
  0-7645-6941-4
- England For Dummies
  0-7645-4276-1
- Europe For Dummies
  0-7645-7529-5
- Germany For Dummies
  0-7645-7823-5
- Hawaii For Dummies
  0-7645-7402-7

- Italy For Dummies
  0-7645-7386-1
- Las Vegas For Dummies
  0-7645-7382-9
- London For Dummies
  0-7645-4277-X
- Paris For Dummies
  0-7645-7630-5
- RV Vacations For Dummies
  0-7645-4442-X
- Walt Disney World & Orlando
  For Dummies
  0-7645-9660-8

GRAPHICS, DESIGN & WEB DEVELOPMENT

0-7645-8815-X

0-7645-9571-7

Also available:

- 3D Game Animation For Dummies
  0-7645-8789-7
- AutoCAD 2006 For Dummies
  0-7645-8925-3
- Building a Web Site For Dummies
  0-7645-7144-3
- Creating Web Pages For Dummies
  0-470-08030-2
- Creating Web Pages All-in-One Desk
  Reference For Dummies
  0-7645-4345-8
- Dreamweaver 8 For Dummies
  0-7645-9649-7

- InDesign CS2 For Dummies
  0-7645-9572-5
- Macromedia Flash 8 For Dummies
  0-7645-9691-8
- Photoshop CS2 and Digital
  Photography For Dummies
  0-7645-9580-6
- Photoshop Elements 4 For Dummies
  0-471-77483-9
- Syndicating Web Sites with RSS Feeds
  For Dummies
  0-7645-8848-6
- Yahoo! SiteBuilder For Dummies
  0-7645-9800-7

NETWORKING, SECURITY, PROGRAMMING & DATABASES

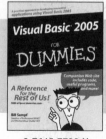

0-7645-7728-X

0-471-74940-0

Also available:

- Access 2007 For Dummies
  0-470-04612-0
- ASP.NET 2 For Dummies
  0-7645-7907-X
- C# 2005 For Dummies
  0-7645-9704-3
- Hacking For Dummies
  0-470-05235-X
- Hacking Wireless Networks
  For Dummies
  0-7645-9730-2
- Java For Dummies
  0-470-08716-1

- Microsoft SQL Server 2005 For Dummies
  0-7645-7755-7
- Networking All-in-One Desk Reference
  For Dummies
  0-7645-9939-9
- Preventing Identity Theft For Dummies
  0-7645-7336-5
- Telecom For Dummies
  0-471-77085-X
- Visual Studio 2005 All-in-One Desk
  Reference For Dummies
  0-7645-9775-2
- XML For Dummies
  0-7645-8845-1

HEALTH & SELF-HELP

0-7645-8450-2

0-7645-4149-8

Also available:

Bipolar Disorder For Dummies
0-7645-8451-0

Chemotherapy and Radiation
For Dummies
0-7645-7832-4

Controlling Cholesterol For Dummies
0-7645-5440-9

Diabetes For Dummies
0-7645-6820-5* †

Divorce For Dummies
0-7645-8417-0 †

Fibromyalgia For Dummies
0-7645-5441-7

Low-Calorie Dieting For Dummies
0-7645-9905-4

Meditation For Dummies
0-471-77774-9

Osteoporosis For Dummies
0-7645-7621-6

Overcoming Anxiety For Dummies
0-7645-5447-6

Reiki For Dummies
0-7645-9907-0

Stress Management For Dummies
0-7645-5144-2

EDUCATION, HISTORY, REFERENCE & TEST PREPARATION

0-7645-8381-6

0-7645-9554-7

Also available:

The ACT For Dummies
0-7645-9652-7

Algebra For Dummies
0-7645-5325-9

Algebra Workbook For Dummies
0-7645-8467-7

Astronomy For Dummies
0-7645-8465-0

Calculus For Dummies
0-7645-2498-4

Chemistry For Dummies
0-7645-5430-1

Forensics For Dummies
0-7645-5580-4

Freemasons For Dummies
0-7645-9796-5

French For Dummies
0-7645-5193-0

Geometry For Dummies
0-7645-5324-0

Organic Chemistry I For Dummies
0-7645-6902-3

The SAT I For Dummies
0-7645-7193-1

Spanish For Dummies
0-7645-5194-9

Statistics For Dummies
0-7645-5423-9

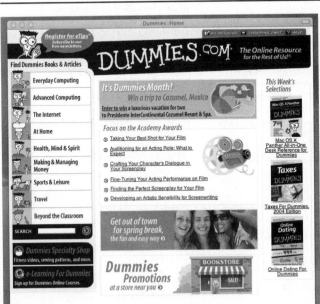

Get smart @ dummies.com®

- Find a full list of Dummies titles
- Look into loads of FREE on-site articles
- Sign up for FREE eTips e-mailed to you weekly
- See what other products carry the Dummies name
- Shop directly from the Dummies bookstore
- Enter to win new prizes every month!